A People that Dwells Alone

A People that Dwells Alone

Yaacov Herzog

Edited by Misha Louvish

Sanhedrin Press
New York

A People that Dwells Alone was first published in Great Britain in 1975 by Weidenfeld and Nicolson, London

First American Edition 1975

SANHEDRIN PRESS,
a division of Hebrew Publishing Company

Printed in the United States of America

Contents

'lo, it is a people that shall dwell alone,
and shall not be reckoned among the nations.'

(Numbers 23 : 9)

Foreword

I am infinitely beholden to his widow for this privilege of identifying myself, in a personal foreword of homage, with an anthology of utterances by my lifelong friend and mentor Yaacov Herzog. The legacy that erosions of peripatetic duty, of unheralded delivery and of fortuitous recording have left behind of his addresses in conference and pulpit, in dialectic argumentation and in public gatherings is little enough and fragmentary at that. Still, it adds up to a brilliant and compelling performance, mirroring the credo and convictions of this many-faceted Jew – philosopher and exegete, diplomat and theologian, jurist and administrator. *Nihil tetigit quod non ornavit* – He touched nothing that he did not adorn.

We were Dubliners by birth and were destined to be, together, servants of the Third Jewish Commonwealth. In calendar and chronology, I was his senior, and, indeed, on furlough in the Irish capital as a fledgling member of the Palestine Secretariat, I attended the ceremony of his entry into the Covenant of Abraham. But in pan-Judaica, in political acumen, and in governmental responsibility, I was his pupil, instinctively and rewardingly. No encounter with him but I gained from his wisdom, expounded with a delightful Celtic lilt, in taut and lucid accents. His was a universalist and associative knowledge. He had an especial talent for lighting up his themes by deft analogy, swift inference, shrewd analysis : his, I make bold to say, were the insights of a neo-prophet endowed with a benignant majesty of mind.

Studying this vestigial distillation of what Yaacov had to say on the nature of the Jewish people and its destiny, the problems of Israel's foreign policy and of the hurly-burly in the arenas of international affairs, the reader will surely be persuaded of the tremendous loss that his untimely death has meant to the chronicles and literature of Jewry and Israel.

It was an arduous task for his widow to rescue even this small sampling of Yaacov's 'confessions of faith' as made known in the United States, in Canada and in South Africa in the course of many a representative and ambassadorial pilgrimage. On her behalf, I thank all who responded so helpfully to her appeal for whatever surviving material was accessible to them : it must be an anonymous acknowledgement, for space forbids individual listing.

Apart from a section that concerns the origins of the Balfour Declaration, the anthology is derived, in the main, from speeches recorded or transcribed there and then. Our Sages ordained that it was unbecoming to write down a man's spoken word – and how rightly this holds with a man like Yaacov, his intellect an ever swelling and enriching fount that strove always towards perfection of substance and style. His thought processes were so lucid, in so orderly a marshalling, that, I surmise, the editors rarely needed to re-cast his extemporaneous phrases into the conventional patterns of planned authorship : thus the printed word here illumines and gladdens precisely as did the vibrant syllables that fell from his lips.

It is my belief that the anthology will encourage us to sense aright the wonders of our people and to share the vision of its future. Of those wonders, of that vision, Yaacov, loving and teaching, was an interpreter and – perhaps a little – an architect. His was a tragically brief span of life, but it was, in requital, a life fully and creatively lived, in selfless nobility.

Max Nurock

Jerusalem, August 1974

Yaacov Herzog

by Shneur Zalman Shazar, President of Israel, 1963–73

A fine stone has been wrenched out of our national edifice, a whole and perfect stone, for he was whole and complete in his talents – in his knowledge of Israel's Torah and the world's wisdom, in his natural charm and in his mastery of the complexities of our time. He was at one with himself and the tasks he undertook, at one with his generation and the generations of his fathers, and – so rare in our generation – he was at one with his Maker. Despite his perception of the obvious fragmentation of the Jewish people, he never ceased to marvel at its wholeness. He saw the modern State of Israel as a logical consequence of the vicissitudes of preceding generations, both from the viewpoint of the spiritual heritage with which the soul of the Jew in our generation is interwoven – whether he knows it or not – and from the viewpoint of the destiny of our national survival in spite of the inexplicable tribulations that come upon us.

Although committed to his religious convictions, he was a rationalist of Lithuanian Jewish stock, a man dominated by the rule of reason. A disciple of Anglo-Saxon culture, he did not wish to give way to mysticism and would not admit that he was under its sway. Deep in his heart, however, he knew and felt the hand of God that protected His people. 'It's not so simple !' he would say at the end of what seemed to be a logical and analytical conversation. And, as he was a remarkable analyst, he was always wonderfully heartening : far-sighted in perceiving perils in the offing, merciless in warning against them, but at the same time a great comforter. He was so able to give comfort because his soul was at peace.

Once he told me, as if revealing a secret, that his name was not merely Yaacov, but Yaacov David, after Rabbi Yaacov David Ben-Ze'ev of Slutsk (Ridbaz), later head of a *yeshivah* in Safed, just as his elder brother was named after Rabbi Hayim of Brisk. His father, the Chief Rabbi of Israel, not only wanted to implant in his sons respect and honour for their ancient ancestral heritage, but also to see their souls anchored in the tradition of the greatest rabbis of their own age.

I met him in the evening of my days, and I found in him a revelation of friendship ; a welcome boon that came from a far distance, yet at the same time from the depth of my spirit. We could never have enough of our conversations, both on the affairs of the day and on questions of eternity, which for him were intertwined.

He was a master of the mysteries of present-day problems ; he studied international relations and became a real expert – in so far as such expertise is possible – in the perplexities of this generation. Still in his youth he learned to be a gifted interpreter, an intermediary between the innermost experience of his people and the heart of the world's rulers. His first literary work, a translation of the Mishnah into English, was an omen of his future role as mediator between the source of Jewish law and those Jews who had been exiled from the spiritual heritage of their people, as well as friendly non-Jews who wished to delve into its secrets.

At the end of World War Two, he set out to accompany his father on his mission to deliver Jewish orphans who had remained in the hands of their Christian saviours. It was then, apparently, that he first sampled the meaning of devoted service to his people, service that involved danger, that required much thought and resourcefulness, profound compassion and rapid adaptability and the capacity to win the trust of strangers and overcome intrigues. He learned to walk with statesmen, princes and cardinals and to serve with utter devotion, without any publicity, in a kind of permanent secret service to his people.

He served the State of Israel before it came into being. During the mandatory period, he was already a member of the Intelligence and a confidant of the founders of the state. Even then he provided invaluable information and won the hearts of men who were previously unknown to him, even as he was to them. The State of Israel was everything to him and precious above all else. He served it faithfully in all circumstances and under all governments from the time of the late Moshe Sharett until our own day. He had no desire for publicity, no interest in ceremony ; he sought only to serve efficiently.

Logically and rationally he perceived the continuity of our generation with the generations before us. He himself was not a man of compromise, but he regarded no Jew, however strange to his viewpoint, as alien, and he was not repelled by any differences within his people. Thus he commanded trust even when controversy raged within the community, and even his most extreme opponents had confidence in him. Just as he felt at home among the Jews of Ireland, so he later formed close ties with the communities of Canada ; just as he could call East London Jewry his own, so he won the confidence of Jewish notables in Washington and New York.

When he served as the Ambassador of Israel to Canada, he was roused to indignation by the verdict that the world-famous historian Arnold Toynbee passed on the essential nature of Jewry since the overthrow of the Hasmonean dynasty. In fact, the entire life of the Jewish Diaspora from 132 years after Jesus of Nazareth until our own day was arbitrarily defined by this historian of world civilization as a fossilized relic of an obsolete culture that no longer had either the power of continuity or the right to exist. He could find no parallel to the Jewish people but the heirs of the Assyrians in our region and the surviving remnants of the Zoroastrians in India. He also injected another, this time vicious, political parallel : the attitude of Zionism to the Arabs in Palestine is comparable to the attitude of Nazism to the Jews in Germany. This was the double indictment that was lodged against the Jewish people from an academic rostrum of world repute, with an air of quiet certainty, without any anti-Semitic wrappings, relying solely on the authority of pure philosophical objectivity.

The gauntlet had been thrown down before the entire Jewish people and the truth of history, and the young ambassador picked it up on the public platform, confronting the professor as an equal in McGill University. Even today it is quite impossible to read the verbatim report of this spiritual contest between the English professor and the Israeli ambassador without profound emotion. One feels as if confronted by a modern chapter of medieval disputation. The young ambassador armed himself with all the civilized, academic detachment of an English university graduate and avoided any emotional excitement, persisting in his cold, conclusive and convincing demonstration until the professor had to grapple with it and was compelled to admit that his analogy was exaggerated.

When Herzog spoke out against the theory of Jewry as a 'fossil', all his pride in the heritage of his people came to the boiling-point, and like a flow of lava came a long list of the creative achievements of his fathers and fathers' fathers over 2,000 years. Like Weizmann, when he declared at the Zionist Congress following the *Kristallnacht, 'Mein Judenblut iz mir in Kopf gestiegen'* ('My Jewish blood came to my head'), so did Herzog's inherited pride cry out when he recounted the creativity of his people over the generations – the Talmud and the Midrashim, *Paytanim* and scholars, Kabbalists and moral philosophers, Hasidim and thinkers. He took the affront to them all as a personal insult, set out to defend their honour with relentless logic and did not desist from the professor, his senior, until his audience could clearly see that he held the upper hand.

Later, both of them realized that they had barely touched on matters of the deepest import, and they agreed to meet again, in the presence of a secretary, to put down in writing, as a permanent document, the entire text of the renewed debate. Herzog was certain that this theoretical discussion was necessary both for our world interests and for our own younger generation, and he started to prepare for it. But his cruel illness came and put an end to this plan, just as it brought to a sudden close other aspirations of his.

I was a close witness to his perplexities when he was offered the Chief Rabbinate of Great Britain and he was faced with the choice of which comes first – even from the point of view of Israel itself – the post of Chief Rabbi in the greatest Jewish capital in Europe, or the leadership of the Prime Minister's Office ? I said to myself at the time : who else among the Jewish people has ever been confronted with a choice of this kind ? For he was truly fitted, in talent, knowledge and innermost being, to fulfil either of the two functions – so distant from each other – with the same measure of complete success.

After being entrusted with the post of adviser to the highest and most responsible authority in the country, he rose to still greater heights by employing his extraordinary familiarity with the complexities of diplomacy in our day, his understanding of the catalytic personalities involved in it and the ideas that influence its processes. He was a partner and a friend to those who sought his advice and tried to help them in their efforts and activities ; but he never imposed his opinions - though neither did he conceal them. He made an immense spiritual effort to know those whom he had to advise and to understand their spiritual motives. He was unfamiliar with their Zionist motivations, and their political background was likewise novel, but he decided to study them from primary sources and personal impressions rather than to rely on popular opinions ; he tried to know them intimately and penetrate their innermost thoughts as well as the innermost spirit of their mentors. He took upon himself a profound study and approached his subjects first as an expert and then as a devoted admirer.

He regarded the centrality of the State of Israel to the Jewish people as the source of its strength, and therefore he never tired of teaching the country's leaders to pay close attention to what was happening in the scattered Diaspora communities. It was thus that he regarded himself at the peak of his mission when he suggested to the late Prime Minister Levi Eshkol to convene the representatives of the Jewish communities in a conference ; he felt the full force of the responsibility when Eshkol charged him with the conduct of the operation and control of all the arrangements. This conference was to determine both the organization of the Diaspora's assistance to Israel's consolidation and continuing struggle and Israel's readiness to take on a material and spiritual commitment to educational work in the Diaspora. He planned to build systematically a structure of mutual help between the State of Israel, as the centre, and the Diaspora Jewries. He was well aware of the difficulties involved, but with the aid of his analytical reason he delineated for himself and those he advised the boundaries of the possibilities without giving way to illusions or ignoring any important factor. Here, too, he was only able to trace the beginning of the road. Like a skilful architect, he was to show his talent again as he prepared to supervise the arrangements for the celebration of the semi-jubilee of Israel's independence. And here, too, death cut him down at the beginning of the plans.

And just as he never wearied of studying the architecture of national unity - with the State of Israel at its centre and Jerusalem at its innermost heart - so too he hoped to see the State of Israel acting in concert with its Arab neighbours, developing variegated ties by mutual agreement and drawing strength from distant world powers. He did not minimize the difficulties in the way, but he knocked indefatigably, over and over again, at every gate that seemed to be opening the slightest crack. The time has not yet come to speak of this, but perhaps in the not too distant future it will be possible to tell the story of his innumerable efforts, of his diligence and persistence, of his undespairing determination. It is to his credit that he was among the most persistent in weaving these plans, but he was happy to find that those he advised shared his aspirations ; despite all the differences in age, and sometimes in opinions as well, he won willing cooperation and mutual confidence.

He was a man of open reason by virtue of both his education and character, from the beginning of his journey until he reached his zenith, but he was not privileged to reach the evening of his days. The thread of his life was severed at noontide. But over all his skies – clear and shining – spread a strong and sacred radiance of implicit faith. And in that veil of mist – as was said in the days of King Solomon – God dwelt for him. He was a unique kind – had we been fortunate enough, the first of his kind. On the brink of what the future held in store, he was gathered to his fathers. May his precious memory be a blessing and a glory to his people.

Yaacov Herzog – A Tribute

by Sir Isaiah Berlin, President, Wolfson College, Oxford

Yaacov Herzog was endowed by the Creator with gifts seldom found in combination ; he had a cool, subtle and powerful brain, a pure and warm heart, nobility of character and a simple and untroubled moral vision that sustained and preserved him in the inner conflicts that must, sooner or later, afflict all sensitive persons caught in the problems of public life.

No doubt he owed this ultimate tranquility in large measure to the deep and unswerving religious faith in which he was brought up by his loving and saintly parents, a faith that never abandoned him, but, if anything, grew deeper and stronger with the years. All that he did and thought and felt was rooted in it, and his life of fervent and selfless service based on total devotion to his people and to the State of Israel was an act of profoundly religious self-dedication.

In this service he literally wore himself out. His life and his death seem to me to possess the heroic quality of a man who gives all that he is and has to the cause that absorbs him entirely. This cause was Judaism in all its aspects – religious and secular, historical and contemporary, personal and political. Above all it was embodied in the State of Israel, which for him (as for many of us) was the spirit of Judaism in its most real historical incarnation. For it he laid down his life.

In appearance he was gentle and unassuming ; but within that frail body there lived a firm and powerful spirit which, armed with a sharp, critical brain, fine perceptions, inexhaustible patience, a great and perpetually growing store of beautifully ordered, accurate knowledge, made him intellectually formidable. As a political analyst and observer he had few equals and, I should guess, no superior. But he was more than this. Because he understood and loved everything connected with the culture, the history and, above all, the religious experience of his own nation, he understood the quality of other nations and customs, and the inner life of individuals who belonged to other faiths. They, in their turn, felt this and responded to him as they did to few public servants or political officials of Israel.

His freedom from vanity, his genuine modesty and sweetness of nature, his unpolemical and deeply constructive character that impelled him always to seek for points of agreement, for ground on which something positive could be built to forward whatever plan he was seeking to realize, disarmed the suspicious and competitive. Politicians and journalists, civil servants and ecclesiastics, academics and industrialists, found him neither aggressive, defensive, nor anxious to impress them with his knowledge, his intelligence or to score points. They found he was willing to understand them and their purposes and to discuss controversial or emotionally sensitive issues in a lucid and rational fashion of which he was master. This predisposed them towards him and caused them to trust him – rightly.

If he was an effective public speaker, it was principally because he had something to say and marshalled facts and arguments with calm, intelligence and precision ; this often left a more lasting impression than the words of many speakers of greater eloquence. Yet behind his plain words there was always a reserve of disciplined passion. He was not a detached *rapporteur*, fascinated by his own powers of exposition ; for the life and security and well-being of his country and of Jews everywhere meant more to him than his own. This came through, and no matter how quietly he talked in his agreeable, slightly Irish brogue, the words had moral, as well as intellectual, weight. His obvious integrity and uprightness achieved as much as, or more than, his restraint and intellectual grasp ; people, both Jews and gentiles, whether they knew it or not, were moved by this and believed him.

In private life he was a marvellous friend – tender-hearted, tactful, sensitive, loyal, utterly dependable, and, when he felt at ease, light-hearted and highly entertaining. He had great charm and understood the nature of personal relations. His ideal vision of what the Jews have been, and could be – when he abandoned his natural reticence sufficiently to reveal it – was deeply moving. He truly loved the Jewish nation and was a patriot without being a nationalist ; this alone is surely one of the rarest of human virtues. He loved his people as such and was tolerant of their foibles. He had devoted friends among Jews of all persuasions – or lack of them – pious and deviant, Zionist and non-Zionist ; provided they were content to be Jews at all and did not seek to evade or bury that which made them Jews, he found good in all of them.

Others have testified to the quality of his service as Ambassador and as adviser to four Prime Ministers. I can only say that he was one of the best and wisest, most attractive and morally most impressive human beings I have ever known, and I shall mourn his passing for the rest of my life.

On Myself

From a radio interview, November 1969

Since my childhood I have been attracted to two worlds, and I believe that in the State of Israel these two realms are completely integrated. During my childhood I became familiar with the world of the Talmud, but I was also deeply interested in international relations. When I was thirteen years old I met Mr Clement Attlee, then Leader of the Opposition in the British Parliament, and he encouraged me to pursue the study of international problems. In this country I continued to study both the Talmud and law.

I entered political life quite by chance. In 1946 I was initiated into the Haganah to help evaluate international affairs and to take part in intelligence work. During the siege of Jerusalem I came into contact with the staff of the Jewish Agency's Political Department, with the late Moshe Sharett, Mrs Golda Meir and a number of other persons who hold central positions in Israel today. When the state was established, Sharett proposed, with the agreement of the late Rabbi Maimon, then Minister of Religious Affairs, that I should deal with the Christian communities on behalf of the Ministry and, at the same time, the problem of Jerusalem – namely, the struggle against external pressure for the internationalization of the city. As a result, I found myself involved in the world of international politics, and I am not sorry for it.

I do not believe in the distinction between the secular and the spiritual realms ; I do not think it has any place in Judaism. I, at any rate, cannot grasp nor understand the significance of the return to Zion against the background of historical continuity without a spiritual conception. There is no doubt that my father, of blessed memory, and his strong faith that the return to Zion in our days is the beginning of the Redemption of Israel had a great influence on me. In 1941, when Rommel was at the gates of Palestine, my father was on a visit to Washington and President Roosevelt warned him not to return, for the country was about to be conquered by the Germans. My father replied that the Prophets had foretold only two destructions and had said nothing about a third. A week after the Six Day War, the late Levi Eshkol reminded me of my father's answer.

One of the other men who has left an indelible impression on my life was the great scholar, Rabbi Issar Zalman Meltzer, with whom I studied Talmud. He was very old by that time, about eighty-five, and he appeared to me as one of the last of the Great Assembly, perhaps the last of a great era in the Jewish Diaspora. Somehow, he was linked in my imagination with the period of the Gaon of Vilna, and he personified that world that existed in the time of the sages of the Mishna and the Talmud.

In the political sphere I was deeply influenced by David Ben-Gurion and particularly by his behaviour in times of crisis. I was also impressed by Mrs Meir when I saw her confronting world leaders to put our case. In the literary field I have been very influenced by Marcel Proust, as an innovator in world literature. I am no expert in these matters, but I believe that Joyce, Kafka and Proust symbolize a new era in world literature. I think there is some connecting link between Proust and Agnon, though Agnon, when I asked him, told me that he had never read Proust nor, I believe, Joyce.

In Proust I found the dimension of the influence of events on memory : even events that have vanished continue to affect the personality, and memory, which lives in the consciousness despite changed circumstances, influences one's daily experiences. Somehow, I connect this with what I call 'the timeless identity of the Jew' over the generations. Among the Jews, for instance, if Rabbi Akiva, Rabbi Johanan Ben Zakkai, Bar Kokhba - or any great man of any generation - rose from his grave and came to life again, it would be as if he had never died, because we could talk to him as if all that had occurred in the meantime had never been, as if Jewish experience had been uninterrupted until this day. Among other nations it is different. For an English child, for example, the Duke of Wellington and Nelson are historical figures - albeit valorous and powerful leaders, but historical characters all the same - not figures that live in his inner consciousness. The same applies to Napoleon for a French child.

I have discussed this with various thinkers from abroad. Some of them questioned this theory in regard to China and I agreed that from the ethnic point of view there is no doubt greater continuity among the Chinese than even amongst us. The Chinese of today no doubt resemble the Chinese of 3,000 years ago more than the Jew of today resembles the Jew of 3,000 years ago. But I was referring to the continuity of memory, to an identity that stretches across the generations, and I asked whether Confucius rose from his tomb in Peking, the Chinese people of today would feel any immediate identification with him, as if he had never died, as if he had continued to live amongst them. After some consideration, their collective answer was No. Confucius in Peking today would be like Plato or Aristotle in Greece - a sublime historical figure, but not really part of the everyday experience and consciousness of the people amongst whom he once lived. On the other hand, I am convinced that if Rabbi Akiva were to come to life today, Jews would not only talk to him but question him as well - about his attitude to Bar Kokhba's war against the Romans, about his personal relationship with Bar Kokhba, about his view of the destruction of the Temple and so on. They would talk to him - about the character of the Jewish people, his dialogue with the God of Israel, his dialogue with the

Gentiles, the historical experience, the continuity of the Jewish people and its future – as if he had never disappeared from our midst.

Part One : Israel and the World

The Herzog – Toynbee Debate
McGill University, Montreal, 31 January 1961

Ambassador Herzog : First let me clarify that I am here in a personal, and not official, capacity. Indeed, over the past forty-eight hours, since Professor Toynbee agreed to this debate, I have done very little in the nature of my official capacity and have been more or less traversing a few thousand years of history, back and forth, in space and time, trying to disentangle civilizations – and fossils.

In this hall last week, an analogy was made, a comparison was drawn, and a word was invoked – a word enshrining a concept, the word 'morality'. Morality is a word of great significance touching the destiny of individuals, of nations, of the international community. But it was invoked by Professor Toynbee on an even broader canvas, the canvas of history, in terms of history's spiritual coherence and purpose.

I agree fully with the remark made by Professor Toynbee and reported in the press as to the nature of the world crisis at the present time. All agree that this crisis lacks adequate definition. The common man, like the statesman, realizes that in mankind's hand is reposed the crucial alternative of self-destruction or redemption, of a new insight into history's purpose or oblivion. And all realize that only through a decisive leap forward in the spiritual consciousness of mankind can the answer be found to this human dilemma. In the attempt at civilization in our time – and I am using a phrase of Professor Toynbee's – this leap forward must come from a deeper sense of morality. Before the body last week, Professor Toynbee, according to the newspapers of Montreal, compared, from a moral standpoint, the attitude of Israel to the Arabs in 1947 and 1948 with the Nazi slaughter of six million Jews. I must first say that the Professor clarified that he was not comparing the two events statistically. But he insisted, so the papers say, that the moral comparison is valid. Secondly, he is quoted with having said that the Jews have no historical right to Israel.

Now as far as one aspect of this analogy, the Nuremberg International Court found that in the summer of 1941 plans were made for the final solution of the Jewish question in Europe. This final solution, as we all know, embraced, in fact, the putting to death, in circumstances of unprecedented cruelty, of six million of our people, including over one million children. It is a crime that human imagination still finds difficulty in grasping and, as in the biblical phrase, 'The earth cannot cover the blood in which it is soaked.' This was cold-blooded planning, with governmental responsibility, and an execution in the magnitude of six million. And the result was that one-third of the Jewish people was wiped out, the great centres of its religion, of its thought and culture, of social and national movement, were obliterated. Professor Toynbee himself has denounced this crime in incisive terms. Indeed, mankind will brood to the end of days on the significance of this factor, unprecedented, of man's inhumanity to man. As for my people, our mourning is endless. It is a mourning for eternity.

Let us take the other side of the analogy. In 1947, over two-thirds of the members of the United Nations took a decision on the partition of Palestine into separate Jewish and Arab States. The Arab representatives on the spot announced they would resist, and within days an armed attack began against the Jewish community in Palestine. Writing of this period, the then United Nations Secretary-General, Trygve Lie, in his book *In The Cause of Peace* (page 163), says : 'From the first week of December 1947 the disorders in Palestine had begun to mount. The Arabs repeatedly asserted that they would resist partition by force. They seemed to be determined to drive that point home by assaults upon the Jewish community in Palestine.' On 21 January 1948, the British representative at the United Nations, Sir Alexander Cadogan, told the Security Council : 'For the Arabs in Palestine the killing now transcends all other considerations.' On 16 February 1948, the United Nations Palestine Commission reported to the Council that : 'Powerful Arab interests, both inside and outside Palestine, are defying the Resolution of the General Assembly and are engaged in a deliberate effort to alter by force the settlement envisaged therein.' Again, in April 1948, the Commission referred to 'continued threats and acts of violence'. Upon the expiry of the British Mandate on 14 May, the Arab armies invaded, informing the United Nations that they were intervening in Palestine with the object of restoring right and order in place of chaos and disorder. The nature of this right and order was immediately defined by the Secretary-General of the Arab League, Azzam Pasha. Speaking in Cairo – I am quoting a BBC broadcast of 15 May 1948 – he said : 'The world would now see a war of extermination and momentous massacre which will be spoken of like the Mongolian massacres and the Crusades.' It was a war of heavy suffering on both sides – military and civilian. Through this war, large numbers of Arabs in Israel were uprooted. At the same time, through this war, large Jewish communities throughout the Middle East were uprooted. Large numbers of Arabs left the country in order to come back in the wake of victorious forces. No international authority had defined responsibility for the Arab refugee problem. It is our contention – and we can sustain it from Arab and other, including British, sources – that the refugee problem was the result of the war proclaimed by the Arabs and a result of an appeal [to the Palestine Arabs] by the leaders to leave in order to return. As an Arab newspaper in Jordan put it : 'They told us to get out, so that they could get in. We got out ; they did not get in.'

But let us look at the results of the analogy in terms of morality, Professor. There are now 200,000 Arabs in Israel, enjoying equality and every right side by side with Jewish fellow-citizens. I represent these Arab citizens, just as I represent Jewish citizens, because they are all Israelis. In the refugee camps, it is true, there are large numbers of Arab refugees. At the same time, quite a considerable number have been absorbed into the economy of the neighbouring countries. But even of those in the camps, despite their suffering, there are many working, and over the past thirteen years their number has increased. In any event, there is a difference between a parasitic existence and total extinction. They continue to suffer because the Arab governments, who originated this suffering, refuse to relieve it by cooperating in the settlement of the Arab refugee problem.

Professor, there is a relationship between the two events to which you refer. In both cases the Jewish people was assaulted. In one case, one third of our people was destroyed ; in the other, we resisted, in self-defence, and, under a merciful Providence, we succeeded.

The second point of relationship is that through the experience of this Holocaust in Europe, our will was strengthened to do everything in our capacity so that never again would such a tragedy befall our people. But how can the two events – the destruction of one third of our people and the Arab refugee problem created through a war started by the Arabs themselves – be mentioned in the same breath? Should we pass an amendment to Article 51 of the Charter of the United Nations on the right of self-defence : an amendment to say that if you are attacked you may resist, but remember, no matter what you suffer in the process, if the man attacking you suffers, you will be condemned by history as having been affected by Nazi influence. You speak, Professor, with respect for Gandhi, and for his concepts ; you relate them across the span of history to Rabbi Johanan Ben Zakkai, one of our great masters of the law at the time of the destruction of the Second Temple. But I would say this : as far as I have read, Gandhi, whilst opposing activist self-defence, never denounced those who pursued it. What should we have done? Allowed the Nazi experience to be repeated? Now, the criterion of moral defensibility, I submit with all respect, sir – is in this case vague and indiscriminate. Morality unless specified and clearly defined does not strengthen morality, it weakens it. Indeed one might say it creates a neutral moralism. Ernest Renan said, *'La verité est dans les nuances'* ; but here you do not even have the nuances. You have two entirely different contexts of right and wrong.

Professor Toynbee : Professional boxers shake hands before they fight. Now let us set a good example for ambassadors and professors. I am afraid that we shall not give such an entertaining performance as boxers might do, but still this is a very important and serious occasion.

As the Ambassador has said, there are one or two other questions that he and I both want to discuss in your presence. The first one is this question of the parallel that I drew, in the book that I published in 1954, between what the Nazis did to the European Jews and what the Israelis did to the Palestinian Arabs. This was brought up, as the Chairman said, in one of the questions that was put to me at the meeting the other day, and I observed : yes, I had written that. I said yes, and in the terms that I stated in print, in this book of mine, I still held to it.

Now, the Ambassador has really anticipated one point in telling you, very kindly, that when I originally made this statement, and when I repeated it the other day, I did say at the same time that I was not making a numerical comparison, because obviously there is no numerical comparison between figures that run into millions and figures that run into three, or, at most, four figures. The second set of figures I am talking about is the massacres of Arab civilians behind the lines during the war between the Arab states and the Israeli forces in 1948. Of course, every increase in numbers produces an increase in suffering, but it is impossible to be wicked or criminal more than 100 per cent. Let me put the point bluntly : if I murder one man, that makes me a murderer ; I do not have to reach the thousand mark or the million mark to be a murderer.

I wonder if there are any Egyptians in the room. I know there are a number of Egyptians in Montreal ; is there any Egyptian present? Perhaps not. Let us suppose that some of the Egyptians of Montreal were here at this moment and say to me : 'How do you, being an Englishman, defend the slaughter in the fall of 1956 of civilian inhabitants of the Egyptian town of Port Said by bombardment from the air, which ran into four figures on the admission of the British Government itself ; and afterwards when somebody was sent to investigate, he could not get it down below four figures, if I remember right?' Now, supposing I were to answer : 'Why, that's not murder : we only killed people up to four figures. Now to be a murderer you must reach the million mark. Now those Germans over there, they reached it, and they murdered several million people. They were murderers, but we, the British, were not murderers.' Now, what would you think of that answer? What would Egypt say, and what would the world say? Now I think that applies all round to all cases. Now as to the massacres – I must use the word – to which I am referring : I was not, in making this comparison, referring to the fighting between the armed forces of the Arab states and the Israeli forces. The situation was, as you know, that Arab states from outside Palestine made war on Israel. I do not defend that. And, at that time, what is now the territory of Israel was inhabited by the local Arab population who had been there for many centuries and by the Israelis who had come in ever since 1917. The victims were the local Palestinian Arab population.

Now we come to this point of morality. And I utterly agree with the Ambassador that this is the essential point and the point that concerns the future as well as the past. Now I have mentioned this British case of

1956 to show that I can look at the things that my own country has done, as well as what other people have done. But I do think that if there is any point in what I have said about the numbers, then in point of morality some of those massacres by Israeli armed forces in Palestine do compare in, so to speak, moral quality with what the Germans did. What we hate in what the Germans did was that it was planned beforehand, carefully carried out cold-bloodedly with tremendous cruelty and with a purpose. Now I am afraid that all these points applied to the massacres that, in numbers, don't compare, but in quality do compare, with what the Nazis did, and that were done at any rate by certain Israeli armed forces – the Stern gang, for instance, and the Irgun. I don't know how far the Haganah was also implicated. I have heard it stated, and I have never heard it denied, that after at least one of those massacres – that of the civilian population of all sexes and ages at Deir Yassin to the west of Jerusalem – the Israeli armed forces – I don't know if it was the government forces or one of the unofficial armed forces – went round in cars with loud-speakers, speaking in Arabic, and said : 'We have done this to the people of this place. If you don't want this to happen to you, get out.' Now every civilian population that is in a war zone and in danger of death very wisely does get out. Happily, after Hitler came to power in Germany, a minority, unfortunately only a minority, of the Jews in Germany did manage, with difficulty often, to leave Germany in time. Now the Germans couldn't take their lives any longer, but they could, and did, seize and hold their property. No one thinks that the European Jews who got out of Germany at that time forfeited their legal rights to their property as a result of having managed, by prudence and foresight, to save their lives by getting out in time. Let me take another case. In 1940, when the Germans invaded France, several million French people from northern France fled from northern France to the south for the same reason that the Arab population of the war zone of Palestine in 1948 fled from Palestine. No one, I think, would dream of saying that by fleeing, as all civilian populations do try to flee from a war zone, those French people forfeited their title to their land and property, in northern France. And if the Germans were to put in a claim today : 'As we invaded the country, and these French people were ill-advised enough to run away, we have a legal title to this property, and it is really rather a shame and illegal that we don't possess it now,' that would seem pretty fantastic. But, as you will realize, the position in Israel today is that by far the larger part, I suppose, of the land in Israel is legally still the property of that civilian Arab population of Palestine that fled from Palestine during the war between the Arab states and the Israelis. The property that does rightfully belong to the Israelis is the property that they bought during the thirty years of the Mandate and long before that – I think, if I am right, the first agricultural Jewish settlements in Palestine went back to the 1880's – the Rothschild settlements. Now, they paid a handsome price for the land, and that land is obviously – legally, morally and fairly

– their property. But it is, if I am right in my figures, a small proportion of the total lands in the area now held by Israel ; by far the larger proportion – the houses, rural property, the trees and so on – are still the rightful property of the Palestinian refugees who are now living outside their homes, though often within sight of them, under conditions of misery and, at present, of hopelessness.

Let me make a general point, which concerns not Arab human nature or Jewish human nature but, I am afraid, human nature of all of us. As I say 'of all of us', let me begin again with my own country. I think it is one of the nastiest sides of our wretched human nature that we are very much tempted, whenever wrong or injustice or suffering is inflicted on us – 'tempted' is perhaps too conscious a word, because this is partly a kind of subconscious psychological reaction – but, whatever the reason, we often do the same thing to other people that are weaker than ourselves. Let me illustrate again by an example from the recent history of my own country. In World War Two the civilian population in my country, Britain, was severely bombed. What did we do within eleven years of that, in 1956? We bombed, in an aggressive attack on Egypt, without declaration of war, and, condemned by the world for having done it, the civilian population, of particularly, Port Said, to some extent of Cairo, I think, as well, and slaughtered certainly more than 1,000 innocent people, probably rather more than were slaughtered in those massacres by the Israeli armed forces in 1948.

Now this is a tragedy of human nature. What is really tragic is that people who have suffered a thing and had experience of it should inflict that suffering on other people, because human imagination is a very sluggish thing and it is very hard to realize at second hand what it means to suffer these things. But of course the British people suffered this bombardment only in one war, just for a few years ; the Jewish people have suffered murder, robbery, expulsion from their homes, not just for a year or two but for centuries running into 2,500 years. The more experience one has of what this means, I would say, the more it is morally incumbent upon one not to do the same thing again. The temptation to work off one's exasperation is no doubt greater, but the moral duty to resist that temptation is at its maximum.

One curious feature about the effect of this comparison – I hope I have now explained as exactly as I can what was and is in my mind in making it – is that I have been surprised at the vehemence of the reaction to it in the Jewish community. I have wondered myself why, if it is a preposterous suggestion, as you obviously feel it to be, you haven't said : 'Here is a silly man, saying this silly thing. Why bother about it? If it is so silly we should leave it alone.' But the reaction has not been like that. It has been, as we know, very vigorous. I think I am going to say rather a controversial thing : that any psychologist would tell you the reason. I would say that, inadvertently, in this comparison I have drawn, I have given the Jewish people a piece of what psychologists call 'shock treatment'. I have said aloud in startling words, something I think your consciences – each of you who belong to the Jewish community of the world – are whispering inside each of you. Now, let my voice fade out and listen to another voice that I will quote. 'I am certain that the world will judge the Jewish State by what it will do with the Arabs.' They are the words of a man famous in all your minds – Chaim Weizmann, whom I had the honour to know when I was a young man ; they were spoken, I believe, or written, in 1949, after the war between the Arab states and Israel, when Dr Weizmann was the first President of Israel. But I would ask you, let my voice fade out, let even Dr Weizmann's voice fade out, and listen to your own inner voice. Because, after all, who was the first to wake up the human conscience? I would say it was the Prophets of Israel and Judah. I do not believe that any person of Jewish religion can ever escape from his own conscience. What is more, I don't believe any Jew ever wishes to escape from it, and I believe this has been the glory of the Jews since the time of the Prophets, and perhaps before : that in all controversial questions between Jews or between Jews and the rest of the world, there have always been Jews who have had the spiritual insight and the moral courage to stand up and criticize their people. We wouldn't know about the criticism of the Jews in the eighth and seventh centuries BC had we not received the writings of Jewish critics who had criticized them. I would say : be your own critics, which is one of the greatest things in your Jewish tradition. And so I would leave you to your own consciences and with the existence of these Arab refugees – who now number 900,000, because many children have been born in exile.

I had the good fortune that my own family was not murdered, that my property or their property has not been robbed, that I have not been driven out of my country, so I don't know these experiences at first-hand. Just the strange inequality of human fortune. But in England, since the time that Hitler came into power, I have seen and met and talked to and sympathized with many European Jewish refugees. And since 1948 I have been in the places where the Arab refugees are now, and I have visited and talked to them, just as in the same way I talked to the European Jewish refugees, so I do know at second-hand what being a refugee is. Now many of you, Canadians of Jewish religion, have, I believe, come from Central and Eastern Europe rather recently, so that in your family tradition, in the time of your parents and even your grandparents, you have living family memories of this thing being done to your families, so you do know more vividly than I do what it means. So, as I say, I leave it to you to think over in your own conscience what is to be done about this situation. We have presented the problem but we have not yet solved it.

Herzog : Professor, first of all let me say that I fully agree on the virtue of self-criticism. If I may sum up your words : I think there are three main points. In the first place I understand that you agree that the Arab armies assaulted Israel when it came to life ; in other words, what Israel was doing was purely self-defence.

Toynbee : Well there is more to be said for it than that because, of course, the cry for independence was for the Arabs a provocation.

Herzog : This provocation was the basis of a United Nations decision and every United Nations record attests to this, including those I have quoted. On 15 July 1948, the Arab position having reached what it did in terms of a threat to the peace, the Security Council considered the situation in the category of a threat to peace. But you will admit, Professor Toynbee, that it is a fact that the Arabs attacked us. I mean in that context. You argue that facing up to this attack our people committed two great atrocities : one the Deir Yassin incident, and the other, driving out the Arabs and turning them into refugees. Very central to your thesis is that the Nazi impact of persecution on the Jewish people brought them to commit such atrocities, and you have mentioned the British action in bombing civilians in Port Said in 1956. Now, Professor, in Volume IV, page 128F, of your *Study of History* you say : 'In the history of man's attempt at civilization hitherto there has never been any society whose progress and civilization has gone so far that in times of revolution or war its members could be relied upon not to commit atrocities.' And you quoted here the behaviour of the German Army in Belgium in 1914, the British Black and Tans in Ireland in 1920, the French Army in Syria, the German National Socialist Storm Troops born in 1933 before World War Two and the Italian Blackshirts. Am I correct, Sir, in assuming that you feel that this is the record throughout history? Now you said that because of the bombing of Britain by the Germans a certain state of mind, some impact, some scar, had developed in the British consciousness that reflected itself in the bombing of Port Said. (The Black and Tans were well over thirteen years before Hitler came to power.) Would you agree with me that all these incidents have an element of cruelty, which is quite comprehensive in your terms, whether it be the bombing of Berlin in World War Two, whether it be the Black and Tans earlier, whether it be Hiroshima, whether it even be the treatment of the early American Indians? Right through this you feel that there is a sense of atrocity. Now how do you relate all this to Nazism?

Secondly, you agree that there were also Arab massacres of Jewish civilians. I can give you details. If you will come to Israel I will show you their graves. Blatant cruelty, and long before Deir Yassin. Were these also in the category of Nazi atrocities? And if so why don't you say both sides did this in such a category? Why do you choose to single us out? Why don't you say that Britain and almost every country in the world falls under that definition? Finally a word on Deir Yassin. It took place after a series of massacres such as the destruction of fifty Jewish labourers in Haifa in December 1947, the well known convoy to Yechiam in which we lost forty people, the blowing up of Ben Yehuda Street in Jerusalem with fifty killed and seventy wounded. And all this, Professor, with a city under siege. In your own survey of international studies written by Dr Kirk under your editorship, he quotes the commander of the Irgun as having said that his men suffered appreciable casualties, that those responsible for that action had claimed that the Arab residents of the village were warned to leave their houses, that this tragedy developed through hand-to-hand fighting, and, indeed, the commander of the operation was killed. But be that as it may, this action was condemned in most vigorous terms by the Jewish Agency at the time, and a message of regret was sent to King Abdullah. We heard no such expressions of regret for Arab massacres, although they were undertaken within the category of armed offensive against us. So to sum up, Sir, I would ask you : do you agree that there is a line linking every act of atrocity committed by soldiers in various countries down the ages? If so, would you agree that this odium of a Nazi impact would be attached to all such nations, not only Israel, including the Arabs who attacked us while we were operating in self-defence?

Toynbee : Well I suppose the Arabs could match atrocities. You could cite many more instances of massacres of Jews and they could give many more massacres of Arabs by Jews.

Herzog : At the end of the first week after the 29 November Resolution, 105 Jews were killed and many more injured. Right after the Resolution in November 1947. All this is on record.

Toynbee : There were things on both sides. Now about my own country. In my books published between the wars I had mentioned things that my own country had done during this time, and if I had not published this volume two years before the invasion of Egypt I would have mentioned my country in this context. The thing that the Indians call Karma, the chain of moral evil, is a generalization of what I tried to suggest before. There is something in human nature that makes us pass on to other people the evil that has been done to us. I agree with the Ambassador that this is a very general and a very powerful thing in human life. But I also feel very strongly that, as Buddha felt when he emphasized this chain of Karma, it is not an excuse. We might just say that this is part of human nature or that everybody does it or has done it sometime, therefore we can all get away with it and mutually, so to speak, condone what each of us does. We have to break this chain.

Now going back to the Israel case. I know very well that many people, no doubt the majority in Israel, were horrified by the massacre done by the Israeli armed forces, and the Israelis are a rather small minority of people in the Jewish world, and I am sure that the majority of Jews in the world, as far as they knew about this, were horrified and felt it as their responsibility: one has a slight responsibility for one's co-religionists. I feel a slight responsibility for my Protestant Christian co-religionists of European race for what they are doing at this moment in South Africa, and a much greater one for what my English Protestant co-religionists are doing in Rhodesia and in Kenya. But these degrees of responsibility are limited. I would make the point that all Israel has indicted itself, so to speak, as a result of that flight, or partial expulsion, and to a small extent in the massacre of the Palestinian Arabs because it has taken and held the land and the property that is legally and rightly still that of the Arabs. Now, to put it bluntly, this is robbery, and I am sure that this is on the Jewish conscience, and this is a continuing thing that has to be cleared up first of all by the Jews themselves, primarily the Israelis. But it is also the concern of Jewish communities all over the world who make Israeli's existence possible by their financial, moral and political support, particularly the Canadians and the United States citizens who are Jews by religion and who have the greatest financial power and the strongest political say in this matter. So we have this continuing question of how to break the chain of Karma, how to prevent the wrong that has been done – which was bred, I agree, by previous wrongs – from breeding further wrongs in its turn. I have been in the refugee camps in the Gaza Strip and I have heard the songs that the children sing in their schools. If you want to see what it was like to be a Jew say thirteen or fourteen years after Nebuchadnezzar exiled the Jews, go to the Gaza Strip and you will study the experience and the state of mind of the Arabs there. They are saying just the same things that the Jews felt then and have continued to feel later : that this was their country and they needed to return.

Herzog : You will pardon me if I come back to the original issue. The issue was the question of comparison : what we did as morally compared to what the Nazis did to us. Now I think it has been established that there was a war of aggression against us. I have given some background to the Deir Yassin massacre. But from what I understand from the quotation I gave and what you have now elaborated, would you agree, Professor, that this stigma of comparison applies not only to our people but to those Arabs who were responsible for massacres, for the ones I detailed and the many more I could list? Most of the nations of the world who at any time had their soldiers in war, even in self-defence, have been guilty of atrocity.

Toynbee : I distinguish sharply, though this is difficult, but it is one of the necessary and valuable conventions of human society, between suffering, death and mutilation caused in fighting between organized uniformed forces and a massacre by people or civilians behind the front.

Herzog : When you talk here of atrocities you did not mean acts between combatants, you meant atrocities committed by military people against civilians and you quoted certain allegations against us. But suppose, from your standpoint and the extreme Arab propaganda claims, that we are guilty of atrocity in that form, do you admit, Sir, that a similar guilt attaches itself to nearly every country in the world? For at some time or other, as you yourself have said in your book : 'No society can rely on its members not to commit atrocities in time of war or revolution,' and again I say, even in self-defence.

Toynbee : I agree that most societies have committed atrocities, but I do not think I have condoned atrocities.

Herzog : We do agree that this comparison can be applied on the universal level to any country whose soldiers have committed atrocities against civilians.

Toynbee : Yes, but atrocities are atrocities and murder is murder whoever commits it.

Herzog : And would that also apply to Arab atrocities against Jewish civilian populations, and the Black and Tans?

Toynbee : Of course.

Herzog : By the United States against Indians? There is a whole realm ; it is limitless. In other words, you were saying, if I now understand it, that, within the general category of denouncing violence or atrocities by military against civilians, Israel, in your opinion, was not separate from the rest of mankind and was guilty in the same way?

Toynbee : Of course, I don't think that the Israelis are different from mankind. I am not an anti-Semite.

Herzog : You claim that Israel cannot claim to stand above the rest of mankind because of what they have done in times of self-defence in war.

Toynbee : It is curious of me to defend the Germans and the Nazis of all people, because my country suffered in two wars of aggression by the Germans, but they, too, are human and what the Nazis did is not peculiar . . . in the sense that the Ambassador has explained that this unhappily is something that is in all human nature and we have to break it. Now why I have brought up the case of the Israelis in this connection was simply the actual fact that I was writing about the Palestine question and about the question between Jews and gentiles in the world.

Herzog : But this would apply to any other nation too.

Toynbee : And as the Ambassador has quoted, there are cases in my book where I brought up examples from the British and the French.

Herzog : May I just say, in a more academic sense, that I feel that in analysing atrocities in history there are graduations. The Nazi onslaught was something quite specific. Can it be compared to any other atrocity in human history? But you, Sir, disagree. Let me explain. Take the people in Israel who went through the hell of the Nazi death camps in Europe. On coming out of there they tried to get to Israel – Palestine at that time – and many who came on ships were held up by the British Navy, arrested or sent to camps in Cyprus. Let us take a man on a ship like that. He had gone through the hell of what the Nazis did to him. Now you would be surprised, Professor, if you speak to these people today. Although they felt at the time that the British attitude was one of cruelty, and certainly political blindness, they did not equate it with the Nazis. These same people who went through the Nazi experience, the Holocaust, and escaped from it, their soul was not so shattered as to equate further evil as being on a Nazi level. And it is these same people that you say were so influenced by the Nazis that they did similar things to the Arabs. I think the fact that you have said this in a universal context shows that this is a distinctive view of yours, and that Israel is only one, or rather, if I may quote the point, that Israel is not separate from the rest of the nations of the world.

Toynbee : I said that Israel is not different from other human beings. Yes.

Herzog : In other words, the Nazi power lies across the world. But even before the Nazis came, this business of atrocities and cruelty was here and even after they have gone it has remained.

I must add here one slight observation on the question of landholdings. I would say that any study of the British Land Register would show that seventy per cent of the land that is now Israel was government-owned : it belonged to the government of the Mandate and formerly to the Ottomans. It never belonged to any separate Arab political entity in Palestine through the ages. The only time Palestine was a separate entity was twice under Jewish rule and once under the Crusaders.

Toynbee : But what about private property?

Herzog : For the private property that was taken through the war we have promised and are ready to give full compensation. This has been promised time and again at the United Nations and in this respect I can speak officially. But, Professor, let us come back to the question of the historical connection to which you referred. You are quoted as saying that the Jewish people have no historical right to Israel. May I produce some facts? For one, the continuity of Jewish residence in the land of Israel never ceased at any time in history, and I can quote you records on that century after century. Secondly, the return to Israel has been central to our religious fate – in our prayers, in our festivals and in every aspect of our national aspirations. Thirdly, the international community has recognized the validity of that right through the Balfour Declaration, the League of Nations, the United Nations. Fourthly, even the Arabs in the beginning did. There is a message from Emir Feisal to Dr Weizmann. He headed the Arab delegation to the Peace Conference in Versailles, and there was an agreement between them, and another letter on that agreement in which Emir Feisal writes that he 'welcomes the Jews home'.

Toynbee : Yes, I was there.

Herzog : So I hope that I have not misquoted. At least there is very clear testimony of that, so you cannot put it into the category of a title that became obsolescent in AD 132. There has been a continuous link and aspiration towards Israel century after century. Some of our greatest religious thought and works were produced there : the Mishnah, the Jerusalem Talmud, the Midrash, the Targum, right down to the Shul-han Arukh, which is the basic code of Jewish law. All these were pro-duced in century after century of continuous residence there, and time and again our people hoped to achieve independence. In 1917 a new motive began the momentum towards Israel, but it was there all the time. You speak of the first settlement being in 1881. I can show you docu-ments of Jewish settlements and towns in Palestine of those days from the tenth century.

Toynbee : The sixteenth century.

Herzog : Even earlier : Saadiah Gaon, Benjamin of Tudela in the twelfth century ; Maimonides, Judah Halevi in the twelfth century ; Nachma-nides early in the thirteenth century – continuous residence. Rabbi Estori Ha-Parhi, author of *Kaftor va-Ferah,* shows continuous resid-ence all the time, and the whole motive of our life was linked up with it. We feel that the present revival of the Third Commonwealth in Israel is a vindication of immortal prophecy. We have traversed the Valley of Death, and now, under the grace of Providence, we have come to fulfilment. That is how we see our history. You feel we are a fossil that went off somewhere and sort of fell into the skating rink, in Montreal terms. We didn't. We remained vital and alive and creative. And may I, Sir, at this stage express some surprise that in your book you do not refer at all to that line of Jewish creativity – to which Einstein also belongs.

Toynbee : The Ambassador raised two points : one about the Jewish claim or title to Palestine, and the other about the word 'fossil' that I have used, not only about the Jews but about quite a number of different people, for instance the Parsees and various Christian sects, and to some extent the Greeks.

Herzog : You do differentiate between fossilism and archaism. The Parsees and we are in the fossil category, as archaic you have the Greeks, the Turks, the Norwegians and the Irish. I am not going to deal with the Irish problem, as I have a feeling they will be able to look after themselves.

Toynbee : I think the Israelis can too. Now back to this question of Jewish title. Now what is remarkable about the Jews was, I suppose, mainly the Jewish community, which exists today, as the Ambassador says, and the fact that they did not lose their homeland. In this way they were exceptional among the people who were uprooted and deported by the Assyrians and Babylonians in the eighth, seventh and sixth centuries BC. The Kingdom of Israel did not, like the Kingdom of Judah, manage to maintain its corporate identity in exile. As we know, the Ten Tribes disappeared – unless the British Israelites are right in saying that the British are one of the lost Ten Tribes, and I do not think they are. Today the Kingdom of Israel is represented only by a few hundred Samaritans, some in Jordan, and some in the present State of Israel ; and all the other peoples of Syria, contemporaries of Judah and Israel, have completely disappeared, whereas the Jews have kept their own identity. They have kept it through the memory of Palestine. I mentioned just now that I think the Jews of today and tomorrow are going to be like the Palestinian Arab refugees because they, the refugees, are in just this state of mind in which the Jews were immediately after the exile by Nebuchadnezzar. Palestine seems to play some magic on people's minds ; once they have lived in it, as the Arabs have more recently than the majority of the Jews, their emotions can never let go of that land. But, at any rate, what about this claim? I would say that if one is that historically minded and emotionally related to a country, one has a certain claim to have the freedom of that country, but on the one condition that one does not carry one's state to a point where it is going to cause hardship, wrong and injustice to the existing inhabitants of the country. This appears in all forms of law, and there is a statute of limitations, which, for the sake of producing the minimum amount of hardship and suffering, provides that a legal claim does expire after such and such a time. Now if we take AD 135 as the time when, except in parts of Galilee, the solid Jewish population in Palestine was uprooted by action of the Romans – and I don't have to refer to the Emperor Hadrian fortunately – if we take that date and say that the statute of limitations does not apply even to people who lost their homes in 1835, then what happens in Montreal? The Algonquins had it only three or four hundred years ago – is that to go back to them? It is much less than AD 135. Has England to go back to the Welsh? It would cause much hardship to deport all the British from England and turn them into refugees. Now here I come to the Balfour Declaration. I mentioned just now that as a young man I was working for the British Government during World War One. The Turkish Empire included Palestine and so I had inside knowledge of what happened at that time. I am critical of the Balfour Declaration and I am still more critical of the conduct of the British Mandate in the next thirty years, because I think we never took a line or made up our mind one way or the other, and that was extremely hard on both the Jews and the Arabs. But anyway, the Balfour Declaration really is central to this point of title. It was a short document. I don't remember it by heart so I don't remember the exact wording, two sentences really : the first is that Britain undertakes to uphold and support – something like that – a Jewish national home in Palestine ; the second clause provided that nothing is done to harm the interests of the existing inhabitants of the country, which at the time of the Declaration in 1917 were more than ninety per cent Arab. I blame the Balfour Declaration because the word 'home' was vague. But it was made very clear (as I know directly from seeing the documents at the time, having been a temporary official in the British Foreign Office) and accepted by Dr Weizmann at the time that 'home' did not mean 'state', because if home meant state then the first clause of the Balfour Declaration would have been incompatible with the second clause. So it was an equal obligation of equal power and validity incumbent on the British government that made the declaration that no harm should be done to the rights and interests of the existing inhabitants of the country. I do think – as anybody would think – that the Jews had a claim to a national home, but I also think that that national home has to exist without caus-ing harm to the existing inhabitants of the country (now 900,000 Arab refugees) and that it should not take the form of an exclusively Jewish state. It might have taken the form of a Palestinian state that included both Jews and Arabs on a footing of equality. That was a theoretical possibility. But once the country was open to Jewish immigration on terms decided not by the existing population themselves but by the British Government, the situation was eventually going to get out of hand. It is true that I can think of régimes and peoples in Palestine since AD 135 who have tolerated and recognized the rights of Jews to live in Palestine. There have always been pious Jews in Jerusalem. Jews study-ing the law in this most sacred place of all to Jews in the world. The Turkish régime tolerated that. I don't know what the Crusaders did. But throughout history on the whole that has been so. And the national home was to be an enlargement of that study of the law by the 50,000 Jews in Jerusalem at that time and the 12,000 agricultural settlers, I think, in 1917. That was rather an old-fashioned form of the Jewish national home. The intention, I think, of the Zionist movement as led by Dr Weizmann and of the British Government as represented by Mr Bal-four, was to broaden the basis and to modernize the Jewish national home by allowing more immigration, letting the Jews, as of right, but in limited numbers, settle in Palestine : limited numbers because of this other obligation undertaken not to harm the interests of the existing inhabitants of the country to have a university, to have all the apparatus of modern civilization. Now I blame the Balfour Declaration in this sense. I think a lawyer could prove that the two obligations undertaken in it were incompatible, but perhaps it is only hindsight. Perhaps you cannot blame the British Government too much for not having foreseen this at the moment. Both communities were going to interpret this in ways that were incompatible with each other. Palestine was meant to enter the so-called A-class of territories that were to be prepared for self-government and complete sovereign independence, and the Arabs, numbering more than ninety per cent, naturally thought that when Palestine became independent it would be an Arab state with a Jewish minority. Some of the Jews, and there was much controversy among Zionists over this, interpreted this 'national home' as merely a half-way house towards a Jewish state. Some of them, I am afraid, even said that this meant 'we were going to use this as a lever to having a Jewish state in the end.' Very human, but, anyway, I think that the Balfour Declaration was right in putting this limitation. Without detriment to the ninety per cent of the Arab population, you could not have a Jewish home, certainly not a political one. I think those were the conditions accepted by the Zionist Organization at the time as laid down by the British, which gave the Jews something of their hearts' desire and had, on paper, safeguarded the interests of the existing inhabitants of the country, which on all grounds of law and morality one should do.

Herzog : I would like to answer a few of your remarks on the statute of limitations, which have certain legal connotations ; they also have in this context a connotation in history. I would like to quote you, Professor. In your study you say 'the Jews are living on as a peculiar people long after the Phoenicians and Philistines lost their identity like all the nations. The ancient Syriac neighbours of Israel had fallen into the melting-pot and been reminted in the fullness of time with new images and super-scriptions, while Israel has proved impervious to this alchemy formed by history in the crucible of universal states and universal churches and wanderings of the nations.' This is an eloquent description, if I may say so, of Jewish survival. The statute of limitations was not recognized by history. We are the only people today in the Middle East speaking the same language, practising the same religious faith, living in the same category of aspiration and spiritual continuity as our forefathers thousands of years ago and those who were exiled from there. There is nobody else from AD 132 in that category or in that continuity.

Toynbee : In 1917 ninety per cent of the population of Palestine was not Jewish. That is the work of history *de facto.* Another work of history *de facto* is the continuous memory of the Jews for Palestine and for their return.

Herzog : I appreciate that.

On the question of historical association you have recognized, Professor, that there was a continuous Jewish residence in the Land of Israel, and the return became the goal of the national life. There is also the fact that down the ages the Arabs never had Palestine as a separate political entity. It was controlled from the remote caliphates for a number of centuries. It passed from hand to hand – thirteen conquests down the ages.

As the Middle East came to life in terms of the development of new nations – a process beginning after World War One and which has continued to our time – the international consciousness recognized that the Arab peoples deserve nationhood and deserve independence, deserve to achieve independence from the torpor of centuries and conquests, and eight Arab states came into being, covering an area close to two million square miles. They've achieved independence of status without precedent even in the 'Golden' days of the caliphate.

Within that category of the Middle East it was recognized that the Jewish people, having longed and lived for its return, should establish itself once again in independence and freedom in the Land of Israel. Now you have an interpretation, Sir, of the Balfour Declaration, based on your association and work at the time with the British Government. But surely you will acknowledge, that Lord Balfour himself, Lloyd George, the Prime Minister of the Government, Winston Churchill surely knew what was meant by the Balfour Declaration, and they have clearly stated so over the years. And indeed Emir Feisal, whom you met at the Peace Conference, also recognized implicitly this whole approach. In any event, those responsible for the Balfour Declaration have clearly defined its purpose. There is talk there of religious and civil rights of other inhabitants, and on that there has never been any question. But the basic issue here is that the Arab peoples, having achieved a patrimony over eight countries in independence, millions of square miles, should not begrudge the Jewish people a state of 8,000 square miles, which can work in peace and cooperation with them.

Originally, the Mandate related to both Palestine and Transjordan. In 1921 four-fifths was cut off and Jordan became independent as the Emirate of Transjordan. So you had a further attempt to satisfy the Arab approach. So over the years the situation developed as it did. Now, if you look at it today, we hold neither land nor resource, water or any other resource, that our Arab neighbours need for survival or advancement. The only blessing can come from cooperation – not only for us, also for them. But history has set certain principles in the approach to the whole problem of the Middle East.

Through the ages we have prayed and believed that our restoration would come, that independence would be restored, that within that context of independence we could again make our contribution to mankind. This has taken place in our time. We believe that there are among the Arab circles, people who subconsciously appreciate this, but they have to be encouraged.

Toynbee : The fact that those eight Arab countries are now happily independent does not affect the fate of those Arabs who lived in what is now Israel, because that is not part of the Arab countries, and the fact that other Arabs have their independence and can make their own future does not make the former Arab inhabitants of what is now Israel any less refugees and expatriates than they are at the moment.

On the Balfour Declaration I must say explicitly that I know that it was clearly understood at the time that the national home was not intended to be a Jewish national state, and this was clearly stated to the Zionist Organization by the British Government at the time that the Balfour Declaration was issued. The declaration was accepted on those terms, and the Mandate was given by the League of Nations to Britain on those terms. I think Britain made an awful mess of the administration of the Mandate. We had taken on something perhaps beyond the capacity of any country to take on. Never mind. The Jews could not have made the mistake at the time of believing that the Balfour Declaration promised them a Jewish State.

Herzog : But it is a fact, Professor. Again I say that I've read the interpretations given by those responsible for the Balfour Declaration, the consensus of world opinion at the time and the unfolding years after that ; certainly you will agree that the United Nations took a decision in November 1947 that there was to be a Jewish State in Palestine

Toynbee : It also took a decision that the Arab refugees were to be returned to Israel.

Herzog : No, they did not take a decision that the refugees have to be returned to Israel. You are mistaken in this, Professor. The General Assembly of the United Nations in 1948 established the Palestine Conciliation Commission to deal with the whole complex of problems that had arisen between Israel and the Arab states. They were to serve as mediators, and the parties were asked in the Resolution to negotiate directly and find a solution to all these problems. Within the context of this Resolution the refugee problem is referred to and the Commission was supposed to study the possibilities either of repatriation or of compensation, but all this within the general context of a peace settlement. The Resolution talks of the return of refugees as soon as practicable and it also talks of those refugees who wish to live in peace. This resolution has been dead since 1948. It died because the Arabs have never announced that they will live in peace with Israel. They refused to negotiate directly and the Palestine Conciliation Commission in fact has been defunct for many years now. And what is our position on this? The Arab refugee problem is one of a whole complex of refugee problems. I believe that since 1940 some forty million people have been uprooted across the world : Korea, Vietnam, Germany, Finland. Nearly all of these problems either have been solved or are approaching a solution. In no case has a solution been through repatriation, but rather through absorption. And what have we said? We have said we were prepared to pay full compensation ; we have said we were prepared to consider a limited repatriation within the framework of the reunion of families. But the problem will never move unless the Arab governments are prepared to cooperate in alleviating the sufferings of the refugees. And the fact is – our figures, by the way, of refugees are about 550,000 – that some 160,000 have been absorbed. This is a unique problem. There is no economic difficulty. Money is being voted by the United Nations, and the United States Government promised backing for an international loan. There is no social problem because they are living among their people. The Arab living today in Transjordan is not a Pole living in Britain. He is living in his own surroundings, in an environment of rising Arab nationalism, religious, cultural identity of background and psychology. The problem will never be solved until the Arab governments are prepared to cooperate in a humanitarian solution. I notice, Professor, that you yourself have criticized the Arab governments : you have said very rightly, in talking of suffering in the first part of our conversation, why don't they take them out of this parasitic existence? Why don't they set them up in farms, villages and homes? Why keep them as a political weapon? You who scan history over thousands of years, do you have any other case or precedent of holding hundreds of thousands of people as political hostages in camps – parasitic, no future, quenching every sense of creativeness in them – so that they can be ready as a political pawn for some ultimate programme to exterminate Israel, God forbid. Is that a moral approach? Have you read the Secretary-General's report of last year? He views the solution in terms of economic integration within the area. Of course we will play our part in it. We are very upset at this continuing humanitarian problem on our hands, but it can be solved. In Israel now there are ten per cent Arabs (200,000). They enjoy every right with their fellow-citizens. But you want us to take back people who have been nurtured on hate for thirteen years on the basis of a Resolution of 1948 talking of those wishing to live in peace. But these have been nurtured on hate, vengeance and destruction, and if we take them back they can rip us apart. Take them out of a totally Arab environment where they live, where they can create economically, socially and religiously and bring them in to be a minority in the Jewish state – this will help the problem of the Middle East? There is money, there is land, there is water. All that is needed is part of that humanitarian benevolence and a sense of duty to which you have referred.

Professor Toynbee, in 1948 the war of aggression was unleashed. It created two refugee problems : one related to some 550,000 Arabs ; the other related to some 400,000 Jews and 70,000 Arabs. We have settled the second problem. We have absorbed over 400,000 Jews from Arab countries who were there of longer standing than the same Arabs in Palestine. We have settled them ; we have taken them in as brothers. We have settled 70,000 Arab refugees in the country. The only Arab refugees who have been struck off the UNRWA rolls are those whom we have taken into our economy. The other problem has not moved, not because there is no money or because there is no possibility, but purely because the humanitarian problem is being put into a context of animosity and hatred. And the feelings of these poor people, their future, their very life is being sacrificed for what? For some demagogic ambition to control and rule the Middle East. Every international body has recognized this, every report has recommended a movement in the direction of economic integration, of broadening economic possibilities. We will play our part. There is no question of that. We long to see the problem solved as you do. But it will not be solved by formulas ; it will not be solved within the context that they refuse to talk to us ; it will not be solved if the refugees are prepared to destroy us. Only last month, Professor Toynbee, a representative of the Arab refugees appeared at the United Nations. What did he speak about? The destruction of Israel, the extermination of Israel. He was probably told to do so by certain governments. He said so. So you tell us now that in 1948 they talked of coming back in peace. Now to take them back after thirteen years, after he says plainly he wants to destroy us. Why not, indeed! Shall we let them come in and rip us apart? Please commit suicide so that the Arab armies won't have to overwhelm you from without. That, Sir, I think, in the scan of history, you will find no nation prepared to do, and since you said earlier that in certain respects we belong to the category of all other nations in our behaviour, in this respect, too, we will not commit suicide.

Toynbee : I think there are two points : one is repatriation and the other is using the refugees as pawns. There is an inconsistency in the Israeli stand. Your claim for Jewish repatriation into Palestine goes back as far as AD 135, though there has been no solid Jewish population in Palestine, though I agree that there have always been Jews in Palestine as a small minority. And since 64 or 63 BC there has not been a Jewish state in Palestine. Its claim for repatriation now is in terms of the Balfour Declaration for a Jewish national home, not a state, but at the same time you deny to the Arabs who were forced out of Palestine as recently as 1948 the very thing you claim as the central claim of the Jewish people. That is inconsistent. Think about it.

Now as regards using the refugees as pawns, I have had the opportunity of talking to representatives of the Arab states within the last few years, and, by the way, I think the Zionist Organization and the Israel Government are rather living in a glass house about using the refugees as pawns. I think some pretty telling comparisons could be made between the use of Jewish refugees as pawns and of Arab refugees as pawns. I think both the Zionists and the Arab states have been guilty of this, and it is a disgusting thing to do. When I talked, as I have had opportunities of talking, to the Arab states, I have pointed out to them the policy of West Germany since the war. As you know I am not partial to Nazis, but I have pointed out that the West German Government since the war has been more wise as well as more humane – it is more important to be humane than to be wise. The West German Government received some nine million refugees from East Germany and their territories, which were formerly German before the war and are now part of Poland and the Soviet Union. The West German Government, as far as I know, has not relinquished its claim to one inch of the territories that belonged to Germany. I am not going to question whether the German aim is to recover these territories and whether this is good or bad. That is not the point here, but the point is that the West Germans have separated – and in this I think they were thoroughly right – the question of claims to territory from which the refugees came and what to do about the refugees meanwhile. It is to West Germany's great credit that her heart and her head have taken the line of absorbing the refugees without renouncing claims for these refugees' territory, absorbing them into her own life and into her own industry, and that is one of the reasons why Western Germany is so prosperous and powerful now. She has given these refugees a chance at happiness. And her voice is powerful among the nations because of that, and I have said to the Arabs : why don't you do that? You don't have to relinquish the Palestine Arab claim to Arab Palestine, you can press it later. If you absorb them into your industry you will have a stronger claim. I am sorry they didn't take this line. I think it is silly of them, but I am much more concerned with the humanitarian side. But I think that Israel is living in a glass house by drawing attention to this particular side of its policy because I think of the time, immediately after the end of World War Two, Jewish refugees were directed for political and not for humanitarian reasons to Palestine, when they could have had immediate homes and a much better future, say in Australia or on the North American continent. But I think politics were played with the Jewish refugees just as they are being played now with the Arab refugees. I condemn both.

Herzog : On this question of politics and refugees, I see criticism of the attitude of the various governments after World War Two, that they had no room for our refugees. I believe you yourself mentioned it in some context that they did not open their gates to refugees, but I must – and this I do on the basis of personal knowledge – reject emphatically any suggestion that they were used as political pawns. The fact is that tens of thousands came to other countries : the United States, Canada, across the world. Those who came to Israel came because they sought independence and freedom and restoration, and they felt they could only overcome their experiences at the hands of the Nazis in a life of creativity with their own people. You have not referred to the fact, Sir, that we have taken in one million refugees. These include over 400,000 refugees from Arab lands. There was an exchange of populations – very much like the exchange between the Turks and the Greeks after World War One ; we have taken in over 400,000 Jewish refugees and absorbed economically over 70,000 Arab refugees. You cannot turn back the clock of history. You cannot feed refugees with hatred year after year and then expect Israel to take them in to destroy us from within. But I would suggest, Sir, if I may in this respect, that in view of the deep humanitarian interest you take in this problem – and I see from the suggestion you have made to Arab leaders, and I fully understand your motive, at least this form of parasitic existence, basic debasement of humanity should cease ; rights are one thing, but also life as it is lived is another – I would suggest that whenever you are free you come to visit Israel so that we can show you on the spot how we have absorbed them, both Jewish refugees and over 70,000 Arab refugees. When you are there and have seen the area and have gotten a sense of the region and what we have done with it, when you see the vast area of the Middle East, and this is part of it, and the endless opportunities to solve the problems in the neighbouring countries, I would like very much then to hear your judgement.

I suggest that, as time is running short, we go on to the famous fossil thing, as I am sure the audience would like to hear about it. As you have said, Professor, the title 'fossil' has become parpart of the national vocabulary since you used it in the context you did and as I understand from reading your works in the past few days – and nights, I might add. There are fossils and also people in the archaic sense. We seem to be in both. We are fossils with the Parsees of India and archaic with the Norwegians, the Greeks, the Turks and the Irish. Well, at least in the archaic angle I have associations since childhood with Ireland, but as far as the Parsees are concerned I am afraid I have no acquaintance with them.

Toynbee : They were a very interesting people.

Herzog : I am not a historian, but your thesis has been challenged by historians of great eminence and writers. There is quite a vocabulary of reply to the 'Toynbee Thesis' or the 'Toynbee Heresy'.

Toynbee : Don't I know it! Aubrey Eban calls it the 'Toynbee Heresy'.

Herzog : And there is also the 'Professor and the Fossil', and others. As a diplomat representing my country, and my experience in this field is in contemporary times, I have not studied history as deeply as you have. I would ask you in all objectivity as a historian : our concept of our life down the ages – I could sum it up in a verse from the Psalms, *'Lo amut ki ehyeh va'asapper maasey yah,'* 'I shall not die but I shall live!' A fossil does not die, but he also does not live. Here we part ways. And as we live, and through our survival down the ages we see the hand of Providence, we have the sense of survival under Providence and we move ahead as we pray for spiritual fulfilment. Here lies the basic difference between us. You say : 'You do not die (why is not clear) but you do not live. No continuity in terms of creative life and thought. You sort of slipped out of the stream of civilization to some remote island and got stuck there. Now and then your voice is heard as it shrieks at the passing ships.' We say : No, we have been in the stream. We have been in the stream in a distinctive sense : in our survival, in our prayers and in our hope, in our attachment to our land and in our belief in the fulfilment of immortal prophecy. But that is an issue and I am not a historian. As I say, others are debating this with you. But I would ask you, as a modern Israeli representing my country and one who has seen the country coming to life and independence, from the academic historical analysis point of view, as you scan the pages of history, is there no significance in the following facts, which cannot be denied :

Number 1 : Of all the ancient peoples of the Middle East, we are the only one living in continuity today in the Middle East, speaking the same language, practising the same religious faith.

Toynbee : With the Parsees.

Herzog : Rabbi Johanan Ben Zakkai, to whom you devote much attention, he and Rabbi Akiva and Bar Kokhba – if they were to come to life and could live with us – would not find a dichotomy that snapped them asunder. There is a continuity of experience.

Number 2 : After this passage through the Valley of Death down the ages – and you yourself have described in your book the corpses and ashes of the Diaspora – we have come to life in our time. We have come to life without rancour, despite all the past, between us and our Arab neighbours. I can assure you that you will see this if you come to Israel. There is no rancour, there is no hatred. There is grief, but there is a hope for peace every day, and there is a confidence that it will come. Nor is there rancour to nations across the world. This very vitality of life, of survival without rancour, this too, I would submit, has a certain significance in terms of historical analysis.

Number 3 : After these thousands of years we have assembled people from seventy lands. The Yemenites from the remote deserts of the Yemen, who were cut off from the main stream of civilization for over 2,000 years, Jews from Morocco, Jews from East and Western Europe's Nazi death camps, Jews from the remote hinterlands of India have all come together, and they have founded a common nation spontaneously.

Has that link no vitality? Was that a fossil? Is that how a fossil reacts? All these particles of the fossil have come together. We feel as one.

Finally, the question of democracy. After all this experience we are the only viable democracy in terms of the Israel-Arab complex in the area. The fact is that today many new nations from Africa and Asia look to us for guidance and cooperation, and they find in our experiment and in our enterprises something that draws them. So we do have a message for the world and not, Sir, as you suggest, that our message ceased some 2,300 years ago. What I am trying to say is very vividly expressed by Professor Lewis Mumford in *Conduct of Life*. He says : 'The binding force of an ethical force based on purpose has been dramatically confirmed in the history of the Jews. Its practical consummation in our time perhaps merits our special note.' We believe that our survival is an index of the supremacy of spiritual over material value. We believe in all humility and thanks to a merciful Providence that it has a relevance to the broad experience of mankind today. I would ask you, Sir, in all respect, if you don't think all these elements have any basis on which you could possibly reconsider your concept of us as a fossil, non-creative, but which suddenly fell out – neither dead nor alive these past 2,000 years?

Toynbee : It is rather a curious point about this fossil. I have never used it of the Jewish people alone. I have always used it of a whole class of peoples. It is rather an academic point. Sorry to inflict my theory of history. I tried to map out a kind of picture of civilization, and I found there were several civilizations or series of civilizations, some of which died out perhaps several thousand years ago ; others are alive today. But I did find that of all the civilizations that died out quite a long time ago were – with exceptional communities such as the Jews, the Parsees, one branch of the Buddhists and certain rather obscure Christian sects – civilizations that had become extinct not in the sense of human beings but had become absorbed into other civilizations, races, peoples and so on. The Ten Tribes of Israel are the classic example. There are many others of course. What I wanted to express by the word 'fossil' was that these exceptional communities had survived from a previous age, just as fossils are a surviving record of forms of life that existed in a preceding age and have survived by encasing themselves for many centuries on end. I think this does apply to the Jews as well as to the Parsees and some of the Christian Diasporas as well. They have encased themselves in a very rigid religious organization, particularly in keeping a very minute system of laws, but also in social customs. Those were the two crude conceptions that I wanted to convey by the word fossil. Now none of the other people I labelled as fossils have ever complained. They found it rather complimentary. The only complaints I have had have been from Jews, and they have complained as though I had stuck the Jews with this label alone and not the other people. I do not know why this is particularly so. I think a fossil is a label, and, as all labels are imperfect, so is this.

It is quite true that it does not convey the idea that communities surviving from previous civilizations are after all still alive because human beings of their survival are still alive. I have a longish section about this word fossil in a forthcoming volume of reconsideration and second thoughts and a great deal about Jewish history. I said if we could take some word for a living creature – in South Africa they found an antediluvian fish called the coelacanthes, I would substitute the word coelacanthes for fossil – would that mean any more to people I have named fossils? It would not, and, after all, the coelacanthes is a very archaic form of life and the present-day Jews are not archaic and are in the full stream of life. But is it not true that from the time of the Romans, from the time of Philo of Alexandria, or at the time when the Christian Acts of the Apostles were written, we see the position of the Jewish communities in the Greek and Roman world as they are today in the Western world? They were living there very much in the stream and common life of that civilization. Under the shock of the Roman wars I do think that the Jewish communities withdrew into a kind of shell, gave up writing and speaking Greek and went back to Hebrew, or rather Aramaic, and for many centuries they remained encased partly by their own will, partly by the bad treatment they received from Christians, especially the Western Christians. It is only since the Napoleonic wars you can say, except in some very early European countries like Holland in the sixteenth and seventeenth centuries, that the doors were opened to the Jews and they were brought back into the full stream of life. The tragic point about this again is, on both the Jewish side as well as on the gentile side, there have been certain reservations about forming a single community. I suppose Jews feel that the gentiles have not really entirely received them into their community, and the gentiles feel that the Jews have not entirely come into the gentile community. The comparison with the situation, say, before 1800 and the Jews in present times is that the latter have, of course, become part of the present stream of life and have played this enormous part in it.

Herzog : You mean we have become defossilized, Sir?

Toynbee : Israel has become defossilized as you can defrost a car. I have not found another word to express what I mean. This is a particular category of communities and, from the scientific and sociological point of view, it needed a name. Find me another name and I will use it. That is all I can say really. It is no insult.

Herzog : As far as I have read in this category of fossils I do think, without wishing in any way to offend the Parsees in India, that if you think of Jewish civilization in terms of its impact on world civilization down the ages, the terms of its creativity – and, Sir, you will pardon me if I observe that in your work you do not mention any creative Jewish activity since about 2,300 years ago, actually since Rabbi Johanan Ben Zakkai. You do not mention the academies of learning in Palestine : in Jerusalem, Safad ; learning in mysticism, Mishnah, Talmud, Jerusalem Talmud, Babylonian Talmud, Targum, Masorah, poetry, the first Paytanim, who laid the basis for modern Hebrew poetry, right down the ages, and Hasidism and the whole movement of a living body of people. These are not mentioned by you. And then the interaction of this influence in terms of relationship with the nations of the world and, after all, you yourself admit that Christianity and Islam owe something to Judaism. So I think that the comparison with the Parsees is not a good one, and we are very happy that you have agreed today that the fossil has become defossilized, and the problem is not so much now finding an alternative term for the fossil, but to find a term for a new creature that has been defossilized.

Toynbee : Remember, I said with some reservations. I am afraid that there are reservations on the Jewish side, as well as on the gentile side, and these are serious, and one has to remember them.

Herzog : Do you accept that the considerations of vitality I mentioned earlier relate to Israel's return and restoration? Have they anything to do with the defossilization? Are they signs for you, historically speaking, of vitality?

Toynbee : The Western gentile races invented nationalism, which I strongly dislike, and the Jews caught this disease from the gentiles, which is very unfortunate.

Herzog : Well, it has been a long, long disease with us and many physicians have tried to cure us down the ages, but we have refused to be cured. I know that you are opposed to the modern state. There are many people also in Israel who feel we must move towards more world cooperation without giving up independence. That is a different matter. What I am saying is : the attributes that have been shown now by the people in Israel - and I am not talking of the state in the formal sense - the attributes of survival and vitality of democracy and lack of rancour, of a sense of peace and cooperation with the new nations of the world after 2,000 years of exile - do you think historically this has some significance?

Toynbee : But I have never denied that the Jews have always been alive. I have criticized some forms of vitality that Israel has taken, but I never denied their vitality. Nearly all of us in this room are Westerners, whether Jews or Christians, and we have the natural Western egocentrism and therefore, of course, the Jews have remained in the West, and because Christianity is derived from Judaism, the Jews loom large. If you went to Southern and Eastern Asia, the picture changes, and the Parsees, who have also been defossilized just about contemporary with the Jews as a result of the reorganization of India, will play an important part in the history, which may surprise you, because India has been playing an important part and they are to India what the Jews are to the Western world.

Herzog : I have no objection at all, Sir.

Toynbee : Well, don't mind being compared with them.

Herzog : Well, I would say this, that I have, as an amateur historian, some concept of approach and I think that analogy can be very sensitive and a very complex business. But, as I say, historians debate that with you. If I may say in conclusion, just at this point, that I do hope, Sir, before you pass another judgement, before your new book comes out, if possible, that you visit Israel and weigh the process of defossilization in your context and see this vitality and compare it on historic span, and then let us have your conclusion. I hope you will be able to come, and I am sure our people would be very happy to show you the country and to answer any questions ; and we have no objection at all if you visit neighbouring countries and have a broad Middle Eastern view.

Toynbee : Thank you, of course. I tell you, there is not enough morality if it has come back to that.

Herzog : On the morality issue, you yourself have agreed that we are like other peoples, and that again can be looked into when you visit Israel.

Toynbee : Thank you very much, Mr Ambassador.

The Meaning of Israel's Resurgence

From an Address to Representatives of Religious Kibbutzim on the Occasion of Israel's Twentieth Anniversary, 4 June 1968

I have no intention on this occasion to try to analyse all the progress that has been made during the past twenty years in various fields – political, economic, social and spiritual. For all or most of us have been living here and each of us has experienced these years of redemption in his own way and according to his own understanding. All I want to do is to draw attention to a few basic features in the development of Israel during these twenty years in the perspective of history, including, of course, Jewish history.

Let me start with a talk I had about three months ago with Professor Raymond Aron, who is known at one and the same time as economist, sociologist, political commentator and thinker – especially in the field of the philosophy of history. He is one of those border-line Jews, one of those multitudes all over the world who were shocked by the Six Day War and the sudden isolation they felt despite their conscious attempt to divorce themselves from Jewish tradition and Jewish history. They were in the process of emerging into the broad channels of world history, outside the distinctive bounds of the House of Israel, and suddenly they were gripped by that experience of the Six Day War, which shocked them to the depths of their souls without their being able to define what had happened to them. And they were drawn to the lodestone of reunified Jerusalem in the search for their own true selves.

I mention Aron because he is an example of a man with a world-ranging intellect, a particularly penetrating mind, one who thinks deeply and scrutinizes the ways of men and peoples. I could give you a list of scores, perhaps hundreds, like him all over the world – this wandering, forgotten tribe of assimilated Jews, perhaps the last remnants of the assimilation that started about a century and a half ago in Germany and Eastern Europe. I believe that now, in the winding course of history, these people have come to a crossroads.

He came into my office after talking to many people all over the country.

'I am oppressed by one fundamental question,' he said. 'It refers not to your policies today, or even during the past twenty years, but to the fundamental problem of the State of Israel's right to exist. In other words, is it not true that the traditional Jewish belief in the Return to Zion – which you believe is realized in the establishment of the State of

75 - 101

Israel – and the expression of that faith in the twentieth century, namely the state itself, are in flagrant opposition to the twentieth-century concepts as they apply to the Arab peoples, or, more accurately, the Palestinian people ? For no matter how you explain the War of Independence, the 1946–8 period and the three wars that have taken place since, and whether the Arabs left because they ran away or because you expelled them, it remains a fact that in 1913 there were 600,000 Arabs and 60,000 Jews here. In other words, before the Balfour Declaration, during the last period of Turkish rule in the area called Palestine, the southernmost province of the Syrian régime that ruled in Damascus – under Turkish suzerainty of course – there were only ten per cent Jews as against ninety per cent non-Jews. Surely this involves a flagrant contradiction ; it arouses a fundamental moral problem, which is at the root of this complex system of relationships between Israel and the Arabs. And the longer it continues, there perhaps are the possibilities of great achievements and developments, but also of more acute dangers of havoc and destruction, not only in the Middle East, but throughout the continent, in fact from the Atlantic Ocean to the Persian Gulf.'

'You have asked me a very penetrating question,' I replied. 'It might even be called an audacious question, since you are now sitting in Jerusalem, the capital of Israel – but that is your privilege. But if you take it upon yourself to pose questions of this kind, you should not be surprised if you get some penetrating questions in return.'

Actually, I told him I did not know how to answer him. If he had clearly defined himself as a Jew, I should have been glad to reply to him in the age-old communication of all the generations and tried to explain the meaning of the mystery that he had so logically presented. If he had presented himself as a non-Jew, then I might also have had a reply. But the difficulty was that he was an assimilated Jew, that he regarded himself as a Frenchman ; although, in the last analysis, in the moment of truth, he was regarded as a Jew, even though he did not know it.

So I quoted some of the maxims of the sages, who said that although a Jew could deliberately try to leave his people, he would have great difficulty, in the deeper sense, in becoming integrated into any other people. That did not mean that Jews could not live in comparative security. For over 2,000 years, apart from two terrible episodes in human history – the massacres of the Crusader period and the European Holocaust in our days – and perhaps the expulsion from Spain as well, although it did not involve the extermination of our people, it was a fact that most of the Jewish people had lived in relative safety, though in many cases incarcerated in ghettoes. What the sages meant, however, was that inner security and spiritual tranquillity could not be achieved by the Jew through any degree of assimilation that he might attain. These facts had not been understood before. We had lived so long in the grip of illusions, entire communities had believed in false slogans – of which the falseness, foolishness and baselessness had become more acutely obvious in the course of the years – but today I believe that the understanding of this fact is steadily penetrating the soul of the Jew.

However, I told him that I did not regard him in this light. Because of a kind of spiritual schizophrenia, he regarded himself as a representative of France, but France did not accept him as such and never would. That was why I found it difficult to regard him as a representative of twentieth-century France. In that case, he replied, who represents France in the twentieth century ? I said I could enumerate five men who, in their collective thinking, represented France in terms of the twentieth century : the Cardinal of Paris, who represented Catholic France ; François Mauriac, who represented liberal Catholic France ; De Gaulle, who represented and embodied all the concepts of historic France ; Malraux, who represented French culture as such and in its universal character ; and Sartre, who represented agnostic, existentialist France. If all these men, whatever each might say, arrived at any common line of thought on any national or international problem, it might be said that this represented French thinking on the subject.

Now, I continued, what do these five really think about the Israel-Arab problem ? I believed that they all thought that the Arabs had a pretty strong case, as Aron put it. The general contention is that here was a people who, but for the process of Jewish redemption, would undoubtedly have developed into the Palestinian nation on its own land. They would undoubtedly have achieved independence in this country, or they might perhaps have joined up with Transjordan. There might have been a British Mandate for them as in Iraq, or the mandate might have been entrusted to France, but this people would have united and found a common expression. The fact is, however, that this was never a nation – and this is one of the most extraordinary things about the Land of Israel. During a debate we had with the Arabs in the United Nations five years ago, our old friend Ahmad Shukairy, head of the Palestinian Liberation Organization, lectured the Assembly about the Palestinian personality. We wanted to prick the bubble in this forum of the nations, and we asked him : when was there ever a Palestinian people here ? Now, this is really an extraordinary thing. If you read all the histories of the Middle East up to 100 years ago – accounts of the travels of tourists, thinkers, archaeologists and orientalists – you will find that they wrote : I saw the peoples of Kurdistan, I saw the Persians, the religious sects of Iraq (though it was not yet called Iraq) ; I saw the Shi'ites and the Sunnites ; I saw the Turks and the Syrians, the Yemenites, the Egyptians and the Sudanese. But they never saw a Palestinian people. Not only did they never see a Palestinian people but they could not even testify to any tribe in this territory of which it could be said that it was geographically attached to the area in which it was living. In other words, this country was never distinguished by a bond with any other people in the sense of a real, spiritual, geographical, political, national or tribal tie since the Jews were exiled from their land.

But this is not a conclusive argument. It could be argued, as Toynbee and his school did – and this was really Aron's question – that this was perhaps true of the past, but what has the twentieth century decided ? It has decided that a nation living in a particular territory is entitled to independence from any colonialist régime. Such independence has been given today even to islands with a population of twenty or thirty thousand. They all get independence ; why not the Arabs who lived in Palestine ?

I said to Aron : what do these five great Frenchmen actually say ? They say that the Arabs certainly have a right. If the Jews were an ordinary nation, a nation to which the normal historical laws of life and death apply, the Arab claim would be much more weighty than it is ; but they all agree – not only the Cardinal, who is bound by the Pope's statement a year and a half ago that the Jewish people is, after all, a chosen people, but even Sartre, in a book or a brochure he published before the Six Day War, said : I cannot judge the Jewish people by the accepted rules of history ; the Jewish people is something beyond time, and we cannot pass judgement on this dilemma of Israel-Arab relations without taking this into account.

In other words, I continued, as long as the external world agrees that the Jewish people is a unique phenomenon in human history, that its course in history is separate and distinct from all other historical processes, that it is both a stranger and a sojourner at one and the same time – belonging to world civilization and yet distinct from it – that wherever it has gone – whether in agony, in prayer and hope, in tragedy or in creative activity – it has always followed its own way, involved in the paths of history but never swallowed up by them and that this is truly the essence of the Jew, it cannot deny the Jewish claim to the Land of Israel in favour of the twentieth-century claim of the so-called Arab nation, which was allegedly expelled from its land. At most it can argue that the right to independence in this territory is divided.

We now come to a most delicate and fundamental point. In so far as the Jewish character continues to be understood and accepted in terms of twentieth-century concepts, then the other twentieth-century concept, the so-called right of the Arabs to self-determination, cannot prevail over the Jewish claim. This, I believe, is a basic element in any survey of Zionism or of the twenty years of the State of Israel. And here we find a tremendous paradox. It was classic Zionism – in fact, basically, political Zionism – that established the State of Israel, but I believe that it never grasped two fundamental problems. It understood neither the Jewish people nor the Arabs. When you read the speeches of the Zionist leadership in 1917–18 and in the 1920s, you find that they really thought that we would return here along an ordinary twentieth-century road. Scores of peoples had started to get some kind of independence after World War One and we too would win independence here. The world would recognize this independence, and we would become a normal people, liberated from the burden of exile, accepted all over the globe. We held out our hands to an arid territory, crying out for development, and together we would establish a productive human society in the area of the Middle East.

But the facts refuted this theory – I doubt whether any other theory has been refuted in such a short time – and today the facts are there for all to see. What was wrong with the theory ? It was the belief of political Zionism that the idea of a 'people that dwells alone' is an abnormal concept, when actually the concept of 'a people that dwells alone' is the natural concept of the Jewish people. That is why today, twenty years after independence, this one phrase still describes the totality of this tremendous phenomenon, which has startled the whole world. If one asks how this ingathering of the exiles, which no one could have visualized in his wildest dreams, or how the State of Israel has endured such fundamental trials in the field of security, or how it has built up a flourishing economy, or how the unity of the Jewish people has been preserved throughout the Diaspora, in the final analysis one must come back to the idea that this is 'a people that dwells alone'. And not only in order to understand how it has managed to survive, but no less from the point of view of its right to exist, must one invoke this phrase.

Today, in the twentieth year of the State of Israel, after the great miracle of the Six Day War, as we examine our position one year after that war, we see that channels of dialogue have been opened all over the world. What do we see ? We see four channels of dialogue, which merge into each other. First there is the renewed dialogue with the Arab peoples. This is a dialogue that cuts very deep. It is really bound up with the question of right. This is not a political struggle ; in the final analysis it is the question of right that counts. We know the Arabs today much better than we knew them a year ago, for we meet them here and all over the world. The iron curtain of blind, undying hatred has not disappeared, but they are prepared to look us in the face.

There are a number of gradations in a situation of this kind. The Bible tells how Joseph's brethren 'could not speak peaceably unto him' (Genesis 37 : 4). The commentators asked why it was necessary to say this, when we had already been told that they hated him. Rashi explains that this was said to the credit of the brothers : they were not hypocrites ; since they hated him they could not speak to him. I would venture to interpret the story as indicating three different stages. The first stage is envy ; the second is hatred. But we find that even when people hate each other they may continue to talk to each other ; for example, in the period of the Second Temple, opposing groups sat with each other, spoke to each other and ate together, but when they spoke to each other it was 'with swords in their tongues'. The third stage is when a man cannot physically endure the presence of another, cannot even speak peaceably to him. This is the highest degree of hatred.

As the world in general is concerned, we have always been witness to the second degree. In the struggles between nations – Russia, America, China – there has been hatred, but not to the extent that they could not speak peaceably to each other. When it came to the Arabs, on the other hand, one had only to watch them at the United Nations to see that when an Israeli representative passed near them, they could not even bear his presence. This was a kind of undying hatred, which, I believe, was the most disturbing feature of this entire complex. This was no mere struggle over refugees or over frontiers, but a struggle against what they regarded as the intrusion of a foreign body into an area in which it did not belong ; as if, by the very fact of our appearance, we had destroyed the basis of their equanimity for generations to come ; as if this were a force that not only had no right to be there, but was liable, in that it had no such right, to deprive them of *their* right to exist, in the profoundest sense of the term.

Today we speak to the Arabs. We talk with them, examine what they are thinking. But I believe that they are still hampered by one fundamental obstacle : the bond between the Jew and this country. It is not easy to explain this point to the Arabs. After all, it is only a few years since the Jews themselves began to grasp the nature of this bond. When access was opened to the Western Wall, when Jerusalem was reunified, we saw with our own eyes how a new kind of communication emerged among the Jews the world over. Assimilated aristocrats and millionaires, children of mixed marriages, came to that stone wall and shed tears, without rhyme or reason.

Even our old friend Toynbee seemed to have changed when I met him three months ago during a visit to London. 'What have you to say now ?' I asked him.

He replied : 'What can you do ? You can adopt a mystical approach ; I have to find a logical explanation.' But he continued : 'When I heard your soldiers at the Western Wall on the radio, I began to grasp the nature of your bonds with this city of Jerusalem and this country.' I asked him : 'How did you understand ? After all, the BBC broadcast the event in Hebrew ; the soldiers didn't speak English. How could you understand them ?'

'In such things, I have historical antennae,' he replied. 'I heard the voices and I understood.'

He spoke more or less in the same terms as Raymond Aron. There was a people here, and it fled or was driven out. He asked me if the Vikings, who came to England 1,000 years ago, or the Gonquil Indians, who were driven out of Montreal 300 years ago, should come along and say : 'Montreal is ours,' whether I would expect the world to support them.

I replied : 'As a man of science, you know that whenever there is a single exception to the rule, one obvious and glaring exception, you cannot apply the rule to that exception. You would be perfectly right if the Vikings actually claimed England and the Indians claimed Montreal, in fact the whole of the United States. But this is not actually so.

There is only one such phenomenon in history, and you cannot argue about this phenomenon on the hypothesis that the whole world might be plunged into a contradiction. There is only one place where, in this respect, there appears to be a contradiction that you cannot grasp.'

But the debate continues, and I believe that among the Arabs, on the same level of dialogue, there is a tremendous soulsearching. They are trying to understand what the State of Israel means. In this connection it is interesting that, during the past year, Jerusalem has become a focal point for the Arabs. They had always regarded Jerusalem as an Islamic centre ; today it has become an Arab centre, as if its loss has irreparably degraded the Arab world and there can be no remedy for the degradation unless they regain the city. Anyone who talks to the Arabs finds this most remarkable development. They speak of Jerusalem and there are tears in their eyes. They say to each other : now we understand the Jews, who cried out for twenty years for freedom of access to Jerusalem ; now, for the first time, when we are cut off from the city, we can understand them. This is a most remarkable thing. What is it all about, after all ? A few mosques and some other buildings – and this has shaken the world of Islam from Morocco to Indonesia !

I believe that, from the political point of view, we may expect that the central struggle will be about Jerusalem, and it is only beginning to develop. But the Arabs have begun to understand, for the first time in twenty years, that this is not just some nation of homeless, persecuted refugees that has won a foothold here, some nomadic tribe spewed out by Western civilization, which, for lack of an alternative, has found a refuge in Palestine. They are beginning to wonder whether, after all, it is not something much deeper. I believe that the prospects of peace or war depend on this Arab perplexity.

In the final analysis the problem comes down to the question of right, to which I have already referred. It goes back to the problem raised by Rashi in his commentary on the first chapter of Genesis. If the nations of the world say to the Jews : Ye are robbers ; you have stolen this land, then the Jews can reply: 'In the beginning God created the Heaven and the Earth': all the earth is the Lord's and He gave this land to Israel. Now this argument is very convincing for the Jews, but why should the rest of the world accept it ? The answer is that the problem is intimately connected with one's outlook on history : whether it is an outlook of faith or a materialistic conception of history. If the latter, then there is some point to the charge : 'Ye are robbers !' If the former, then the world will simply have to accept the fact that the concept of Providence and the place of man under Providence came from Israel, and that that concept has no validity without the Land of Israel. I believe this is the basic problem : whether the debate continues on the basis of 'Ye are robbers !' or there is an understanding of the unique quality of the Jewish people and its separate path. If this becomes understood, there is a prospect that we will be accepted as part of the Middle East. In my view, this is the key.

It all seems unpolitical and irrational, what I am telling you, but I, who have been engaged in foreign affairs for twenty years, am more convinced today than ever before that this is the key to everything.

I have spoken about one level, the Israel-Arab level. There are other levels on which one hears the beat of the wings of history, senses them at every step. Shortly after World War Two, I went to the Vatican to talk to the representatives of the Church. As one who was dealing with the problem of Jerusalem in 1948-53, I was very much concerned about the reaction of the Vatican. In the early years of the state, the Vatican roused the Catholic world against us. Resolutions were adopted at the United Nations and there was a great deal of pressure. Many countries did not want to recognize the transfer of the government to Jerusalem – and still refuse to recognize it to this day. The source of all this was pressure from Rome.

I remember how I arrived there with a colleague in December 1948. I was received by a distinguished representative of the Vatican, and he said to us : 'Gentlemen, I hear that you came from Palestine three days ago.' I replied : 'We came from *Israel* three days ago.' The words literally stuck in my throat ; I absolutely lost the power of speech when I understood what I had just said. After 2,000 years we were privileged to be the first to enter that world fortress and tell them : Gentlemen, something has happened in history. There is a change !

And twenty years later, when I came to Rome at the end of June 1967, I met with the cardinals, and there was a great debate about the future of Jerusalem. I saw that something had changed in them. They tried to convince me that, after all, they had saved Jews during World War Two ; they had saved the Jewish community in Rome. They were trying to make an impression of moderation ; they were trying to find a way to our hearts. I sat there and marvelled : here was this mighty fortress, ruling over 600 million Catholics, whose fiat crossed the boundaries of nations and continents, and yet they did not complain that ancient Jerusalem was now in our hands. I do not know whether it was a result of pragmatism or concern for their immediate position – in case some harm may be done to their institutions or we might prefer the Eastern churches to the Vatican – but this was their attitude.

In Jerusalem I have an old friend who has given us a great deal of help ever since 1948, the Greek Patriarch Benedictus in the Old City. In 1949-50, when Rome was pushing us to the wall, he came to our assistance. First of all, he sold us perhaps one-sixth of the area constituting Jerusalem at that time. Secondly, he notified the United Nations that in Jerusalem it was the status quo that counted.

Now he sent me a message in order to remind me that he, too, had the same status as the Pope. This was a gentle hint, as if to say : 'Is this the way to treat a friend ? You have taken over Jerusalem, but you don't come to me, you go to Rome.' So I went to see him in his palace on the Mount of Olives, the Palace of the Greek Patriarch. He reminded me of days gone by, how he had stood by us. He sat there on his throne, surrounded in a circle by his acolytes. He read out a document, which said, in effect : My dear sir, if you want to discuss Jerusalem with the Christian world, you must know the right address. The address is not where you were a week ago ; it is here. 'Here I have the rolls of my ancestry,' he said. 'I am the ninety-fifth Patriarch of Jerusalem – the first Patriarch was appointed in 451 by the Council of Chalcedon – and as Patriarch I hold the place of primacy in Jerusalem.'

As he talked the sun was setting, and as its last shafts were piercing his priestly palace, my mind drifted far from the relationship of Israel and Jerusalem re-united and the Greek Orthodox Church and all the importance that we attach to it. My mind also flashed back to 451. I thought : where were my people at that time ? At the time that the Christian Patriarch was appointed in Jerusalem, it was in order to underline that this city – to which Jews were denied access – was not only to be physically torn asunder for all times from the Jewish people, but also spiritually to be outlawed from its patrimony. That was the inner meaning of the appointment.

At that time, the last communities in this land were almost coming to an end. The Mishnah had been edited 200 years previously ; the Jerusalem Talmud was completed fifty years before. The spiritual kingdom of the House of Israel had passed by Babylon – except the right of *Semikhah,* the ordination of rabbis, which remained in Palestine. The academies of Sura, Pumbedita and Nehardea had been in existence for centuries ; Ravina and Rav Ashi were on the point of completing the Babylonian Talmud. Jerusalem was still Aelia Capitolina, closed to the Jews. The Jews came to Mount Scopus and looked down on the city from there. The scattered Jewish communities in Palestine continued to exist for another century or so, until they were expelled by the Persians. Then the Land of Israel ceased, in practice, to be a Jewish centre, except for the lodestone of the Jewish faith and the Western Wall of Jerusalem, which became more of a concept than a reality.

At that time, in Byzantium, the political Roman Empire had combined with the Christian Church. It was an accumulation of power unequalled in history. If we want a contemporary parallel, we must imagine Moscow, Washington and the Vatican combining into one great centre. And that gigantic fortress of power decided it is not enough to give Christianity to the entire world ; it is not enough to rule the known globe ; now they would cut off spiritual Jerusalem, as a historic entity, from the Jewish people. So they appointed the Patriarch of Jerusalem.

And I thought to myself that if, at that time, a Jew had come into a synagogue in Rome, or Crete, or Alexandria, and said to another : 'Have you heard ? They want to seal the doom of Jerusalem, to cut us off forever from this city. They have appointed a Patriarch,' and the other had replied : 'Despair not, my friends, because 1,500 years hence a Jewish official of the Government of Israel will visit the descendant of the Patriarch now appointed, and the ninety-fifth descendant will say : "The city is yours ; it is reunited under Providence. You have found the new road. All I ask is that you recognize my rights as well. Do not wash me off the tablets of history. If you must come to terms on the city, remember that I am the arbiter, I am the proper representative, because I have been here – I and my ancestors – since 451" ' ; those who heard such a statement would have thought the speaker a madman.

There is also our dialogue with the statesmen of the world, both in the East and in the West. I would define it as the struggle between imagination and insight, on the one hand, and political realism, on the other. In every one of the world's chancelleries, ever since 1917, they have been asking who is this handful of people in the Middle East and what is going on here.

You cannot blame them. I know them ; I have worked with them for years, and I do not accuse them of anti-Semitism. What can you expect of an American official who has never studied the Bible, and certainly not the sayings of the sages or the history of the Jews ? He comes to the State Department in Washington, and what is his task ? His task is to defend American interests the world over. He is sent to the Middle East Department, and his duty is to protect American bases and American influence in the Middle East. That is his responsibility.

On his first morning he looks at the map and sees the Arab world from Morocco to Persia, from the Atlantic Ocean to the Persian Gulf, over sixty million souls. Then he sees the Islamic world, numbering hundreds of millions, extending to Indonesia and Pakistan. And all that world cries out in one voice : 'Why did two million Jews come into this country to disturb our peace and unsettle our stability ?'

Then he listens to the other side. We tell him that we are a bastion of democracy, that in the whole of Asia, from India to Tokyo, there is no other democracy. We talk to him about the Bible, but he has not studied it. He is confused, and it is only natural that he resents us. This has been going on since 1917, when the British Foreign Office was opposed to the Balfour Declaration, until this day, when the American State Department – or at least some of its officials – is opposed to the attitude adopted by President Johnson.

On the other hand, there are statesmen with great vision like Lloyd George and Balfour. Lloyd George explained his attitude very well. He admitted that he had been in favour of issuing the Balfour Declaration only because he had no alternative. He saw that Britain was in deadly danger during the war. His only hope was that the United States would come into the war and that the Russians would somehow stand up against the Germans. He was told that the Jews, both in America and in Russia, might be the key to the situation. As in all human affairs, he explained, there was the egoistic aspect, without which nothing can be done, but there was also the sublime idea. That also attracted him. He knew the Bible as he knew no other book. He knew the villages of

Palestine and all the historic biblical places better than he knew the villages of Wales, where he was born. Balfour suggested that this might be an atonement on the part of the Christian world for all its persecution of the Jews.

That is how it goes, from Lloyd George and Balfour to President Johnson of our time. There is a constant struggle between some kind of mystic obligation not to clash with this very special people and the natural professional view that the more one supports this people, the more one rouses the antagonism of a powerful current that, at least in the coming years, carries the key to the struggle between East and West, between freedom and oppression, between Communism and the free world. But in the last analysis, at the moment when the Jewish people reached the point of total challenge, it was vision that conquered – not only among us, but in the hearts of the nations of the world – and thus the dialogue continued with the leaders of the Western world.

For the first time, I believe – if I can trust my antennae or my perceptions, and I speak with many people, Arabs and others – they have started to consider whether this is not something deeper than the superficial view of the situation. Perhaps, they wonder, the bond is deeper than we have read in the propaganda of our leaders. Perhaps this picture of a people of persecuted refugees, which has come here for lack of any alternative, perhaps it is only part of the truth, but not the whole truth.

So it is, too, in the dialogue between Rome and Jerusalem. There has undoubtedly been a shock to the soul of Christendom throughout the Christian world. They are trying to understand what has really happened here : have the principles and concepts to which they have clung for almost 2,000 years been shattered, or is it something that will be crushed between the wheels of history ? For the first time, they have started thinking, for until the twentieth year of the State of Israel the assumption was that this matter was extremely temporary. Our permanence was always in doubt, even when we won. This time, political, security and spiritual elements have been combined in such an extraordinary structure that they have begun to wonder – from Damascus to Cairo, from Pakistan to Morocco, in Rome and throughout the Western world. Again we have the same struggle between the professional policy-makers and the inspired statesmen. Some of them have begun to ask whether there was something unsound about their political assumptions during the past twenty years ; perhaps their evaluations were mistaken.

Now we come to the last level – which I believe to be the fundamental one – the level of the House of Israel. Here, too, a dialogue has been reopened. Anyone familiar with Diaspora Jewry is aware that there have been ups and downs. There has been a falling away. They began to regard Israel as something normal, and as soon as it became a matter of normalcy, it lost its power of attraction. They looked for all kinds of excuses to soothe their consciences, and a considerable portion even began to loosen its ties. Neither Zionist propaganda nor the Jewish

Agency, with all its power and influence, nor even the State of Israel, with all its ambassadors, institutions and a supreme effort encompassing the whole of Jewry and all its economic resources, could have achieved ten per cent of what one hour of prayer at the Western Wall did for the Jewish soul. This is one more indication of the fact that among the Jewish people, in the last analysis, it is the spiritual, not the material, aspect that counts. I am therefore convinced that, in the process of the redemption of Jewry, a new future, the course of which we cannot fore-see, opens up before us. True, it is a future with many dangers, but it also enfolds many possibilities unimagined by our forefathers.

The State of Israel is a paradox. All the normalities have been proved baseless. This is a nation that lives by faith ; however it is expressed, faith is a part of its foundation. It is a nation that lives in the present, but its rights go back to the past. And everything is integrated and intertwined in a process of redemption that, I implicitly believe, lies before us in this new era of Jewish history in which we have the privilege to live.

Israel and the Soviet Union

In Answer to Questions at a Seminar of the Religious Kibbutzim, 4 June 1968

I believe that the Six Day War has shaken some parts of the Communist world that seemed unshakable before. The Soviet Union started its penetration into the Middle East in 1946 and was halted at Azerbaidzhan in Persia. It tried again in Greece and was halted once more. In 1955 it succeeded in jumping over the wall of the Northern Tier of the Baghdad Pact with the arms deal between Egypt and Czechoslovakia.

Since then the Russians have been trying to make the Middle East an area of influence. They regard Israel as an obstacle – not so much from the Middle Eastern point of view, because Israel has actually given them an excuse for their penetration, it has enabled them to gain a foothold among the Arabs with their arms and incitement – I believe it is the Jewish aspect that counts with them.

Three weeks before the Six Day War I was in the United States. I had a talk with an assimilated Jew who enjoys a very exalted status in his country. As I sat and talked to him, it came to mind that perhaps the day would come when this man might hold in his hand the key to the future of the State of Israel, as he is in control of a complex of security and political affairs in the higher echelons of the administration in Washington.

I tried to bring up the Jewish question. I spoke to him about the Middle East, and he spoke to me like any other courteous and sympathetic American official. At this stage he showed a polite interest in what I was saying, but I could not get very far with him. No matter what ideas I put forward, he replied as if he were some non-Jew whose ancestors had been born in Texas 200 years ago and who had never seen a Jew.

This went on until he asked me : Can you improve your relations with the Soviet Union ? I replied that, in my view, we could, insofar as it concerned the Middle East, for the Russians, in their penetration, had achieved such influence that an improvement in their relations with Israel would not be any obstacle to the continuation of the Arab-Russian *rapprochement.* But there was one thing we could not help, the burden of 4,000 years that stood in the way. He said : 'Four thousand years ? I don't understand you. We're talking about what is happening now.'

This was a consequence of Jewish unity, I replied. So long as Moscow understood that the Jewish people in Israel could not cut itself off from the Jewish people in the Soviet Union, it could not agree to a fundamental improvement in relations with us. Communism cannot permit any other world movement that claims to represent a human ideal to exist in its midst, in its very heart.

If you examine the ways of history very closely, you will find that the Jewish people has arrived at either a close relationship or a severe clash with every state, idea or movement that has claimed to represent a universal ideal – whether it be Christianity or Islam, Nazism or Communism, the British Empire or, now, the pretended empire of De Gaulle. Wherever any nation or group has arisen and said that they will guide the ideals of humanity, they are bound to meet us, for that is a fundamental feature of historical experience.

So we came face to face with Communism. I remember that my grandfather, of blessed memory, who was a rabbi in Brezhnik, a very small town in Russia, told me that in 1905, when the news spread throughout the country that the first, unsuccessful revolution had broken out, and in the little towns they heard that revolutionaries had risen throughout the length and breadth of Russia, a band of Jewish revolutionaries burst into his synagogue one Sabbath eve and said : 'Stop all your prayers ! What do you need this Jewish separatism for ? The revolution is succeeding all over Russia and we shall become part of the awakening Russian civilization, part of the world of the revolution.'

The congregation tried to drive them out, and they resisted. He quietened them and called the young men into his house. There he told them in Yiddish : 'Perhaps you are right. The Czar may vanish from the world and all his régime of oppression may vanish with him. A new revolution may arise and appear to transform the world. But you should know that you, who have helped to bring it about, will not be a part of it for long.'

I think this is the basic point for Moscow. I see no possibility of an improvement in relations at the moment. I think the Soviet Union and its satellites believe that enhanced Jewish prestige in the Middle East not only endangers the position of the Soviet Union, not only has struck a severe blow at Soviet prestige, but it also shakes the foundations of the Jewish community inside Russia.

That is why I do not, at the moment, see any prospect of improved relations. However, it is not impossible that this shock in itself may lead to a breakthrough in the thinking of the Kremlin, for even there, during this wonderful year, extraordinary things have happened.

Bucharest has broken with the Moscow line. Tito has emphasized his independence. In Poland there is continual unrest. Prague is slipping out of the ring. Moscow faces very great problems. There is a threat to the monolithic character of the system and it cannot tolerate democracy within it. This structure is either monolithic, totalitarian and absolutist, or it breaks up and disintegrates. There is no middle way.

It is possible that something will happen there, which we cannot foresee, and it may lead to a momentous turning point. They may let the Jews leave. We cannot tell. I would say that perhaps the prospect of Jews leaving the Soviet Union is in the nature of a paradox. It seems to me today that it is closer, though not immediate. I cannot prove this in any logical way, but it seems to be closer than a year ago, before the Six Day War.

I think that the deeper breach, the more the Jewish bond in Russia is strengthened – and it is growing stronger without an Israel Embassy in Moscow – and the greater will be these prospects. But all this is in the field of conjecture. I do not foresee immediate possibilities, unless we withdraw from all the territories as the Soviet Union wants us to do – and perhaps even then it would not change.

The Soviet Union admits today that we do have a right to be in the Middle East. That is something it never said before – or, rather, it said it once, when in 1947 Gromyko voted in the United Nations for the partition of Palestine. Since then, there has been no approval from them on Israel's rights in the Middle East – neither in words nor in thoughts. Now they say it. But they say : first you must give back the territories, and then you will live in safety. Whether this change will lead to a basic understanding is wrapped in the mists of a future that I cannot foresee at this moment.

The Permanence of Israel

From an Address in Durban, South Africa, 18 May 1971

As we survey the scene today, in the twenty-fourth year of Israel's independence, four years after the Six Day War, I believe we can note a change among the Arabs – subtle, incipient, as yet not too deep, but at least an agonizing reappraisal, a questioning : were they indeed right in assuming, as they had, that we were temporary ? This is the result of the miraculous, phenomenal stand of twenty-three years ; of three wars successfully fought by Israel ; of the fact that vast armies numbering tens of millions look through telescopes and know that facing them are small forces of young men on the Suez Canal, on the Golan Heights, along the Jordan Valley, who look into a vast unknown without fear. And they must ask themselves in this intuitive dialogue : whence this sense of total confidence ? whence this innate faith ? whence this assurance that all their dreams are not for nothing ?

Surely it must have a relation to permanence. Only a people in their home, after a recent homecoming, in total stability, in total security, in total assurance of their future, could stand as we stand and face them as we face them.

And the impact of this dialogue proceeds continuously. Despite the shooting that fortunately has ceased – we hope not temporarily – despite the bitterness, despite the tangled wires that divide us, despite the blaring of propaganda on both sides, it is there ; and, for the first time, in recent months Arab capitals have at least begun to say the word 'Peace'. I will not, at this stage, enter into a semantic analysis of what peace means to them, what reservations they have for the future, whether they have not merely pushed aside their dream of vengeance for a better day. But the fact is that they can utter the word ; the forbidden word 'Israel' can be said day in day out on their radios and by their leaders. For the first time they are acquiring a glimmer of balanced assessment, a realization that the Middle East may well have to be a mosaic of different peoples, faiths and communities, and perhaps this phenomenon, which they considered a passing phase and an aberration in the Arab Middle East, enjoys a permanence and roots that stretch back beyond the existence of the Arab race.

This agonizing reappraisal has not yet found emotional expression in a drive, in a thrust, for peace, but it has found calculated expression in more realistic assessments of the balance between war and peace, of the dangers to the Arab world of renewed war and in a questioning with regard to the wisdom of their course until now.

The process, my friends, is slow, but we can say, *'yesh sachar life'ula-teinu'*, there is a reward for our labours. Not in vain have our defenders lived – and died – not in vain have we asserted our faith and belief in the future of Israel, whatever the odds. The dialogue continues, and from it let us draw encouragement.

But this dialogue is essentially not a question of territory, of refugees or of usual problems between states, which can be solved round the table. Essentially it refers back to the crucial roots of continuity : have we a right to assert that throughout history we have maintained a metaphysical link with this land, and, consequently, this give us the justification to claim it as our own in the twentieth century ? This is the unique debate, which likewise explains the vagaries surrounding it, the endless rims of dialogue throughout the world.

Not only is the Arab world beginning to change its assessments, but, across the world, the strategic capacity of Israel, its permanence on the Middle Eastern scene, and its position as a major factor in Middle Eastern strategy, is accepted today. This was not necessarily the case ten or fifteen years ago. I remember discussing a loan with the American Secretary of State in Washington in 1958. When we questioned him about repayment in ten or fifteen years' time, I can recall a slight smile appearing on his face. When we asked him what it was he was smiling at, he replied hesitatingly : 'Do not ask me. Surely you do not intend to ask me what will be in the Middle East in ten years' time !'

The rims of dialogue proceed to the great centres of thought and religion across the world. There they ask : what is the inner meaning of all this ? How has this people, a third of whose sons and daughters were led to slaughter only a quarter-century ago in endless humiliation, in unmitigated cruelty, who were at the nadir of their fortunes, flung to the abyss of a cruel and merciless fate, whence do they rise again, phoenix-like, with force, with vigour, with faith and regain the capital of their eternity, Jerusalem ? What is the meaning of all this ? As cardinals and princes of the church have asked me : what is the enigma, what is this mystery of your revival ? And the debate goes back and forth across the world on the nature of this revival.

Indeed, the Jew today – not only we in Israel, but our brethren throughout the world – is no longer a subject of humiliation nor of contempt, but of a spiritual scrutiny that can touch the very essence of vast theologies, philosophies of thought, indeed entire historical trends.

The leaders of Islam, representing 600 million Moslems, upon meeting in Rabat, Morocco, in September 1969, asked themselves what this is all about when we said Jerusalem is ours. Indeed, in the words of the prophet, 'mine house shall be called a house of prayer for all people' (Isaiah 56 : 7). We have never denied that ; we have offered, and we give, every religious freedom to every group in Jerusalem. But they could not tolerate that the sovereignty in Jerusalem is ours.

This dialogue, my friends, has its core in the Middle East, with the

Arab world, beyond it with the great powers and beyond even that with the major spiritual forces of the world. But ultimately, as we analyse the assessments, as we analyse the new posture of the Jew – his new dignity, his force, his firmness, his new perspective – we come back to the change of assessment in the soul of the Jew himself. And they are interrelated. The dialogue between Israel and the nations of the world spans recorded history ; as we feel, they react, and as they react, we feel. It is an interlocked dialogue, ambivalent, often marred with blood and torment, but also uplifted, in a higher cooperation, in a search for a messianic period for mankind.

Within the Jewish soul a revolution has also taken place. In 150 years of emancipation, the Jew sought to obliterate his identity, to escape into the abyss surrounding him, to be Germans of the Jewish faith, then socialists, communists and part of world revolution.

But the Mekhilta gave the answer 1,900 years ago. On the concept of a Jew sundering himself from his people, *karet*, it says : '*Yachol tikaret miyisrael vetelech lah le'am aher ? Talmud lomar : "Milefanai ", bechol makom shehu bireshuti'*. The Jew can leave his own people, but he can never become integrally or spiritually part of any other.* This is the nature of Jewish distinctiveness through the ages. This is not only our inner identification, this is our distinguishing mark in the eyes of the world. As such, we make our contribution to the supremacy of spiritual over material values in human history. And this characteristic of the Jew links up with the nature of Jerusalem, which, in a desolation of over 3,000 years, has maintained its timelessness, awaiting the Jew and remaining part of the Jew.

A revolution of Jewish consciousness started in 1967, when Jerusalem, in the words of the Talmud, '*shehubra lah yahdav*', as it became reunited, '*osa kol Yisrael haverim*', it makes of the whole of Israel one great family, from one end of the world to the other, far surpassing any physical contact. It started, '*kimedurat esh*', as a beacon of fire, in the hills of Soviet Georgia, when the mountaineer Jewish villagers suddenly came down from their perches after half a century and said to the Soviet authorities : we feel strange here ; we want to be in Jerusalem. And they wrote remarkable documents, which will remain for all time in Jewish literature, saying : we have nothing against the Soviet Union ; we have nothing against the régime ; but we were born in Jerusalem, we belong there. Even as Agnon, our Nobel Prize winner, told the King of Sweden : I was born in Buczacz, but only in a dream ; in reality I was born in Jerusalem and exiled by Titus.

*The Mekhilta, the Midrashic commentary on Exodus, discussing the verse 'whosoever eateth that which is leavened [on Passover], even that soul shall be cut off from the congregation of Israel' (12 : 19), writes : 'This might be understood to mean that the soul will be cut off and go to another people. Hence it is written [Leviticus 22 : 3] : "that soul shall be cut off from my presence [literally, from before me], I am the Lord", *i.e.*, in every place that is under my authority.' Using the age-old Jewish hermeneutical methods, Herzog builds his own interpretation on the foundation of the ancient commentary. [Ed.]

And so these Jews of Georgia, with inimitable heroism and bravery, put themselves in danger and raised the call of Jerusalem in that vast system of slavery, of ideological uniformity, of mental coercion. They said : 'We wish to return.' And as they spoke, their message got across to the universities, to the heirs of Trotsky, to members of the Communist Party, and the whole of Russian Jewry stared. Those who had never been to a synogogue, to a Hebrew school, were seized by something inward, something eternal ; and they said : let us go, for we find no fulfilment here.

And across the Arab lands, in the torture cells of Baghdad prisons, Jews said the same thing. They refused to yield : come what may, let us go home !

And in Washington, the capital of the free world, a delegation of all segments of American Jewry - including those who ran down the concept of Zionism a short fifty years ago, raising the irrelevant phobia of dual loyalty, speaking, until ten years ago, of 'Diaspora trends' - appeared before the Secretary of State and argued the case of Israel as the bastion of freedom in an area threatened by the Soviet colossus, and therefore a key factor in American and free-world interest in the Middle East. But as they were about to finish, their leader rose and said : 'Mr Secretary, we must be honest with you, we have spoken until now as American citizens, but before we leave you, we must tell you that where Jerusalem is concerned, we are all citizens of Jerusalem ; without it, we cannot live.'

He was not aware that he was merely echoing what a Jewish delegation answered Caligula, Emperor of the Romans, when he said, 1,900 years ago : 'I have given you your rights as Roman citizens. Wherefore do you link yourselves with Jerusalem this tiny village in a remote province of Rome ? Surely the lure, the force, the dynamism of Rome, conqueror of the world, mistress of lands in Europe, North Africa and the East, is sufficient. Wherefore do you link yourselves, wherefore do you come to us to speak on Jerusalem ?' And they answered : 'We cannot do otherwise, because we can only be fulfilled Roman citizens if Jerusalem is with us in peace. We cannot divorce ourselves.'

This is the essence of the metaphysical union spanning over 4,000 years. It has defied all odds ; and, at the nadir of Jewish history, at the moment of decline, at the loss of identification, at the flight from Jewishness, from peoplehood, from faith, it has suddenly flared anew as a vast beacon that lights up every Jewish path across the world - from Soviet Russia to the Arab lands to the affluent societies of the Western World. And believe me, there is nowhere that my travels take me - to the chancelleries of the great, to the most famous newspapers, to top military headquarters - where I do not feel the electricity of the eternity of Jerusalem.

This, my friends, is the background against which we stand today as we enter the twenty-fourth anniversary of Israel's independence. There is a new perspective ; yet we still face vast perils. I could spend many hours telling you of the half-million Egyptian soldiers from Cairo to the Suez Canal, of the 100 missile sites, of the 1,200 artillery units, of the hundreds and hundreds of planes that are limitlessly delivered to Egypt, Syria and Iraq, of the constant threat of a renewal of war, of those days and nights when we ponder our military assessments - will they try to strike anew or will they bide their time ? I could tell you all this.

I could tell you in detail of our four-year political struggle of insist-ence upon secure frontiers. We have arguments with the whole world, including our friends. But at least with our friends we share a common denominator : the balance of arms is to be maintained and there is to be no movement without peace. Yet, we differ on the territorial question. They tell us that we can never get more territory for security ; geography does not mean security any more, only international guarantees are to be trusted. And we throw back at them - as we did to Secretary Rogers last week - the sordid and bitter experiences of international guarantees over 20 years : the 1949 Armistice Agreement, the 1956 agreements on the freedom of passage. And we ask : shall we again throw all this away ? Not only throw it away in terms of our danger, but, even deeper, shall we abandon the quest to convince our Arab neighbours that we are here to stay ?

As we see it, the area is torn between two conflicting trends : the one pushing to war ; the other urging agonizing reappraisal for true peace. At the moment they coexist : at the same time that Sadat's armies prepare for war, he says the word 'Peace'. We believe that, if we stand firm, they will move from talk of peace to negotiation. And we believe that, if we meet them eye to eye over the negotiating table, we can find a solution even to the territorial problem, for the monster image of Israel and their phobias of us will have disappeared.

And so we urge Western statesmen not to push us, to give us time, to let the process work itself out. We ask them not to accuse us of intran-sigence when we claim that we are realistic, and not to press us, because we will not yield. Even if we have to stand in political isolation we will do so ; just as we stood alone in the fields of battle. We have lived with loneliness throughout history, and we are masters of survival. We will not crawl before it, no matter how unpleasant it becomes.

And so the debate goes back and forth. They ask us what we will do if war breaks out anew and the Soviet Union gets involved. We answer that, with the proper deterrent from the Western World, the Soviet Union will not involve itself in offensive action. And we will face up to the Arab armies ineluctably, if compelled to do so, as before. But we cannot yield at this stage and go back to the miasma of uncertainty. We would be leaving our children and grandchildren a legacy of endless tension and war, and they could rightfully ask us why we abandoned our strategic positions at the crucial turning point ; why did we stand firm for years and then yield ? We are caught in the dilemma of a dialogue with the Western world, of hostility by the Soviet Union and the Arabs and of serious undercurrents of dialogue throughout the world. All eyes are upon us, asking : can you take it ?

As a British statesman said to me some months ago : 'Maybe your analysis is correct, but can you take it, have you the strength ? And who will stand with you ? Are you sure that your people throughout the world are with you ?' I said : 'I have no doubt.' And we in Israel have no doubt.

My friends, the nature of this epoch is so stirring : it has revolutionized an entire people ; it has revolutionized the inner springs of perspective across the world towards us. With firmness touched with generosity, with strength uplifted by spiritual understanding, we can move ahead. We can make this the true beginning of a new epoch of endless vistas. We face perils. No man can guarantee that fighting will not resume tomorrow, that our soldiers will not have to again fight bloody battles. But we know we have the strength to withstand them. The balance of arms is in our favour at the moment. The strategic balance is with us because we have the most advantageous strategic lines.

We may face political isolation and pressures, but we face all this in the knowledge that we belong to a new epoch and that the Jew has changed – in Jerusalem, in Israel and across the world. And though at times it looks dark, the light will reappear. With all the difficulties, with all the pressures, we are the generation of redemption. Let us indeed be worthy of this privilege that defies human logic and supersedes human vistas.

Survival and Acceptance : Aims of Israel's Foreign Policy

An Address at the Jewish Theological Seminary, New York, 8 April 1959

On the fifth of Iyar 5708 [the equivalent, by the Jewish calendar, to 15 May 1948], after a gap of close on 2,000 years, Jewish statehood was resumed. The nature of statehood, the concept of sovereignty, its attributes and forms of national and international expression, had been a constant theme with philosophers, sociologists and political scientists. Their analyses and definitions related to evolving frameworks in varying civilizations, periods and eras ; Jewish statehood formed no part of their study.

Although, in physical terms, Israel's statehood in exile was ethereal, the destruction of the Second Commonwealth had not resulted in the extinction of independence. The Jewish communities of the Diaspora maintained not only an integrity of spirit and unity within themselves and with each other, but also enjoyed, in varying terms and degrees, some of the aspects of statehood : a judicial system, organs of public representation and control, communal taxation, a system of organized philanthropy and an internal national discipline arising from a voluntary acceptance of spiritual authority. The sense of statehood was a measure of identification with the Prophets' message. For if the attribute of continuing prophecy was withheld, the heirloom of the past was preserved intact. As the Sages said, *'Yisrael im ein nevi'im hem bnei nevi'im hem'*, 'if Israel are no longer prophets, they are the sons of prophets.' In contemplating ultimate realization, the generations of exile combined the memories of the past, as enshrined in sacred or secular records, with impressions of the societies of their environment.

This independent survival, in both its conscious and subconscious aspects, was hardly noticed by historians. Certainly its impulse and goal were overlooked. When political Zionism emerged at the beginning of this century, it found difficulty in convincing the world of its contemporary reality, of its ultimate validity and of its character as spokesman of the Jewish people. On the other hand, the masses of Jewry rallied automatically to its summons, for dream and vision had been consistently intermingled with self-expression in terms of internal independence. In the field of external relations, however, a balanced pattern was lacking. In the atmosphere of exile, it was difficult indeed to contemplate the posture of a Jewish state on the international scene and the nature of the relationship that would emerge between it and the nations of the world. No less than the content, the form and climate of conventional foreign relations were obscure and enigmatic.

In 1948 Israel took on overnight the internal forms of statehood. Tradition, the continuous pattern of uninterrupted internal independence, environment – past and present – combined to facilitate a stable and orderly transition from a Diaspora society. There was also a legacy in the field of external relations. From the first exile to Babylon, some five centuries BCE, we can trace an intricate record of Jewish relations with the nations of the world. With the destruction of the Second Commonwealth, the Diaspora character of this relationship became total. Evolving patterns of society, of religious movements, of philosophic analysis, the search after human destiny, political developments, economic and social upheaval, the changes in the balance of world power all had their impact – direct or indirect, positive or negative – on the spiritual, political or economic fortunes of Jewry. In essence, the story of the Diaspora was that of the struggle to harmonize two apparently conflicting trends : the maintenance of the sanctuary of the spirit inviolate, on the one hand, and involvement with extraneous trends, on the other.

With the emergence of the Zionist movement, Jewish external relations became more universal in scope, assuming coherence and direction. With the achievement of international recognition it began to weave a pattern of Jewish relations. Yet, although it spoke the language of imminent statehood, the very nature of the circumstances did not allow it to overcome the anachronism that had characterized Diaspora external relations. These relations never approached the inherent stability and freedom, albeit limited, enjoyed by internal expressions of independence. The latter were, in a sense, self-sufficient, drawing their vitality from native sources of inspiration. External relations, however, were an uneasy dialogue, the disparity in status between the two participants denying it a common basis. The Jewish party to the dialogue spoke for a reality that in the eyes of the other was metaphysical. It was obliged to try to convey in contemporary terms an intuition and experience that bridged the gaps between past and future. In the measure that it affected normalcy, it merely emphasized its abnormality.

At times the cleavage between the internal and external postures seemed to threaten to deteriorate into national schizophrenia. Relations, attitudes and impressions were formed and became part of the consciousness of Jewry from generation to generation. Their objective truth was coloured and frustrated by the subjective experience to which they were related. Immortal prophecy had defined the interaction of a distinctive spiritual and national course with the general human quest for its spiritual destiny. This same prophecy enshrined the teaching that the harmony of relationship would be achieved fully only with the restoration of independent statehood.

The establishment of the State of Israel opened the prospect of achieving a balanced and coherent system of relations with the nations of the world. The struggle for survival and unending international complications have burdened this mission. Moreover, an amalgam of past relationships, political and spiritual, has had to be clarified and defined from the perspective of independent nationhood. Nevertheless, much progress has been made in overcoming the heritage of anomaly and in convincing the world of the validity and permanence of Israel's statehood. Inherent independence has at long last found harmonious expression externally. To analyse the development of Israel's external relations is in essence to trace the course of this process. The development of Israel's foreign policy can be reviewed under two headings : 1) the state's survival, and 2) its acceptance by the international community. These chapters have not been consecutive, but intertwined throughout.

Israel is one of twenty nations that have attained independence since World War Two. Most have been burdened with grave internal difficulties – social, economic, and political. In many cases the relations with neighbouring countries have been marked by tension. All have felt the impact of the global conflict. But Israel is the only state whose very existence has been continuously challenged from birth. The tactics of her neighbours have changed, the acuity of their threats has varied, but the tenor and motive have remained constant. The driving force has been emotional, rather than national, interest, with inflexibility and fatalism pitted against indomitable faith and confidence. The Arab refusal to cooperate initially with the new state, or even to recognize its right to live, could be foreseen ; the attempt to strangle it at birth was not unexpected. That the second decade of Israeli statehood should find the conflict still unsolved refutes in retrospect much of the political prognoses that were prevalent before the rise of the state.

The war of 1948 did not entirely dampen the hope of an early acceptance, inherent if not formal, of Israel on the part of her Arab neighbours. The history of the Arab-Jewish relationship through the ages had been comparatively free of extreme excesses of racial hatred and of lasting religious antagonism. In fact, it contains records of cultural and scientific cooperation. With the Arab masses, hostility to Israel appeared to be perfunctory, dictated by their leaders. Side by side with Israel's attainment of statehood, the Arab peoples were achieving independence. After an eclipse of many centuries, the vista of a new era of Arab nationhood was opening up. Israel held neither land nor water nor any other precious resources that the Arabs required for their survival and advancement.

The failure of the Arab armies would, it was hoped, convince Arab leadership that, with the military resources available to them, the destruction of Israel would not be a practical proposition in the near future. Arab-Israel peace was a primary objective of the international community speaking through the UN. The armistice negotiations seemed to indicate a possibility of clarifying differences through direct contact. The agreements seemed to be the first stepping-stone towards peace, the text of the documents said so in as many words. Shortly after the conclusion of these agreements, actual peace negotiations were undertaken with King Abdullah of neighbouring Jordan. The hope of an early settlement, however, soon proved abortive ; it became clear that the Arab leaders interpreted the armistice agreements not as a preamble to peace but merely as a respite to organize themselves for a future onslaught. The question has been asked whether at this stage Israel should not have put the Arabs to the test of their signature to the armistice agreements. The possibilities and prospects of such an attempt are not within the scope of this analysis.

The relentless and protracted character of the Arab-Israel dispute can be ascribed to a number of factors ; however, two especially stand out : the crisis in Arab evolution, and the involvement of the area in the global East-West conflict. These two processes developed simultaneously, in mutual frustration and tension.

Experts have analysed the impact of independence on the Arab mind after long centuries of subjection to foreign domination. With the passing of the golden era of Arab independence, the momentum of cultural development, scientific discovery and philosophical probing almost came to a halt. In the latter part of the Middle Ages the Arab world and Europe were rivals for cultural achievement. But while the dynamism of the one continued, the other lapsed into stagnation and oblivion. In terms of inherent development, history, in a sense, flowed past the Arab world. The renewal of independence in modern times was more of a gift from outside than the result of indigenous effort. On reawakening, the Arab world found itself lacking the motifs and patterns in the political, social and economic spheres that, over centuries of trial, failure and achievement, have become the accepted norms of the Western world. Frustration at the incapacity to solve these problems overnight resulted in aggressive impulses outwardly. Hostility to Israel became a focal point for the sublimation of internal tensions. Therefore, Arab-Israel peace has to be preceded by the emergence of positive directions within Arab society.

The first winds of the Cold War were felt in the Northern Tier of the Middle East : in Azerbaidzhan in 1946 and in Greece and Turkey in 1950 and 1951. The international tension engendered by the Korean War affected the area in depth. West and East sought to win Arab sympathy and involvement for their conflicting objectives : the former to associate the Arab countries in an overall defence of the area ; the latter, by frustrating this effort, to disrupt the contiguity of Western defence. Seven months after the formation of the Baghdad Pact in February 1955, the Czech-Egyptian arms agreement was signed. External pressures exacerbated inherent instability, diverting Arab attention still further from the task of constructive internal development.

The interaction of external and internal tensions had a critical impact on the Arab-Israel relationship. The pro-Western Arab régimes argued that the Western cause would be enhanced through a weakening of Western ties with Israel. The anti-Western régimes urged on the Soviet Union a policy of hostility towards Israel as a means of winning Arab sympathies. The re-arming of Arab armies became the price of Arab favour towards West and East alike ; it was adequately paid.

With the radical upset in the arms balance between Israel and the Arabs, the hope of avenging the defeat of 1948 flashed anew in the Arab mind. Nasserism symbolized the search for an external outlet to cover up internal failure on the one hand and the exploitation of East-West tension for nationalist advantage on the other. From January to October 1956 Israel faced a growing threat. Eight years after the war of liberation she was obliged once again to take up arms in self-defence. The Sinai Campaign staved off the immediate threat to Israel's security. It brought a measure of relaxation in the Israel-Arab relationship – temporary at any rate. Nobody, however, expected that the military victory would be followed by peace.

The Sinai Campaign showed the Israel outlet to be a costly one for Arab frustration ; at the same time it underlined the peril of attendant international complications. The emphasis shifted to intra-Arab relationships, their intensity sharpened by the East-West conflict. In the past two years violent upheavals and acute tensions have convulsed Iraq, Syria, Lebanon, Jordan and Saudi Arabia, and their reverberations are being felt throughout the area and into Africa. Simultaneously, the Cold War in the Middle East has almost reached a climax. The present conflict between Baghdad and Cairo illustrates the ambivalent nature of the interaction of these two processes.

What of the future of the Arab-Israel dispute ? On the one hand, as but one of an amalgam of interlocked tensions, its solution has become dependent on developments beyond its native context. Yet, in terms of the Arab attitude, there may be some ground for the hope that the Arabs will ultimately realize that hostility to Israel deepens rather than alleviates their crisis. Militarily speaking, the prospect of overcoming Israel by force is less today than it has been in the past. Israel's proven defensive capacity, her developing economy and her increasing international status cannot have gone without impact on her neighbours. Nor can they fail to have noticed Israel's abstinence from any attempt to exploit to her advantage the storms and stresses within the Arab countries. Although Arab hatred towards Israel has not abated, one has the impression that the Israel issue is no longer the central aspect in Arab emotional reaction. If the intra-Arab struggle and the East-West conflict have deepened Arab instability in the broad sense, there is possibly some compensation in the fact that the Arab mind has been brought face to face with the challenge to its own destiny and with the threat to the integrity of the area as a whole.

I am not suggesting that hatred to Israel has abated. It would be premature to return to the hopes entertained before the rise of the state and for some time after. Yet, despite the radical change in circumstances, some grounds for that hope, as outlined earlier, have continuing relevance. This would more clearly emerge if other aspects of the tension were to subside. It is beyond the capacity of Israel to influence the course of extraneous developments ; it is within her capacity to impress on the Arab mind the impact of her growing stability and progress as well as her peaceful intent.

In the struggle for survival, the effort of Israel's foreign service has been complementary to that of its defence forces. It has been directed firstly to obtaining arms, economic aid, political and moral support for the stand against aggression, but it has likewise countered the Arab attempt to make Israel the pariah of the international community. It has explained to the world the challenge to international order inherent in Arab hostility to Israel and has sought to enlist international influence to curb its intensity. It has invoked the sanction of international law for its elementary rights. But Israel has never believed that indirect action will bring about an Israel-Arab settlement. It has always been its primary theme that a settlement can only be achieved through direct negotiations with the Arabs. The armistice negotiations were the starting-point for this theme ; the failure to bring it to realization has not weakened the belief in its validity. Only when direct negotiations come about will Israeli foreign policy find an opportunity for full self-expression.

In 1947 Israel's right to statehood was upheld by a two-thirds majority of the United Nations, including the USA and the Soviet Union. Within a comparatively short time after her establishment, the majority of the countries of the world extended to her diplomatic recognition ; many exchanged with her diplomatic representatives. In 1950 she became a member of the United Nations and rapidly attained a dignified status in the council of nations. Yet her first ten years have been marked by an incessant struggle for inherent acceptance. Outside the Arab complex, Islamic countries and others have withheld diplomatic recognition ; some countries, having granted it, have refused to exchange diplomatic representatives. Moreover, within the framework of diplomatic relationships and within the United Nations there have been successive stresses and tensions. Arab diplomacy and propaganda have sought to exploit every possible international relationship and development to discredit Israel and undermine her status : these include United Nations deliberations on refugees, utilization of the waters of the Jordan River, Israel's right of passage through the Suez Canal, frontier incidents, the Sinai Campaign, the Bandung Conference, and the Western Powers' Middle Eastern policies.

The attitude of the Soviet Union during the past four years is an outstanding example of the scope and impact of this harassment. In 1953 the fabricated doctors' plot and its aftermath caused a temporary breach of relations with the Soviet Union. However, the restoration of relations did not alleviate a developing tension, arising, on the one hand, from the growing Soviet link with certain Arab countries and, on the other hand, from its reaction to the internal structure of Israeli society and Israel's international position on matters of dispute between East and West.

From 1953 to 1956, US-Israel relations suffered from differences of appraisal of Israel's security situation and her reaction to infiltration and armed incursion. The Sinai Campaign brought these differences to a head. Many of these stresses have been overcome ; others have lost much of their intensity. On the positive side there has been a constant and growing pattern of aid and sympathy. Israel's relations today have reached a depth and intimacy that are in striking contrast to her situation not so long ago. A friendship has developed with France, and it proved itself at a time of isolation and peril. Over the past two years early differences with Britain have been smoothed out. Since the withdrawal from Sinai a new harmony has developed with the US, and Israel is covered by the Eisenhower Doctrine.

Her right to free passage through the Gulf of Akaba has been internationally upheld and Israeli ships sail unimpeded. Close ties and economic cooperation have developed with the African continent rising from the torpor of centuries. Relations with Asia have broadened. The Christian world has come to recognize that Israel has faithfully fulfilled her undertaking to respect Christian interests, institutions and pilgrim rights in Jerusalem. The friendships with many countries in the Latin continent, Europe and the British Commonwealth have deepened. Finally, there is growing understanding throughout the world of the true nature of Middle Eastern tensions.

In the pattern of trial, setback and achievement, Israel's foreign relations have progressively matured. Israel has come to understand the underlying realities of world politics and the reflexes of international approach. The international community has increasingly appreciated the permanence and quality of Israel's statehood. In reviewing in retrospect international support for the establishment of the state, one cannot escape the impression that it has related more to the concept of a home for homeless people and a centre for its spiritual advancement than to political independence and international rights. Therefore, the process of acceptance of the state has involved a progressive balance in perspective.

For the analysis of this development, world reaction to the Sinai Campaign and the appraisal of its motives serve as an interesting laboratory test. The essential point at issue with the international community was Israel's claim to equality of treatment within the framework of international law and the UN charter. The view has been expressed that this experience was a turning-point in the international attitude to Israel. The coming years will bear out the validity of this contention. But the fact that Israel enters its second decade with ever-growing stability in her international status cannot be questioned.

The rise of Israel is an index of the supremacy of the spiritual factor in human history. With the transition from the valley of death to the broad uplands of destiny, immortal prophecy has been fulfilled before our eyes. This is Israel's contemporary message, and this will remain its lasting impact. In these terms, to paraphrase the well-known epigram of a French cleric, its very survival is its contribution. Moreover, this survival has been bound up with the integrity of international justice and order.

This is in the nature of the objective experience as it unfolds in the prophetic interpretation of history. What of the subjective spiritual motif in Israel's external relations ? The answer is that in the immediate sense it has been the same as the political theme – namely, survival and acceptance. But in the depth of the nation's consciousness there lies the legacy of prophetic ideals in terms of world peace and international cooperation, and it is inherent in that legacy that Israel will make its distinctive contribution to the realization of these ideals.

The first stage of Israel's external relations has been almost wholly confined to sheer survival and acceptance ; it has been inevitable that its policies revolved around these themes. However, even as the anomaly of Diaspora external relations did not cripple the nation's objective capacity to regain a balanced relationship with the restoration of statehood, so has the experience of external harassment not frustrated the inner motive of Israel's relationship with the nations of the world. The endless hostility of its neighbours has not dampened its ardour for peace and its conviction that peace and international cooperation will yet come. And along with this belief is the inner conviction that Israel will ultimately make its contribution to the world scale of international relations.

Problems of Foreign Policy

From an Address to a Plenary Session of the World Jewish Congress Executive, Tel Aviv, 11 January 1970

Anybody who has travelled abroad recently will surely feel that throughout Jewry, as indeed throughout the world, there is growing concern as to in whose favour time is working. This concern, this apprehension, takes on various forms. It finds expression at times in criticism of Israel's policies in the territories. It involves criticism of Israel's 'lack of flexibility' in declaring public positions. It involves criticism of Israel's insistence on direct talks as the only means of achieving peace in the Middle East. It claims that Israel is ignorant of the undercurrents in the Middle East that threaten Western positions, that open up the spectre of the entire area falling under Soviet control, with Israel remaining a small, isolated, pro-Western island, with little if any significance in the vast mass of pro-Soviet opinion that would emerge in the area. It argues that we refuse to recognize the development of a Palestinian national personality among the refugees in the area, whose outward and most fanatic expression is the Fatah. But it is my impression from talks with editors, statesmen and military leaders that this criticism is secondary to the central question – which is thrown at you everywhere – what will be the end ? Now this question has also been raised in Israel over the past year, and various answers have been suggested.

Those in Western capitals are, of course, not obligated either by the biblical message of faith, by the sense of Jewish eternity, by all those inner elements of faith and mysticism that have kept our people alive to the present day. Their view is prompted purely from a professional, political standpoint. Our feeling is that the situation is viewed according to the perspective of the person who views it. On the question of time in the Middle East, which is crucial, there are many people with their separate clocks. This problem, in which we have been immersed for two and a half years, has achieved world dimensions, which, with the exception of the two world wars and possibly Vietnam, no other problem has attracted. Certainly no problem in the moral and historical sense has ever torn at the consciousness and the conscience of people across the world for a period of fifty years, as has the conflicting claims of Jew and Arab – the Jew resting his case essentially on a metaphysical point of departure, on a link beyond time with the land, and the Arab claiming to set his case within the context of the twentieth century.

Now we believe that in the struggle for time we will win. We believe that time is with us. This is not a thing you can prove. There is no mathematical, scientific formula by which we can prove it. Nor am I touching now on the issue of faith, without which the Jewish people has no uniqueness and no chance of survival ; I am talking to you as I would talk to a Foreign Office official in trying to analyse time. We believe that time is in our favour in the sense that the war of attrition is eating away at the vitals of Arab integrity and strength far more than at our vitals and strength. We believe that, over the past year, within the Middle Eastern context - and I will say something later on the world context - there have been three trends of the deepest significance.

Firstly, there has been a second war of which people are hardly aware. When you read, day in and day out, of bombings, of artillery, of bombs going off, of soldiers being killed, the whole scenario of the Middle East seems to be a continuing series of bloody films of hostility and death, with no lines of discrimination or planning. That is not the case. In March of this year, Egypt, in fact, went to war without actually declaring it. Egyptian strategy was based upon what they conceived as a second stage leading to a third stage. It was promulgated by President Nasser in April 1968, when he spoke of three stages. The first stage was the defence of the homeland from further Israel penetration, bearing in mind the nakedness of his forces after their defeat in the summer of 1967. The second stage was what he called 'aggressive defence' : his army would be in a position to begin to probe our defences in preparation for a breakthrough into Sinai. His plan was, if not all-out war, at least one action of considerable import where, if he could swing a victory, he would restore the morale of the Arab peoples. As Heykal put it at the beginning of this offensive of March 1969, 'If only we could destroy ten thousand Israel soldiers, that in itself would change the entire perspective of the Arab peoples.' This war began in March of this year with violent artillery barrages across the Canal. It continued until about July, with Israel suffering considerable losses on the Canal ; it was halted around July, and our Air Force then moved into action. Since then it has continued in a desultory fashion.

But the position on the ground is not the crucial point at present ; what is crucial is what has happened in Nasser's mind. Nasser was forced - and this is not speculation but fact - to recast his strategy from imminent action on a large scale to a war of attrition lasting two, three or four years. In seeking to define this war of attrition, he has fallen back on historical terms. He has told his people things that were inconceivable for any Arab leader to declare one, two, or three years ago, certainly before the Six Day War. He has spoken of the possibility, if the Arabs are further defeated, of their disappearance from the scene of history. Those who follow Arab psychology will understand what it is for the architect of Arab unity, for a man who leads a nation of thirty million and claims to lead an Arab world of 100 million, to say this.

The whole Arab world has lived for twenty-two years in a miasma of assessments, of myths, of self-folklore, totally blinding themselves to reality. When they met in 1964 and 1965 at the summit conferences in Cairo, Alexandria and Rabat, everything was cut and dried. It was so simple. All they had to do was organize a unified command, to give Ahmet Shukeiry [former head of the Palestine Liberation Organization] the right to establish a Palestine personality and to prepare their forces. They believed that the preparation itself would rip Israel's integrity to pieces. And again I am not speaking of speculation ; the facts are known.

But today, when the Arab world meets – as they have met twice at summit conferences in the past two months – their language has changed. And believe me, heavy, heavy lie the heads of the Arab leaders in our area. The dilemmas through which they live, which face them day in and day out, are far more crucial and agonizing than those which the leaders of Israel face – though I agree that they too are pretty grim. For the first time something has snapped in the Arab mind. I would say it is the facile assumption of myth. For the first time they are sufficiently shattered to cast doubts in their own minds. And for the first time, in talking with one another as to the correctness and prudence of their assessments over twenty years, they no longer glibly talk of throwing us into the sea. The assumptions of Arab strength, which Nasser proclaimed at the Khartoum Conference of August/September 1967, were not heard, certainly not with the same vibrancy and confidence, in Rabat two weeks ago. There is a doubt, a hesitation, and this expresses itself not only in a weakening of the unity on the Israel issue. Grave differences came up in Rabat which could not have easily been conceived of before. Algeria – Boumedienne, of all people – turned on the Libyans and made fun of their military power. Who are you, he said, to challenge Israel ? And he himself, two weeks before Rabat, came out with a new plan that was conditional on the Arabs rejecting any concept of throwing the Jews into the sea, because their assessment of their future and their course has weakened. The inner fissures within the Arab world, which tore them apart for ten years, have suddenly been resuscitated.

Feisal and Nasser faced each other with deep suspicion in Rabat : it was Feisal who refused to obligate himself to greater financial aid ; it was Feisal who challenged Nasser at the conference to produce the accounts – where had the money gone ? And Nasser, being so dependent on him, was unable to attack him in return. The issue of Libya was central in their thoughts : who gains control of the billion dollars of oil that are flowing from the oil wells in Libya ? And Algeria, for the first time, appeared in deep cohesion with Morocco and Tunis, and with deep suspicion of Nasser, to the point that Nasser's official visit to Algiers was cut to an hour and a quarter.

The whole area of southern Yemen and southern Arabia is again a scene of deep movements and clashes. The British departure east of Suez next year already poses the problem of who will gain control of the sheikdoms of the Persian Gulf, with all their vast wealth : Iran, Saudi Arabia, supported by Iran, or the Southern Yemen Republic, supported by Egypt and by Aden ? Even in Baghdad and in Damascus there is tension. In the north, the Kurds continue to fight the Iraqi government. In the Yemen area, the Southern Yemen Republic hardly controls its own territory. And Libya, too, can never be assured that there will not be a counter-revolution.

I am not saying all this in order to imitate the Arabs and to paint you a facile or simple picture, as if Israel totally holds the upper hand. All I am trying to do is to project the idea that the picture that so many of you have is not a complete picture, there are two sides. This year any Arab hope of all-out war has been knocked out of the realms of reality. And in so far as the Arabs consider regaining by force what was taken from them in 1967, they think in terms of two, three or even four years.

The Russians indeed knew this from the beginning. They told Egypt as early as October 1967, and certainly in July 1968, when Nasser came to Moscow, to put out of their minds any idea that within two or three years they can overwhelm Israel. Russian experts spoke of five years at the earliest, and yet Cairo continued to insist that it would have the power by 1969, the very latest early 1970. And Nasser assured Arab leaders in March 1968 in Cairo, to deliver a blow of such force that at least Israel's morale would reel and Egyptian balance would be restored in the Canal, if not in the Sinai Peninsula. So that clock has been pushed back.

Secondly, the inner cohesion of the Arab world against Israel on the financial, military and political planes has not been strengthened lately ; I would say it has even been weakened. They have failed militarily ; they have failed to mobilize the world of Islam – which, had they succeeded, would have been dangerous indeed – and, within their own camp, they have failed to sustain even that element of integrity and force that they produced at Khartoum over two years ago. Moreover, as I have said, within the Arab world, the fissures and differences that have been caked over for the past two years are now re-emerging, whether around the issue of Libya or in southern Arabia.

Nasser holds power in Egypt through a cruel dictatorship and a police-state system, but in Egypt's intellectual community, there are grave doubts. I would say the mood in Egypt, as far as we can judge it, is to come to some definite decision : either to go to war or make peace ! They cannot accept this endless attrition of Arab fatalism, although, at the same time, there is no force at present that could challenge him. But it is no longer a monolithic world with only one assessment – an assessment that nobody dare deny if he is to remain an Arab patriot. So I am quite sure that even as we sit here today, as at every Jewish conference, wondering in our inner consciousness how long Israel can go it economically, militarily and politically, in every Arab cabinet room, in every Arab embassy and at every Arab conference the same question is being asked.

The great difference is that until 1967 only we asked it. I might add that this did not include all Jews, because until 1967 Israel seemed assured, although this was purely a surface evaluation. In the inner sense, the total failure of the original Zionist conception of what would happen in the Middle East, the total incapacity of men so great in vision and action to grasp the nature of the Middle East, the nature of the Arab people, and, possibly, the nature of the flow of Jewish history brought us to false assessments. I believe that our assessments now are more balanced than then.

I further believe that for the first time the Arabs are beginning to realize that the Israeli experiment in this land is not a temporary pheno-menon ; it is something much deeper. But between recognizing that and accepting it there still remains a vast gap. They have to overcome endless emotional inhibitions. They have to acknowledge that their dignity, the dignity of tens of millions, has been trampled underfoot ; they have to acknowledge that they have shown a momentous incapacity in the mili-tary field and that all talk of Arab unity, indeed all talk of one Arab nation, has been but a farce in twentieth-century terms. This transition is not easy for them. It would not be easy for any people, but certainly not for a people of the East ; certainly not for a people that has lived its history with a sense of its fatalism and the power of that fatalism against every external force.

I would further add that, over the past year, it has become more and more clear that the Soviet Union does not want war in the Middle East. The Soviet Union does not want peace, but neither does it want war : the Soviet Union wants tension. They have certainly applied every possible pressure on Cairo and other Arab capitals against war. They have not tried to dissuade them from frontier incidents. They have not tried to bring the war of attrition to an end. But they have warned them that they will not support them in any all-out offensive, and they have warned them of international complications that might ensue. This, too, is a matter of some encouragement, because until, I would say, July 1968, there was no clarity as to where exactly the Soviets stood.

If, in terms of these assessments, one tries to look back, say, to January 1968, the American political experts on the Middle East at the time feared war. They said that with a great Arab re-armament, 1970 could be the crucial date. Now we are in 1970 and nobody can argue that there is a danger of all-out war this year ; I do not think any analyst, no matter how pessimistic, could conceive of such a possibility. Secondly, they spoke of a collapse of Arab society. They spoke of the loss of those governments that had some element of stability. They spoke of Israel and the terri-tories becoming a second Algeria, with the Fatah driving in even deeper. But, above all, they spoke with deep concern of the possibility of Soviet intervention, with all that that could mean in global terms. And it was a great American who expressed this by saying : 'The Soviets will strike like a snake when they are ready.'

Now, if we review the situation from then until now, I can assure you there are very few people in the capitals of the world who conceived in January 1968 that we would be in a position today where the Arab governments have to reassess the possibility of war and push it off for three or four years. Far from the Soviet Union showing an inclination to intervene, I think her disinclination to intervene has deepened. There are many reasons : the Sino-Soviet conflict ; the ferment in Eastern Europe, with Czechoslovakia as its core ; the endless desire to reach some *détente* on the world scene ; the growing lack of reliance on either Arab integrity or military capacity.

And, with all the unpleasantness that internal terror causes us, nor has the integrity of Israel been affected. Daily life has continued and developed. Immigration has increased, the economy has moved ahead. There is no impact, in the inner sense, on the morale of Israel, either from pressure on the frontiers or from the internal terror. These, again, are facts not laced with speculation.

On the global rim – which is the Soviet-U S relationship – we have had a bad beating over the past few months in what we call the erosion of the U S position. This, by the way, is less related to the Arab-Israel conflict than to the fear of the loss of Western positions in the area. What brought on the fact that the United States found it possible, or necessary, or even urgent, to present her programme to the four Great Powers and subsequently publish it was related to a chain reaction that began in September in Libya, and before that in Khartoum : the abortive revolts in southern Arabia, the threat to Lebanese and Jordanian integrity, and the American feeling, against the background of the vast anti-American campaign, that they had to do something that would somehow regain for them some balance in the eyes of the moderate, pro-Western Arabs.

But I do not think that at this stage there is a possibility of the Soviet Union agreeing to the American proposals. I think the war of attrition will continue not only in the local military field, but in the political field across the world. I think the clocks will continue to tick. I think Nasser will continue to tell his people that time is with him and that Arab fatalism can overcome every external force. I think the United States will continue to find, or at least seek, means to improve her position with the pro-Western countries. I think the Soviet Union will continue with its thrust into the area to gain influence and power. But, on the crucial issue within the Middle East – has time, so far worked for, or against us – I have no doubt that today the answer is positive. It has definitely not worked against Israel so far – and let us pray and hope that it will not in the future. I do not think there is any ground for pessimism, though there is ground for concern because of the development of the Fatah in Arab countries.

But let us not forget that the Arab lands have been involved in revolution and counter-revolution for the past fifteen years. When we hear that the Middle East is about to collapse, we cannot help but remember what was said in 1955. I can remember Mr Ben-Gurion talking to the

American Ambassador in October 1955, almost with a sense of deep presentiment and concern, of the future of Israel as Russian arms flowed into Egypt for the first time ; in the north, the Baghdad Pact was being erected. Israel was totally isolated, both from the west and from the east, in those crucial months that ultimately ended in the Sinai Campaign.

We cannot help but remember 1958, when Hussein was given hours to live. I can still recall the late Secretary of State Dulles summoning me post-haste to the State Department one afternoon. I told him the Ambassador, Mr Eban, would be back from London in a few hours, but he said, 'No, I can't wait an hour.' I asked what happened, and he said, 'Hussein may be assassinated tonight. What will Israel do ?' I can re-member Dulles saying : 'How can I guarantee the integrity of countries in the Middle East against indirect aggression ? After all, tomorrow somebody can throw a tomato at the Shah of Persia in the market-place and kill him. Does the American Government then have to send in the Marines ?' So they were thinking in terms of the monarchical régimes in the Middle East, of pro-Western forces.

Let us also not forget that in Egypt itself there are forces working *against* Soviet penetration. There is a saturation point in Arab fatalism that no foreign element has succeeded in piercing. There is an essential xenophobia that the Russians are feeling for the first time – as the British, the French, the Americans and, indeed, the Turks in their time, felt the lash so acutely on their body politic. There are in Cairo officers and other elements who say that Egypt's residues of sovereignty are being sacrificed to the Soviet Union and that the Soviet Union is not giving them support in knocking Israel away from the Suez Canal.

The Soviets, you will be surprised to hear, are also very worried. The Soviet Union fears that should Nasser be overthrown tomorrow, which is certainly within the realms of possibility, anything can happen in the mad world of Arab imagination. It was not accidental that Heykal last Friday quoted Mr Kosygin as having said to the Deputy Premier of Iraq : 'For heaven's sake, unite, you Arabs, on one thing ; be maximalists or minimalists, but at least say something clear.' Because the Soviet Union – and again I speak not from speculation alone – fears very deeply that if Nasser is overthrown, their investment – by now probably in-volving thirty-five per cent of the entire Soviet foreign aid, running into ten or twelve billion dollars, a vast sum for the Soviet Union – will go down the drain ; their thousands of experts may be expelled from Egypt, and their entire process of penetration into the East, which they have fostered for centuries and seemed on the point of achieving so recently, will go up into the air.

I do not want you to regard me as lacking in realism. Believe me, I could project to you a world of phobias and fears ; I could write a cata-logue of the fears that have assaulted Israel month by month, week by week. Take two weeks ago : there was the possibility that four of our ships would be held up in the Mediterranean. Suppose a French cruiser had ordered them to stop, or suppose a Soviet cruiser had stopped them in the eastern Mediterranean. What do we do, what do we tell the sailors to do – resist ? These are phobias that I could catalogue at great length. I am not trying to tell you that the course is an easy one. I believe that the dangers are great and may become even greater. But I do believe that, if we look back – not only over fifty years, not only over thousands of years of Jewish history, but even over the past twenty-two years and, above all, over the past two and a half years – in terms of the struggle for some small measure of light and realism to penetrate the Arab mind, out of the endless churning of this vast area – through the Arab-Israel conflict, the East–West conflict and the intra-Arab complex of relationships – Israel will ultimately emerge triumphant. This may take long and arduous years, but sustained by the unity and faith of world Jewry, with patience, and, above all, with a sense of balance and with the realization that we are in danger, we will come through and move ahead.

Replies to Questions

Dr Goldmann [Nahum Goldmann, President of the World Jewish Congress] mentioned Mr Ben-Gurion's prognosis over a period of many years of eventualities in the Middle East. But I believe that military experts will sustain the assessment that in 1967 the Arabs did not show much greater capacity than in 1956. I well recall military assessments in the early 'sixties of the Egyptian Army having become a full-fledged army with vast force. I can remember experts who believed that to shatter the Egyptian Army in Sinai, as in 1956, would cost endless casualties and possibly was not within the realm of reasonable prospects. The facts turned out to be different. I do not think any military expert today will claim that within the next few years the Arabs can gain superiority. If you talk of five, ten, fifteen, or twenty years, then we are looking into the distant future.

I can recall in 1948 what people across the world said when China underwent revolution, and they thought of what will happen when Russia and China get together to dominate the world scene. I remember the tremors across Western capitals. Today this is hardly the assessment, in terms of both the internal situation in China and her growing rift with Russia, which, by the way, is probably one of the major factors in Russian restraint in the Middle East.

We could go back. Dr Goldmann is far more experienced than many here, and certainly than myself, in terms of what I would call the Odyssey of Zionist hopes, expectations and fears over many decades. It is not for me to recall to him the situation here between 1936 and 1938, the time of the White Paper ; World War Two, when the Nazi armies threatened Palestine and with it the last vestiges of Jewish hope ; 1946 to 1948, when the British Empire miraculously decided to give up its place on the world scene as an empire with actual territorial power and decided to move to the sphere of strategic communications. But were it not for that, had the clash between the Yishuv and the British Mandate taken place in the thirties, very possibly no Jewish State would have emerged. If you think back to the situation we faced in 1955-6, with vast armaments from Russia pouring into Egypt, I recall that Joseph Alsop, the well-known commentator, commenting on the Czech-Egyptian arms deal in October 1955, said ; 'It is five minutes past twelve, and the Middle East is lost to the Western world.' I recall, as I mentioned earlier, Mr Ben-Gurion's feelings in October 1955 after this Czech-Egyptian arms deal, when the arsenals of the West were sealed to us.

But it is not my function tonight to review the history of Israel or the miracles that, day in and day out, have attended our progress. All I want to point out is that this area is in a constant state of confusion, with three major conflicts, or tendencies, always unfolding : the Arab-Israel, the inner-Arab and the Soviet-American pressures for influence. Nobody can say definitely that the situation will get worse ; all I was trying to say was that there is an element of balance that provides us with a realistic basis for our hopes and expectations.

Dr Goldmann mentioned the Fatah development. I would say that that is the major ground for concern in the Middle East and should affect us deeply. At the same time let us not forget that the Palestinians and those supporting them have been active here for the past fifty years. I would not be honest if I were to say that anything like the Fatah has emerged in previous times. It has impetus, idealism and force ; it carries dangers the like of which we have not known in the past. At the same time let us not forget that, in a sense, these dangers affect the Arab régimes before they affect Israel ; and Hussein of Jordan, the President of Lebanon and Nasser himself are very, very alert to these dangers. It is not for nothing that the Soviet Union has so far withheld direct support from the Fatah and has not given them political recognition. The answer is very simple – and this, again, is not speculation – that the Soviet Union fears Nasser's reaction. The whole Fatah situation, too, is becoming involved in more and more splinter groups. So it is a little early, I would say, to define this as an ultimate danger. But I agree that it is certainly a dark spot on the horizon, which must be closely watched.

Dr Goldmann, speaking of Nasser, said a word of Jewish wisdom : that any heir to Nasser could be worse. That is true. But in the assessment of the Arab world today, we feel that Nasser's charisma is a major force in the thrust against Israel. We saw this at Rabat. We know that Hussein does not agree in his heart with Nasser. We know that Hussein believes the Arab world will never gain in another war, that the continuation of the present trend of Arab policy will bring total catastrophe to the Arab world. We know that Hussein takes seriously what Nasser has thrown out as a challenge : that one more defeat and the world will hear no more of the Arab entity as one of the great entities of world civilization. And yet, Hussein has no alternative – not only because Egypt is such a vast power in the Arab world, but because Nasser, over fifteen years, through a magic of personality and great idealism in terms of Arab patriotism, has managed to impose a certain moral authority on the Arab world. If he were to disappear tomorrow, we believe there would be a certain disintegration – not necessarily that they would make peace tomorrow, but the various elements diffused across the so-called façade of Arab unity would probably assert themselves much more than they are doing today.

And again let us not forget the balance of forces within the Arab world. I mentioned earlier the Maghreb, which is essentially moderate : Tunis, Morocco, Algeria. When I say essentially moderate, I believe, and I say this with full conviction, that neither the King of Morocco nor the President of Tunisia nor, very possibly, Boumedienne today really expect that one, the Arabs will be in a position to make all-out war within the foreseeable future ; two, that they could possibly win the war ; three, that even in a war of attrition they will weary Israel to a point where she will be forced to surrender her vital interests. This is very central in terms of the entire assessment of the Arab world. I believe that Hussein agrees with them, I believe the Lebanese agree with them, I think Feisal in his heart of hearts is not remote from that assessment. This does not mean, and I tried to point it out earlier, that these moderate elements will jump to make peace tomorrow. None of them is ready to forfeit what they feel to be their place in Arab history and Arab patriotism. But it is a long cry from a situation of a monolithic totality of conviction, of an absolute certainty that time flows in their favour. In terms of the Arab assessments, there has been a vast change, and in this respect there is a ferment, the results of which we cannot yet know. But we may at least hold certain hopes in terms of the unfolding scene.

I agree with Dr Goldmann on the Soviet Union. I also believe that they do not want the destruction of Israel. I also believe that it is not impossible that they may reach an agreement with the United States, although if they wished to do so it would be in terms of their direct interests. I believe the Soviet Union would not lose, in terms of her thrust in to the Middle East, from an agreement, and I believe she fears that without a total agreement or some form of settlement in the Middle East – not peace of course, but some form of settlement – that her vital interests may be imperilled by a total collapse of Arab society. This, paradoxically enough, Washington and Moscow simultaneously fear.

Nasser's genius has been, over the years, to convince Moscow that if he fell a right-wing government of a fascist complexion would take over in Egypt and the Soviet thrust would be totally blunted and set back to before 1955. Simultaneously, he convinced the United States that if he collapsed, total chaos would reign in Cairo and Communism would implant its first seeds in Arab minds throughout the Middle East. I am not sure if the United States is still convinced, but I would say that, on balance, American officials fear his downfall because they do not know who will come in his place.

And there is always a possibility of a Soviet-Nasser clash over the Middle East. This is one of the paradoxes of the area : although they march hand in hand in alliance to destroy Western positions, they are both poised to inherit the results of this collapse, and so whenever the collapse seems imminent there are signs of tensions in Cairo. We felt this in 1960-1, in the famous Kruschev-Nasser debates in public, and this has had a certain expression recently. This is another one of the unknowns that we can throw into the bag of future unknowns.

Dr Prinz [American rabbi and communal leader] has raised the issue of 'no conditions'. On the question of 'no conditions', you ask : why we deceive ourselves and the world by saying we come to the negotiating table without prior conditions when, after all, Jerusalem, Gaza and Sharm el-Sheikh are conditions from which Israel will not budge.

I think I know the inner mind of our government - if one can talk of the inner mind of a collective of twenty-four people - and I think I have some background on the thought of the people of Israel. I would say that what you consider to be a paradox is essentially the child of circumstances. In what sense ? The idea of peace is so remote from our consciousness - because of twenty years with three wars, because of the ceaseless propaganda, the constant pressures on the frontiers and the natural complexes and phobias that this situation has created - the idea of peace seems to be such a fantasy, in a sense, that to sit down and attempt to present total logic in preparation for hypothetical circumstances of such remoteness is in itself a paradox.

You say then, if, after all, we come to the table, there can be no negotiation. Why are you so sure ? First of all, many Israeli spokesmen have spoken of a free port in Gaza for King Hussein. What is a free port ? What does it mean ? What are his conditions ? How does he reach his free port ? How does he carry his goods to the free port ? What sovereignty or non-sovereignty would the free port involve ? I could throw out to you a whole series of questions that you could put to any class of political scientists, and I am sure you would get many replies.

You say rightly that we will not yield at Sharm el-Sheikh. But, also, it depends on what circumstances you are talking about. Suppose Nasser were to arrive - and I am talking totally hypothetically ; I represent neither the government, the Prime Minister, nor anybody else, I am just analysing in my mind - suppose Nasser were to get on a helicopter and come to the Dan Hotel and say, 'I made a mistake. The Arab world relents. We wish to liquidate totally the Arab-Israel conflict ; we will unite in a regional covenant across the Middle East.' And with him the entire Arab world moved from a course of hatred to a paean of praise and cooperation. If, at that point, he would say, 'And on Sharm el-Sheikh, I agree, after what you went through, that you must have iron-clad guarantees, and maybe I, Nasser, will even agree that you keep your troops there ; but suppose we say you keep them for fifty years, for 100 years.' I am not prepared to underwrite today – I probably shouldn't say this, but there's no press here, the room is closed, and I trust your confidence and the chairman's assurances – that if Nasser were prepared to allow Israeli troops to remain in Sharm el-Sheikh for fifty years, with iron-clad guarantees, with joint naval patrols, that we would say : 'Under no account ! You go back to Cairo ; there'll be no peace ; we'll fight for 100 years. Over what ? We want a title-deed to the ten square kilometres surrounding Sharm el-Sheikh (or whatever the military say : ten, twenty, thirty, fifty).' So why argue that there is no possibility of negotiation ?

Even on Jerusalem we have said we are prepared to make agreements with the world churches to assure their religious rights and the universal status of the places that they feel are sacred to them. Now this also means certain agreements on Jerusalem. This went through the Cabinet. We offered it to the Vatican. And, by the way, when you referred to the refugee problem tearing asunder the Christian churches and Israel, I would not exaggerate. If you are talking of certain elements in the Protestant churches, you are right. If you are talking of the entire Christian world, I do not agree. The fact that Rome today, in the present situation, can discuss the possibility of proclaiming a Christian duty to recognize Jewish religious rights in the Holy Land is in itself of such phenomenal, revolutionary consequences as to completely wash away, in terms of balance of world power, and certainly in terms of balance of history, the entire challenge in certain circles of the New Left to Israel's essential rights. The very fact that a proclamation of that nature is discussed – unfortunately I do not think it will come about – must have certain repercussions among Catholics in the United States and throughout Western Europe.

But to come back to the question of pre-conditions. The truth is that the exact conditions that we will put on the table are a matter of the deepest concern and, I would say, inner tension in the Jewish community in this land. To try today to work out exactly for what we will press – I suggest leaving that to the future. But to argue today that, because we say 'without prior conditions', we are deceiving ourselves and the world is just not correct. If you lived here long enough, I am sure you would realize that, in this internal debate, the very fact that we can say that shows the measure to which the people of Israel is prepared to go for peace.

If you talk of the Palestinian people, let me ask you : the Arabs sat in

Rabat two weeks ago, and the entire Arab world said to Arafat : 'Proclaim a government-in-exile ; we will recognize you.' Arafat refused. The other Arabs didn't push it. The Palestinians, it is argued, in the West Bank and the Gaza Strip, are under Israeli military control ; but in Beirut they rule supreme. They aren't even blocked by the Lebanese Government. Why on earth don't they get up and proclaim themselves a people ? What is the inner reason for this ? Why have the Palestinians not proclaimed themselves a people ? Their first action should have been – and any logical man would have advised them accordingly – to proclaim a government-in-exile. They could request recognition from all the Arab governments, run up a Palestinian flag, establish embassies and request recognition across the world. Why don't they do that ? The answer is a very simple one. Nasser doesn't want it and Hussein doesn't want it. And the answer may also be that there is not, as yet, the national cohesion for a true Palestinian people. Maybe we are all really mistaken. If you go to the West Bank and speak to the Palestinians, one element claims an Arab people and wants such an entity ; the other element, and not only out of fear of Hussein, says they are part of the Jordanian entity. Yet a third element says there is no meaning to a Palestinian people – one more people to the fourteen-fifteen Arab states – unless this means the destruction of Zionist ideology and institutions and the vanishing of the uniqueness of the Jewish state. It is as simple as that. Why on earth people expect us to recognize a Palestinian people, I cannot understand.

I had a leader of the New Left here from New York two weeks ago. He went around the West Bank and talked to many Israeli intellectuals ; and many Israeli intellectuals also say the only panacea is to proclaim a Palestinian people. Maybe, maybe. But I told him there are two types of people you meet in this land – that is, both Jews and Arabs. One element, which says : 'Recognize the Palestine people,' is not telling you the whole truth. What they mean is : recognize a Palestine entity in Judea and Samaria and then take a few tanks and send the leaders over to Amman to establish a Palestinian people. King Hussein represents only forty per cent on the East Bank ; democratically speaking he does not fulfil the Palestinian people's aspirations, he is the block to a settlement in the Middle East. Give the Palestinians their state, and Israel can come to terms. There are many people who think in those terms also in the Western world. The other element, I told him, is thinking in terms of vitiating the Jewish character of the state. That we cannot do.

So, when you say : 'Recognize the Palestine people,' first of all, it is by no means proven that there is such a cohesion of national character that brings them to consider themselves, outside the unique Israel aspect, as a people, as compared to Jordan or Egypt. Secondly, Arab leadership is violently opposed to them proclaiming that. Thirdly, they are themselves torn, fragment by fragment. However, Arafat's position is very clear : there will be no Palestine entity until it takes the place of the

Jewish entity ! Because he argues – rightly from his standpoint – that if they become an entity in Judea and Samaria, then Israel has won the battle. Under no account, therefore, will he permit it. And I am quoting the Fatah newspaper, *Free Palestine,* two weeks ago, in London.

And finally, I ask you, what about your government, the United States Government ? Its latest proposals envisage Hussein returning to the West Bank and even gaining control of the major part, if not the whole, of the Gaza Strip. The United States is interested in helping Hussein, for crucial reasons of her global policy. If we were to proclaim a Palestine entity, or recognize it or, let us say, treat it as seriously as you would suggest, this means : one, going contrary to American policies, and we have enough differences with them ; two, sealing off the door finally for any settlement with Hussein, and this is an issue that must be seriously considered.

Now you also speak, Dr Prinz, of the encounter of the Government of Israel with leaders of the Jewish people. I agree with you that one should be frank. But I would say on the issue of the refugees – I do not think anybody who has any intelligence can assume that the refugee problem is not one of the major problems of the area – the question is how you approach it. Should we settle the refugees throughout Judea and Samaria ? What do we do with those in the Gaza Strip ? I would say the answer of the government at present is to begin pilot projects on refugees. We believe the problem can only be treated on a regional scale. This does not mean that we do not treat it with sufficient gravity. But you must remember that you are speaking here to a nation that has been under siege now for twenty-two years, that has providentially been saved three times, and that has before it a future of hope but also of great danger. We therefore do not have those sensitivities that you may feel, naturally and rightfully, when criticized on certain aspects of Israel's policies abroad.

But this takes me to the last point that was raised here : the situation and world opinion. Now here, too, we will differ essentially. The question is : where does Israel stand in world opinion ? In terms of Israel's world situation, it is my clear impression that the Arabs, with all their vast propaganda and money, have not gained more support in the West. This does not mean that Israel has increased its support.

There is a remarkable dichotomy. The Arabs have not gone up in the Gallup Polls nor in the admiration of statesmen, people of the spirit, or great journalists. Israel has gone down a little – not so much, I would say, on the refugee issue or the territories, but largely because of the question that has been a major subject tonight : will there be an end to this constant bloodletting ? Is there any hope of peace in the area ? I admit that on this issue we have not presented our case very well before world opinion. I admit that in the whole field of public relations we have been woefully deficient. But I would say that, essentially speaking, on the central issue of who is responsible for the lack of peace, you will still find that the major element of world opinion says that the fault lies with the Arab states, not with Israel. And so we still have a vast host of world opinion in our favour.

It is fantastic to try to judge the gyrations of world opinion, because here, as in the case of the ships from Cherbourg, everybody assumed the world would all say all right ; legally, in the formal sense you are right, but after all it is a fiction. You sent your people there and they gave up the ships, and a Norwegian company took it for oil, and who on earth believes that they are really going to be sent here to dig for oil ? And yet, in the entire world press, it became a fantastic drama, almost a comic drama of ships racing across the Mediterranean being followed by planes and ships, and yet finally reaching Haifa. And Israel, according to all the experts, moved up in world opinion. So where is the denominator, where is the index ?

I, personally, do not feel anything wrong in a frank debate. I think one of our great mistakes is that we do not ask Jewish leaders to debate frankly with us. I think it is a great mistake to try to stifle criticism. I do not think we can expect the Jewish people to stand with us unless we are ready for full and frank debates. I do not mean in the public sense, because we have enemies across the world. And I therefore appreciate the fact that Dr Goldmann, with all his criticism – and he was very fair tonight – has not spoken publicly, but has chosen to argue in Israel, with the leaders of the Government of Israel. This is his right, probably his duty. And I say the same of Dr Prinz. But above all, in viewing the situation, let us keep our balance, our fairness, our capacity for frank dialogue ; and, above all, in addition to our faith, let us base it upon realistic assessment.

The United States and Israel

From an address to the Israel Defence Forces Command and Staff College, 12 October 1969, following Prime Minister Golda Meir's visit to the United States in September

The United States has come a long way in regard to its bilateral relations with Israel, especially in the central sphere of the balance of forces. In a joint statement published in 1968, the United States undertook to follow and preserve the balance of forces in the Middle East, keeping a close and constant watch on the situation. No doubt you remember twenty years of struggle over this subject. Formerly, the United States declared that it would supply no arms to the region, later, that it would supply only defensive arms ; then it agreed to supply small quantities of offensive arms, provided that it should not be the major supplier of arms to Israel – that was the function of France. And now, stage by stage, it has reached the point of undertaking to preserve the balance of forces, with the question of the Phantoms being the crucial and fundamental expression of this undertaking. In this regard, President Nixon has shown sympathy and understanding for the Prime Minister's request for more Phantoms. Thus, the Republican Administration has gone a step further in adopting this doctrine of American responsibility for preserving the balance of forces in the Middle East.

In the second sphere of economic aid, the President promised further examination, and it may be assumed that we shall get assistance from the United States. Israel's needs are many, and time is pressing, especially in view of the position of our foreign currency balances and the tremendous economic pressure that we face. We shall need a great deal of American help in order to close the gap that threatens us. We have reason to expect that we shall not be turned away empty handed (as we have hardly ever been in the economic sphere during the past fifteen years), if we consider the promise of 'sympathetic consideration' against the background of the general sympathy shown by the President to the Prime Minister, the breach in the heavy armour of the Republican régime, and the Prime Minister's success in establishing close contact with the President and the Anglo-Saxon establishment in the United States. By its nature, this establishment is always more favourably disposed to the pure American kernel – free from Jews, blacks, Catholics and groups originating in immigration from the distressed countries of Europe. The Anglo-Saxons are the backbone, the foundation, of American society. While Kennedy represented the immigrant groups, Nixon represents this Anglo-Saxon kernel, which by its nature has never been close to

Jews for many reasons – not always through its own fault, to some extent through the fault of the Jews, but we shall not try at this time to analyse the convolutions of Jewish thinking in the Diaspora, especially in that great community of the United States.

In any case, it is a fact that this President, who always felt a certain distance from the Jews, has now come much closer to them. He has been made aware of a much more favourable attitude on the part of American Jews. For the first time, through the Prime Minister, he has felt that the Jews are, as it were, smiling at him, and presumably he is now very hopeful about the significance and the prospects of this smiling face. He has undoubtedly smiled back ; in other words, a bridge has been established with this man, who has, after all, a great influence on the affairs of the world for another three or, perhaps, seven years.

Nor should we forget the tremendous public reverberations of the Prime Minister's visit, for we ought to realize that, in the democracies, it is the ordinary people who count in the final analysis. As a political animal who has reached the top, the President is well aware that his survival depends, not on the Middle East experts in the State Department or on the professors or the intellectuals who present their opinions to him, but on, what is called in American parlance, the Kansas City milkman, or, in London, the Chelsea busman – in short, the common man. Here the Prime Minister was very successful. Through her great power of getting to the ordinary people in the United States – on TV, etc. – they felt a kind of identity with her and with the case that she represents. There is no doubt that these waves of identification have reached the delicate antennae in the White House. Accordingly, we may assume that, on the bilateral plane, our prospects are not insignificant, and in the course of the next few months we shall get some measure of satisfaction.

There are two other planes – the inter-Arab plane and the plane of relations between the Great Powers – in which the United States is no less vital to our interests than on the bilateral plane, for without the American capacity for deterrence there is not the slightest doubt that the Soviet Union would long ago have overrun the Middle East. The question is, then, whether the United States continues, as in past years, to stand up to the Soviet Union, or whether its capacity or determination in this respect has been weakened. My impression is that the United States is keeping to its commitments.

Vietnam may work on one side or the other. On the one hand, Vietnam is not only sucking America's blood but, even more serious, it is weakening American thinking. You feel as if people there are wandering in dense and, as it were, impenetrable forests. The doctrine that has dominated American thinking for twenty-five years, since 1945, the doctrine of confronting the Soviet Union in every region, has not been undermined from the aspect of commitments, but it has been seriously weakened. The United States is fumbling in the dark ; it is still in the grip of a serious trauma. There are some who believe that Vietnam means a new era in American history, that America will close in upon itself, become a kind of 'Fortress America', and leave the rest of the world to look after its interests as best it can. I do not accept this view, at any rate not with regard to the next two years. There is also another view : if they get out of Vietnam, as presumably they will – and there is no question of getting out with a victory, the question is only the extent of American failure – they will concentrate even more on keeping their commitments in other regions and, first and foremost, in Europe and the Middle East.

In any case, it may be said that the United States is still faithful to its basic commitments in the Middle East. That is one side of the coin. But there is also another side. American thinking has been shocked by what has happened to American soldiers in Vietnam. This means that if ever there is any question of sending American soldiers to any area, not only will they refuse, but they will run miles to avoid the very possibility, even if it means escaping into a blind alley and complete confusion of thought. An American diplomat gave me the example of Libya – a powerful bastion of Western oil interests, an American base that cost hundreds of millions of dollars, of basic importance to the entire Western defence system in the area, and yet, look what happened there. He told me something interesting : in all the reports from American embassies in the Middle East, in all the cables from Washington expressing alarm at the news of Qaddafi's revolt, in all the intelligence reports – in short, in everything that passed through his hands – he did not find from any level in the American administration, either in Washington or in any part of the Middle East, the suggestion that they might try to find out the extent of the backing for the revolutionary junta. No such idea was mooted.

In any case, I found a fundamental change from the America I knew in 1957–60, when I served in Washington, from the America I knew in 1963 and even in 1968, when the late Prime Minister Levi Eshkol visited President Lyndon Johnson in Texas. At that time, President Johnson may already have been thinking of retiring from his post, but nevertheless he still held the fort, when the symbol of holding the fort against the Russians was the American soldier. Today, such an idea is anathema, absolutely unthinkable. This is undoubtedly a change in the American outlook, although it is hard to say exactly what it means in regard to us. I do not mean to say that the United States is ready to stand aside and allow the Soviet Union to take over the Middle East. To our great good fortune, the Soviet Union, at least, does not believe that. However, I feel the lack of that tremendous impetus that I still felt a month before the Six Day War, when I talked to Rostow in the White House in connection with Soviet penetration into the area through the Persian Gulf and the emirates ; at that time, you got the impression that the United States felt that every unit in the area was responsible to it by virtue of its world leadership and that it regarded the Middle East as vital. Even today they will give you routine answers, but you don't feel the fervour.

All the fervour is working in one direction : how to arrive at an agreement with the Soviet Union. Here there are undoubtedly different ways of thinking. That is, they made it clear to us that, for many reasons, the United States would not sell us down the river ; it would not agree to anything less than peace, according to the American version – though that is very far from peace as we see it. If they tell you that time is working against us, what they really mean is that it is working against them. They tell us that if only they can get an agreement with the Soviets, there is still hope. If we tell them that they are admitting the legitimacy of the Soviet presence in the Middle East, they reply that we are just being foolish – after all, the Soviets are already entrenched in the Middle East.

In 1960, David Ben-Gurion came to the United States and suggested to President Eisenhower that America should try to arrive at an agreement with the Soviet Union on the limitation of the arms race in the Middle East. A few weeks later, Ambassador Avraham Harman and myself were summoned to the State Department, and the Secretary of State said to us : 'What's wrong with you? Your Prime Minister, the leader of a basically pro-Western country, proposes that we should bring the Soviets into the Middle East, give them a status!' In Washington today, I believe, the question is not whether to give Russia a status in the Middle East, but how to ensure that Russia shall not liquidate the remaining Western assets in the area and agree to coexistence, in the same way as the United States wants them to agree to coexistence the world over.

Washington is well aware that the Soviet Union is in the grip of an internal crisis no less severe than that of America. It is not only a question of China, Czechoslovakia and the rest of Eastern Europe, but of cracks that have appeared in the entire Communist ideology. There is no doubt that the Soviet bloc has been shaken. Nevertheless, Washington has been showing signs of uneasiness, a kind of urgency, which was not apparent before, to arrive at an agreement with the Soviet Union. It is not, as some people say, just in order to satisfy American public opinion – an anguished cry, because of despair with Vietnam, to get a settlement and get rid of the constant world tension.

I do not believe that President Nixon really thinks in his heart of hearts that he will reach a final settlement. And even if he does think so, I do not believe that he will go so far, whatever may happen, as to abandon Israel. They are still optimistic in the United States, as you have read in the newspapers. But they put the following question to us : it is true that you can stand up to the Arabs, but what will be the end of it all, how will you carry the burden of ruling over one million Arabs, how will you bear the economic burden, how will you overcome this escalation in men and armaments, how will your morale stand up against tens of millions of Arabs?

In the final analysis, however, if you ask me to sum up the reactions in

Washington to the Prime Minister's visit, I would say that the tremendous response from public opinion has undoubtedly greatly strengthened our position in the White House. The increased closeness of the President and his administration both to the Jews and to Israel opens up great prospects : almost certainly, of the supply of arms ; lesser prospects, but still serious ones, for some satisfaction in the economic area ; true friendship from the United States, and the certainty that she will not abandon us. On the other hand, there is an American striving, resulting from a kind of inner despair, for an agreement with the Soviets ; and if the Soviet Union and Cairo approve – and it is our good fortune that they do not – there will undoubtedly be serious differences of opinion between ourselves and the United States.

From time to time I wander over the face of the globe and talk to representatives from the Middle East and Western countries in various places. You arrive at a point where no common view is possible. In the final analysis, I would say, we arrive at a confrontation of Jewish faith with twentieth century logic. This is very basic. The gentile sees the world, in a way, in terms of a balance sheet, of credit and debit. The method used in a Wall Street company, he applies to an international problem. Lord Thomson of Fleet, who owns 124 newspapers and is certainly a clever man, once said to me after he had been visiting in Cairo : the Arabs are certainly badly beaten, but let me tell you, sometimes, in my business, I beat my rivals – newspaper owners in different parts of the world – and yet, when I have forty companies against me, then, although I can beat them once, twice, again, and every time, I still don't sleep nights. They are forty and I am only one. And I want to tell you, on the face of it, you are perfectly all right, yet my Western mind asks you : *Quo vadis?* How can you face this swirling world of hatred? How can you hold your own against forty, fifty or 100 million Arabs? The Moslem world is in a ferment, and the Soviet Union is behind it, as well as China – which cannot be laughed off, as it constitutes three-quarters of the globe – and here is a country of two and one-half million and it says : time is on my side.

The Western gentile mind really can't grasp it. And don't let us give way to paranoia and imagine that every non-Jew who tells us not to insist on a real peace treaty is an anti-Semite. That isn't so : he just sees things in his own way. He doesn't hate Israel ; with all his heart he wants us to live in peace, but he says to us : you are striding forward into an unknown that is beyond the grasp of my understanding ; if you want to go on, do it, but why drag me down with you? This is where a line is drawn between us and the nations of the world, and it is really also a moral line, when it comes to the problem of our right to the Land of Israel. When you argue with them, at some point they question our absolute right. I believe this had been a problem throughout modern times ; for fifty years it has been troubling political leaders, priests and ministers, journalists, thinkers and academics all over the world. Who is right in this dispute? So long as they admit the uniqueness of the Jewish people, they cannot pass final sentence and say that the Jews have no right to this country, but they really find it difficult to decide between the uniqueness of the Jew and the Arab claim. When Israel was in danger, none of them wanted it to be wiped off the map of human history ; they did not want to witness the destruction of this unique entity. And yet, when Israel is victorious over the other side, then the question of the Arabs is aroused ; and they hesitate, pulled this way and that in perplexity by this eternal question.

And, by the way, let no one tell you that anywhere in the Western world a non-Jew has really settled this question. This has been the constant struggle ever since the days of Lloyd George and Balfour. An American President who has had a soft spot for us, has felt that way not only because of the Jew of New York, but because he did not want to deny something that affected his heritage as well. Dulles was pulled two ways by this question. I remember once, at a dinner, he got up and said : What can I do? Israel has only one embassy in this city out of a hundred, but I cannot look on it as just one country out of many. If I do that, I shall be denying the entire Judaeo-Christian heritage on which the whole of this country is built - without that, there is no America. I cannot treat it like Afghanistan, or Guinea, and judge it on that basis. (It may well be that this was what he felt on that occasion, but he was prone to vacillating from day to day.)

After all the political debates, the differences of opinion, the tremendous flood of friendship, when you get down to rock bottom and the question of rights arises, they tell you that you are seventy or eighty per cent right, but there is still that twenty per cent that isn't quite clear ; therefore, we have to give something to the other side. And we say : if we admit that twenty per cent is not clear, then that undermines our very foundation, for we are an eternal people and you cannot slice eternity into pieces. The same applies to a true political evaluation. You can go along with them up to a certain point, with differences of opinion this way and that, until you get to the tremendous, awesome wilderness of the unknown. Then you say to them : I have been travelling in this wilderness for thousands of years, and I just keep going on and on. And they say : not with us ; this is a concept we cannot accept ; this is a logic that is quite illogical ; we cannot go any further. This is where you have to stop and make a compromise. That is really the basis or, I would say, the sum-total of the Western world's attitude. All at once they look at you with tremendous respect. Here is a people that has arisen, in twenty-five years, after six million were slaughtered in the gas chambers of Europe, to become the most important military factor in the Middle East. Tremendous respect - but also perplexity, wonderment, profound anxiety for the future.

Canada and Israel

On the Occasion of the Establishment of the Canada–Israel Chamber of Commerce, September 1961

The theme of this evening is economic. But it has a deeper aspect than the formal development of trade relations between two friendly countries. The presence here tonight of leading personalities in the economic life of this great land of freedom, their sponsorship of the newly established Canada-Israel Chamber of Commerce, the messages from the Prime Minister of Canada and the Minister of Trade and Industry, the very atmosphere prevailing here – are all indicative of the foundation on which rests not only trade but the wider gamut of the international relationship of which it forms a part. This foundation is confidence.

There is not much novelty in Israel's expression of confidence in Canadian development. For this vast land, linking two oceans and serving as a bridge between three continents, is blessed in abundant material resources and its people have forged its nationhood from a diversity of backgrounds. These people, in discerning the inner bonds of man, have achieved through their harmony a new dispensation of nationhood. And dynamism, creativity and faith, having consolidated nationhood, now impart their inspiration to the development of the land on which this nationhood sets its imprint.

But the other partner in the venture we are honouring tonight is thousands of miles away – a small land born to renewed life in heavy travail. People and land, after a separation of close to two millenia, have been united in a unique tapestry in which torment ushered in faith, and which, in its turn, has ushered in achievement. Development – economic and social – has defied the norms of conventional assessment. Yet Israel has had to develop economically while shouldering the burden of absorbing over one million immigrants since its establishment thirteen years ago. Moreover, much of its vital economic capacity has had to be diverted to maintaining an adequate defensive posture, without which its life would hang in the balance. Its three land frontiers remain sealed by barriers of hostility, boycott and blockade.

Could there be a more disparate picture of the elements of partnership than that presented by Canada and Israel in the economic field? Yet this is but the external picture. In reviewing the inner motive that inspires the relationship between Canada and Israel, indeed in considering the motive that underlies this gathering and the endeavour it is inaugurating, I am reminded of a conversation I had with the Prime Minister of Canada on my arrival in Ottawa a little over a year ago. Mr Diefenbaker reminisced on his visit to Israel in 1955 – recollections at once comprehensive and incisive. But his central impression, as he put it, was of the measure of spiritual motive inspiring the activity of rebuilding. Israel is beset with problems today, but in 1955 they were far greater, indeed appeared insurmountable. Yet here I was sitting with the Prime Minister of Canada, a man of public experience over decades, one whose daily life is immersed in the problems of government, and the impact that was fresh in his mind, five years after his visit, was not of the security, social and economic problems of Israel, and not of the manner in which the people were seeking to overcome them ; it was of spiritual motive. From other Canadian leaders with whom I have spoken, indeed from varied groups across Canada, one hears the same impression. They have sought and found the innermost characteristic of Israel reborn. They have perceived the process of a nation's quest to regain its soul, that quest in which it has found strength to renew its life in freedom and independence in the family of nations. Our forum this evening is the forum of trade ; its mainspring is mutual confidence. This in turn touches on mutual spiritual sympathy and understanding.

But we are not engaged merely in an analysis of the motives of friendship. We are studying the expression of this friendship in terms of a leap forward in economic cooperation. And here, two factors become crucial. The first is the factor of stability, a consideration that obliges us to assess briefly the contemporary situation in the Middle East and its prospects into the future. After three years of comparative calm, the area has again come into the headlines of world tensions. If I may be permitted to digress, I wish to say that Israel's policy towards the present clash within the Arab world is one of total non-intervention. As I have had the opportunity to mention in Montreal on a previous occasion, one of the three points of tension in the Middle East is the intra-Arab tension. In the past five years some fifteen convulsions have taken place in Arab capitals from Baghdad to Khartoum. All this must be viewed as an evolutionary process, as a nationalism, subjected over centuries, that searches to define motives and patterns in the political, social and economic spheres – motives and patterns that, over centuries of trial, failure and achievement, have become accepted norms in other world areas. Side by side with the Arab internal crisis, the Middle East has been a focal point for the Cold War during the past decade. For our area is a meeting point of three continents, the repository of vast oil resources and of vital importance in terms of communications and strategic consideration. These two points of tension – the complex intra-Arab relationship and the Cold War – have contributed in considerable measure to frustrating progress towards an Arab-Israel settlement. Yet a deep observation of the course of the Middle East during the past few years will, I would submit, indicate a trend towards stability rather than a retrogression. Underlying the convulsion and tension, there are the beginnings of a sense of area-destiny among the peoples of the Middle East. The Cold

War, which has struck with intensity other areas – the Caribbean, Africa, the Far East and, of course, Berlin – has, in the Middle East, not shown signs of intensification. Indeed, the Middle East in present world circumstances would seem to be behaving outside of its native context.

Arab hostility to Israel has not abated, but there is ground for the hope that out neighbours will ultimately realize that Israel is a permanent factor in the area and that their hostility is not only futile but harmful to their own interests. Israel's proven defensive capacity, her developing economy, her growing international status, cannot have been without impact on her neighbours. Nor can they fail to have noticed Israel's abstinence from every attempt to exploit to her advantage the storms and stresses in the Arab countries. One has the impression that the Israel issue is no longer the central aspect in Arab emotional reaction. If the intra-Arab struggle and the East–West conflict have deepened Arab instability in the broad sense, there is possibly some compensation in the fact that the Arab mind has been brought face to face with the challenge to its own destiny and with the threat to the integrity of the area as a whole. It would be premature to return to the hopes entertained before the rise of the state and for some time after. Yet, despite radical changes in circumstances, certain of the grounds for that hope have continuing relevance. This would emerge clearly if other aspects of tension in the Middle East were to subside. It is beyond the capacity of Israel to bring about such developments. It is within her capacity to develop on the Arab mind the impact of growing stability and progress coupled with peaceful intent.

We believe that peace will come. This belief arises from the deepest springs of faith. We believe that with peace a new era will open up for the Middle East, reminiscent of its one-time greatness and assuring it its rightful and constructive place on the world scene. It may be paradoxical, but it is no less true, that of all the sources of tension in the Middle East – the East–West conflict, intra-Arab disputes, differences within the Western alliance, the great problem of Arab economic and social evolution – the Israel-Arab dispute, though highly charged emotionally, is probably more prone to practical solution that other problems. Israel holds neither water nor land nor other resources that the Arabs need for their survival and development. The matter has been tested twice in the field of battle. It is being placed presently before the bar of world opinion. Surely the time has come for both sides to negotiate directly in a constructive spirit. The present attitude of the Arab governments is not only illogical in terms of their own people, it is not only without precedent in international conduct, it is out of context with basic international trends that, within the shadow of the atomic threat, identify peace with human survival. But the international community must also play its part in bringing about a new era in the Middle East.

What is needed is not appeasement but a new international approach to the Middle East directed to guaranteeing for its peoples peace and economic development. This approach should be based on three principles : (1) The integrity and independence of all countries in the Middle East, freed from external threat and interference ; (2) Peaceful coexistence within the region, with the outlawing of boycott, blockade, subversion and hostile propaganda ; (3) Large-scale economic development, leading eventually to regional cooperation.

The international assessment of the Middle East is unduly influenced by current public attitudes in the area. It is, therefore, marked by a fatalistic acceptance of danger, instability and tension as a permanent feature of the Middle East scene. While the danger of further crisis is ever-present, on a long view the concept of the integrity and independence of all countries of the area and the sense of common destiny are increasingly striking roots. This process is evident not only among the non-Arab peoples in the Middle East ; it can also be discerned in certain Arab circles, whose public posture should not always be taken as an expression of their inherent attitude. World statesmanship should recognize and support this development, which symbolizes the true trend of history in the Middle East.

If the outer rim is, as I have submitted, moving in the direction of stability, slow and difficult to define as this movement may be, the inner stability of Israel has been sustained in unceasing growth. Stability and greatness have gone hand in hand, each enhancing the other. There is probably no area where this interlocking of qualities has found more abundant expression than in the economic field. I am neither an economist nor a businessman, but I believe that the figures speak for themselves. Gross national product has increased almost ten times in the past decade : from IL264 million in 1950 to IL2,470 million in 1960. In 1950 imports were $290 million while exports were $37 million ; in 1960 imports were $500 million, while exports reached over $350 million. Economic development within the country can be judged by productivity and exports. International business confidence in Israel's economic capacity can be judged by the yardstick of investment. In 1960 alone the Israeli Government approved 440 new foreign investments. The total private investment in 1960 was over $100 million.

International confidence finds further expression in the growing network of economic relations with the new countries of Africa and Asia. Israeli companies are engaged in undertakings in these two continents yielding annually some $60 million. From Burma and Nepal in Asia to Ghana and Liberia in West Africa, close to 400 Israeli experts, technicians and business administrators are engaged in technical advice and joint enterprises with the governments of these countries. After initial trial and error, the Israeli economy has, we feel, reached the highway of progress with ever-increasing competitive capacity on the world market. The challenge of economic growth has been central to the process of renewed statehood. If large-scale immigration – over one million immigrants since the establishment of the state – has involved vast expenditure, its effective absorption has in turn created the labour sinews for economic expansion.

Economic relations with other countries – in trade, investment and technical assistance – particularly with the new countries of Asia and Africa, are simultaneously the result of a growing network of international relations and a basis for the further cementing of these relations. The next decade can be decisive in economic growth. If the present rate of progress can be maintained, the objective may be attained of a balance of payments resting entirely on industrial expansion, productivity and exports. As this decade unfolds we must seek out and enlarge areas of cooperation that have not yet been fully explored. One such area is that of Canadian-Israeli economic cooperation.

The background has been outlined : the mutual goodwill and confidence that characterize Canada-Israel relations ; the dedication to democracy, to human dignity and values, to peace and international cooperation, which forms the basic texture of the relationship ; the dynamic economic development in both countries ; the quest for increased trade ; the readiness for partnership.

Against this background the Canada-Israel Chamber of Commerce has come into being. There is a widening interest in business circles in both countries in the development of trade, in partnerships and enterprises and in investments. It will be the function of the Chamber to canalize this mutual interest into the field of practical possibilities. This interest in business circles is sustained by both governments. I will not seek here to analyse the broad picture. However, I believe that one can say that there is considerable prospect of a new era of economic cooperation unfolding between Canada and Israel. On behalf of my Government, I wish to express appreciation to the Chairman of the new Chamber, to his associates and to all who have dedicated themselves to the fulfilment and practice of the hope that is approaching realization.

At the Granting of the Histadrut Award to Prime Minister John Diefenbaker, 7 April 1962

We honour tonight the cause of humanitarianism, the affirmation of the common bond of mankind. We honour a statesman who has toiled incessantly in the vineyards of humanity. We salute Canada-Israel friendship and the Prime Minister of Canada, who, symbolic of this friendship, is the recipient of an award linked with the Israel Labour Federation, a central pillar of renewed statehood. But above all we pay tribute to an insight, to an intuitive grasp of the theme of a small people's redemption, to the understanding that has characterized the approach of the illustrious guest of honour.

The Greek historian Thucydides, over 2,000 years ago, wrote of men ceasing to understand one another because the meaning of words had no longer the same relation to things. In the present age of a possibly decisive crisis in values, spiritual, cultural and humanitarian, the problem of communication – of man with himself, of a people with itself and on the international plane – has become crucial to human survival. For side by side with scientific and technological advances, which in decades have outstripped the discernment over centuries, mighty human forces have been set in motion, the map of the world is constantly evolving, and movements and strivings muffled in the depths of history have sprung to the surface. Indeed, the ceaseless and timeless search for human destiny seems to be vying with time itself.

Against this canvas, as part of the broad spectrum of renewed nationhood across the world, a small land on the east coast of the mediterranean, hallowed in history, repository of religion, but burdened by the desolation of millennia, has sprung to life – its sons and daughters from every corner of the globe gathering to water its parched soil and, with it, the soul of the people whose destiny has been interlocked with the land down the ages.

The trappings are those of modern statehood. The setting is the contemporary regional and world scene, with its burden of power politics and the currents and undercurrents of complexes and rivalries. The method of communication with the external world is that of conventional diplomacy and of contemporary mass media. But even as the inner significance of revival is related to a vindication of the spiritual over the material factor in human survival, even as the assurance that, precarious as is the course, the ship will, by the grace of Providence, reach the haven of peace and security – even as this assurance derives from the confrontation of hardship and torment by faith, which has been the essence of a people's experience down the ages, so the communication with other nations, its depth and vitality, has vibrant spiritual tones. How else can one explain the consistent friendship between Canada and Israel – that link of sympathy and goodwill between two parties so disparate in area, in resources, in capacity ; a link sustained neither by defensive alliance, by powerful economic stakes, by geography, by common experience, yet nonetheless deep and vital and constant.

The guest of the evening, the Prime Minister of Canada, has over decades shown a deeply sensitive appreciation of the spiritual motives of Israel reborn, its rise and onward progress ; he has instinctively sensed its purpose and meaning. In the context of deep humanitarianism and broad international approach, he has extended the hand of understanding and friendship. My government and people are deeply aware and appreciative of this. I am thus privileged to convey to you, Sir, not only the formal greetings but the sincere friendship of Israel reborn.

At the 'Ambassador's Ball', Toronto, 1963

This is the third occasion on which Mrs Herzog and I are privileged to attend the Ambassador's Ball in Toronto, linked with Israel Bonds and honouring Canadian-Israeli friendship. In the Jewish legal concept, an action performed three times becomes a presumption of certainty. It is not necessarily a presumption of the continuing presence of the participants ; it is a presumption of the continuity and deepening of the ideal that is honoured. But presumption is not the correct term. For if this occasion honours an ideal, it itself is the product of the ideal. It is a symbol of fulfilment and, at the same time, an index and promise of the deepening of this fulfilment into the future.

On this third occasion, Mrs Herzog and I are more capable of assessing Canadian-Israeli friendship than on previous occasions. For over the past two and a half years we have travelled extensively throughout this great land and have met and established close relations with many of its leading personalities in the various fields of national life. More and more have we been able to probe the inner springs of this friendship – a friendship sustained neither by geographical proximity, by great economic stakes, by defensive alliances, by vital common interest but nonetheless abiding and ever deepening. Even more than with those who closely follow international events, one is touched to the core by the friendship of ordinary men and women across this great land, who may not follow day in and day out the intricacies of international diplomacy and development. When, in the biblical expression, they pose the question to a foreign representative : 'Whence comest thou? what is thy country?' and he replies, 'I am a Hebrew ; and I fear the Lord, the God of heaven' (Jonah, 1 : 8-9), some instinctive contact, suffused with sympathy, seems immediately to form a bridge defying definition. Its essence reflects the dialogue that has been renewed between Israel and the nations of the world in our time and that finds significant expression in Canada.

Is it the biblical tradition ; is it the sense of equity at the restoration to its land of the only people that, in exile down the ages, has never broken the bond with the land of its destiny ; is it appreciation of the refusal to be daunted by what at times may seem to be insuperable odds and the pinning of survival and ultimate fulfilment, even in the long night of exile, on abiding faith in the new dispensation of revived nationhood? Is this attitude part of the saga of a nation that itself has formed an inner bridge of national consciousness between peoples of differing origins and culture. Or, again, is it an expression of an international approach seeking justice and equity, of an innermost striving for a world in which the inner bond of mankind will be more and more emphasized?

On this occasion we traditionally assess briefly Israel's progress from the time of our last meeting. During 1962, the renewed upsurge of immigration that commenced some three years ago was sustained, and some 60,000 immigrants, refugees from oppression and insecurity, arrived in the past year in Israel. Economic development has enabled their immediate, if not final, absorption without the need for a long and demoralizing stay in transit camps. The gross national product increased by close to eight per cent. Exports rose by fourteen per cent, new exports yielding an income of $35 million, and the entire export reaching $450 million. Within this framework, exports to Canada passed $5 million in 1962 as compared with two and one-quarter million in 1960. The development of the Negev has taken great strides forward, with the building of the new port of Ashdod, to cost altogether close to IL 90 million, with the expansion of the Dead Sea Potash Works, yielding in 1962 160,000 tons as compared with 130,000 in 1961, and the beginning of a large extension of the Timna Copper Works, the survey for which was undertaken by a Canadian company. The vast Jordan water scheme to carry water from the Galilee to the arid wastes of the Negev has moved forward and is approaching completion. Private investments totalling close to $100 million were received in 1962. In all this effort, Israel Bonds played a vital part in setting up the infra-structure for an economic leap forward and in guiding this development. We are happy indeed that this year we can make the first redemption of bonds to the sum of $250 million.

On the other side, the past year has seen the introduction of missiles into the Middle East, with all that can mean for a delicate arms balance. But a deterrent has also been acquired to assure the continuity of peace. The search for destiny within the infra-Arab framework has reached a new stage of crisis and struggle, while the pressures of the Cold War have continued to relax.

Even more important than any practical assessment, however, the past year has been a further layer in the process of redemption. As the years unfold, the fact of independence assumes permanence as if it had never been absent ; a new consciousness evolves as the impact of exile gives way to the sense of revival. Progress is counted in contemporary terms, but withdraw the canvas of faith and historical experience and the state's meaning becomes blurred. It is against this canvas that the deeper significance of every hour, day, month and year becomes more apparent.

Lately, among the eminent historians of Britain, a great debate has unfolded on the nature of history. It can be capsuled as a debate between determinism and free will : is the course of history set by factors – political, social and economic – that will unfold in any event, unaffected by personalities and movements, or are personalities and movements capable of changing its course? In considering the rise of Israel in this context, maybe there is a harmony between these two viewpoints. If there is determinism in the course of the Jewish people, it is timeless, beyond definition in mortal terms. On the other hand, the fulfilment of what we call determinism is a matter of free choice, as has been proven before our very eyes.

This occasion, then, is a further expression of a community which, in dedication and service has shown itself as part of this great effort of choice and free will. Proud sons and daughters of a generation that has seen tragedy without parallel in Jewish annals has also experienced the fulfilment of age-old prayer, vision and dream, a generation that has proclaimed it will not rest until this new destiny is assured for all time and, in exercising its choice, has become part of the destiny is serves. It is an expression of choice ; and, as this choice is exercised year after year, as the bond strengthens, the sense of novelty arises like a perennial fountain. Redemption can never lose its novelty. Its very essence demands that it deepens with time. Arising from an inner Jewish core, at the same time it finds a harmonious setting in a general Canadian approach.

Tonight there is no one personality to be the recipient of the award. But there is a recipient. The recipient is the people of Canada, who, in their collective consciousness, have shown enduring sympathy and interest for the rise to life of the small land on the eastern coast of the Mediterranean.

After the Six Day War

A Confidential, Off-the-record Review for the Follow-up Committee of the Jerusalem Economic Conference, 11 November 1968

From June 1967 I would say that a new epoch has opened in the history of Israel and of the Jewish people. It may not be pure coincidence that the Economic Conference and the vast upsurge of personal involvement in economic terms with Israel has coincided with this new period. We treat you as partners, in the deepest sense, and take you into our innermost confidence as to how we see our situation. Now, our situation can be studied under various headings. Firstly, in terms of the dialogue with the Western world. With these countries we have varying relations of friendship, but on a broad level we can speak of relations of mutual understanding. With them we have had a dialogue, since June 1967, as to whether and how the situation in the Middle East can be radically changed from one of a temporary nature, always on the brink of semi-despair and as if fated for all time to be the focal point of tension, with no hope of a permanent peace and no hope of regional cooperation.

I would say that, on broad lines, there is a meeting of minds, that this is the objective to be sought. I refer here to the United States, to Canada, to the United Kingdom, to the major countries of Latin America. France is an exception to this category at the moment, but, nevertheless, Italy, the Scandinavian countries and the Benelux countries are still to be included. Where do we stand with this group ? I refer to the heads of state, the Foreign Ministers, the officials of the various Foreign Offices and leaders in the political thought of the Western world. As I said earlier, on the basic objective of achieving peace there is a meeting of minds, but in certain areas – not merely in semantics – there are differences. There are differences on whether direct negotiations should be the central framework of the movement towards peace, or whether it should be an ultimate stage before a peace arrangement is settled. There are differences as to whether one should insist on a peace treaty, or whether one should agree to a contractual arrangement binding the parties – something vague, certainly less definitive than clear, total, absolute relations of peace, with all that that involves. In addition, there will – when we achieve direct negotiations in some form or another and we get down to substance – probably be differences between them on what should be considered the secure and recognized boundaries adumbrated by the Security Council in its resolution of last November. I think that we would probably insist, as absolutely essential to our security, on broader boundaries than they will be prepared to concede or could be acceptable to the Arab world. But this last point, which could probably, in certain circumstances, be a major issue of difference, has not yet come to the point of concretization, because we are still in the early throes of the search for peace.

We are not under pressure from the Western world, as is often suggested in the newspapers. I do not think that over the past year and a half the approaches from Washington or London or other capitals can be described as pressure. I would say that they have been trying to coax us into what they consider to be a more realistic approach, but what we consider to be a much more dangerous approach. It may be obsessive, but we live in one central fear that we believe to be realistic : lest we lose an historic opportunity, providentially afforded us, of a breakthrough to final peace in the area, lest we are flung back to this abyss we have known for twenty years of endless uncertainty – always on the brink, always watching the frontiers, as Arab armies build up on the other side. Can we continue in this round of tension, or can we break through to a lasting peace ? I would assume that a debate on this point may become more incisive between the Western capitals and Israel, but at the same time, I do believe that we will succeed in maintaining a common denominator of understanding.

But let us not forget that where vital interests are involved – and they are involved in terms of Judaism and history, of Jerusalem and security, of the whole amalgam of Jewish experience as it marches on us – we shall have to resist, if necessary, even the coaxing – or possibly the pressures – of our friends. As far as public opinion throughout the Western world goes, I think it has had ups and downs, but lately it has improved somewhat ; we are not looked upon as so utterly extremist as we might have been some six or eight months ago. I think that the nature of Arab intransigence, their refusal to give a clear answer to the crucial issue of peace – and by peace I mean what the world and Webster's dictionary mean by peace – has penetrated, more or less, the consciousness of world opinion, side by side with the questioning of Israel's policies that you will meet across the world. I would say that, lately, the balance has been a little restored in our favour, although, of course, one can never foresee how these things gyrate up and down.

If we move on to the Soviet Union – that is, in a way, the source of all tension in the area in that it supplies the arms that create the endless rounds of tension ; which incites the Arabs with dreams of conquest and, when the possibility of war comes nearer, tries to withhold them from taking risks ; which is pursuing essentially a paradoxical policy because of global interests, quite unrelated in the final analysis to the interests of either the Arabs or Israel – I would say that there is no dialogue in the formal sense. We have no relationship whatsoever with the Soviet Union ; apart from talks here and there in the United Nations and the various capitals, there is no exchange of substance with the Soviet Union or with any of its satellites – except Rumania, which maintains good relations with us and which seeks the course of peace in the area.

Now, what does the Soviet Union want in the Middle East? Is she arming the Arabs for further war, or is she arming the Arabs in order to maintain her state of influence? Does she seek a take-over in the area? Is she ready, if a new war develops, to intervene? I would say that this is a great question mark that troubles not only our minds, but those of major Western capitals. One can make, with certainty, a few points. Number one: we have no shred of evidence over the past six or eight months that the Soviet Union is encouraging the Arabs to go to war. As far as we can judge from all the material that flows to us, the Soviet Union is urging patience and restraint on Nasser, who is the crucial figure in this drama. They say to him: no further war, because a further war may involve a further catastrophe for the Arab peoples. They say: leave it to us. Through pressure at the United Nations, through pressure on the West, through a search for an agreement with Washington – maybe through threats against Israel – we will force them out of Arab territories without war. In any event, give us a chance.

The language of the Soviet Union spokesmen over the past month or so at the United Nations, both at the General Assembly and the Security Council, I would say, has been more moderate than that used by them a year ago – not only moderate in its tone, but even more moderate in its demands. They do not claim that Israel must retreat unconditionally from the territories. At least they try to bring their policy closer to their interpretation of the Security Council's resolution. This may sound like small consolation, but I would say that it is an index of the result of our capacity to withstand pressure.   Essentially, we have no grounds to assume that the Soviet Union is planning to intervene in the Middle East in any direct form. Now, as I say this, I must qualify it immediately, because there are vast areas of twilight between a total commitment of Soviet intervention and various forms of indirect intervention.

The question arises: if the Suez Canal flares up continuously, and we have to take very severe action to put an end to the tax on our positions, would the thousands of Soviet technicians – also rooted, by the way, in lower units of the Egyptian Army – with about 100 pilots, sit by and let us hit the Egyptian Army one more time? Let us assume another eventuality. If the Egyptians were to land troops across the Canal in sufficient force to hold a bridge-head for a few days, they would be acting on the assumption that, if we were to push them out by force (after we had assembled enough men), the Soviet Union would not let them be thrown back across the Canal. But what would the Soviet Union actually do?

I think one can say with certainty that the Soviet Union does not want such a situation to develop, but if in Cairo the hotheads – and I refer here not so much to Nasser, who is much more careful, but to the General Staff, which is deeply humiliated after last year's defeat, after the internal breaches in the Egyptian armed forces, after the Amer incident and its aftermath, and which consequently longs for a moment to restore, in some form or other, its military status, at least in the eyes of its people and of the other Arab nations – were to succeed in getting permission to develop attacks along the Suez, to cross over, as they crossed two weeks ago (two units of commandos with thirty men apiece), but with thousands and perhaps also from the air, what exactly would happen ? I would say, in all frankness, that this is an open question. We have no indication that the Soviet Union is clearer, either in desire or intent, today than it was eight months ago, and I would assume that it would be wiser if we stopped talking publicly about what might happen if. I should not criticize my superiors or people in high positions in Israel, but I would personally make the suggestion that this public debate as to what we should do if and when the Soviets, in some form, should wish to intervene, should be treated as academic and certainly should not be pursued with too much intensity.

That is the situation with the Soviet Union. I say that on the political front they are pressing for some solution at this stage. There were very close talks between Moscow and Washington at the beginning of the [General] Assembly, following a pattern that has gone on over the past year. I think that one of President Johnson's greatest disappointments has been that, after the failure in Vietnam, after the breakdown of the 'Great Society', he had pinned his hopes since last January on some *rapprochement* with the Soviet Union on the Middle East, some *détente* at least on the question of limiting the arms race ; and the Phantom decision – at least in negotiation (we have yet to see when and if we get them, but we assume we will) – was taken after the President had become convinced on the basis of the Gromyko-Rusk talks that there was no possibility of a *détente* with the Soviet Union in the Middle East at this stage.

Let me move on to a few other fronts. In the area of Jerusalem, with the Christian world, I would say that one of the miracles since June 1967 has been the silence – I would not say acquiescence – of the Catholic world. Those who remember the clash between Rome and Jerusalem in 1948 and 1953, the vast incitement across Latin America and Western Europe that we faced at every point, the insinuations against Jewish communities in these countries, will wonder today, as we occupy – actually, have united (we occupy in *their* eyes) – the entire area of Jerusalem, as the city is united under the sovereignty of Israel for the first time in well over 2,000 years, that Rome keeps its silence. We have no record, over the past year or more, of any attack on Israel, either on the issue of Jerusalem or indeed on any other issue relating to the territories, to the Arab population, neither from the Vatican nor from any Catholic dignitary, cardinal, bishop, archbishop, statesman, journalist or the entire gamut of the Catholic press. This is a matter of the highest significance, if you bear in mind the balance of the United Nations and what could happen in Latin America and across Western Europe should

Rome take a different position.

As I asked a Prince of the Church in Rome only some months ago, 'Wherefore does Rome keep its silence ? Why does the Vatican, with its vast legions of countries and forces and populations of hundreds of millions, keep its silence ? And when the Jews have returned to Jerusalem, after close to 2,000 years, and when this return has been touched by miraculous developments not foreseen by any political analyst or thinker, nor by any person with power of spiritual analysis, what is the meaning of this silence ?'

He answered : 'After the Six Day War, in Rome, we contemplated this phenomenon, and we came to the conclusion that it is a mystery beyond our immediate capacity to grasp, to plumb its depths, and we decided to wait and see how the situation would unfold.'

I asked : 'But what is your analysis ?'

He said : 'Our analysis is that there are three possibilities : either the Arabs will regain Jerusalem ; or secondly, the Jews will hold it ; or, thirdly, the city may become internationalized. We prefer to wait and see how this will unfold.'

I said : 'As far as I am concerned, there is only one possibility : the city will remain Jewish. But how can I convince you ?'

He said : 'How, indeed ?'

'If I put to you the military balance and tell you that our military experts feel that for the future, Israel, with the grace of Providence, can hold the balance of arms and maintain her deterrent capacity against the Arab armies, no matter what arsenals they develop, you will answer me that you, too, have military experts in Catholic countries, who may think differently, and neither you nor I can resolve this question. If I argue that we feel we can hold our international posture, that there can be no withdrawal without peace, that we have the capacity – with those of our friends who still stand with us – to hold on to this position, that there shall be no decision on Israel withdrawing without peace, again, you will say to me : "Surely, I, who have intimate contacts with some thirty countries, should be able to judge this much better than you !" And finally, if I tell you that in the evolving process of political events, all experience over the past twenty years indicates that we will hold on and stand where we are, again you can dispute it on objective grounds – as you term objectivity.

'If I argue that this is my religious faith, that, after close to 2,000 years, this is the Third Commonwealth of Israel, that the prophets spoke of two destructions – as my late father, of blessed memory, once said to President Roosevelt – but never foresaw a third, that this is the restoration of the Jew to his homeland after an exile of soul and body over millennia, this is our faith, with this we have lived, with this we shall survive ; you will say to me, naturally, "I am not obliged to accept your faith. My faith is different."

'Why, then, do I tell you that we shall stand as we are – and we have the power to stand there – until peace comes, and peace will come ultimately. I say to you, Prince of the Church, in purely pragmatic terms, history knows no parallel, no precedent, to what was said by the prophets of Israel and the masters of the Talmud. Thousands of years ago they foretold this phenomenon of exile, of the break-up of a people into a thousand atoms across the world, to every culture and civilization, yet destined not to yield either to pressure or temptation and one day to return. They took the entire faith of Judaism – its precepts, its history, its destiny – and they said : "We put it to a tangible, clear test. And the test will be that those who believe will see the return, ultimately, in faith and confidence, to that place."

'Now, had the Jewish people, after the Second Exile, diffused into a world church built on the Christian or Islamic pattern, had they given up Jerusalem, had they only maintained it, let us say, as a spiritual concept, but given up the concept of physical return, had the land been occupied by indigenous people and become characterized by their residence in it, had there been a new link across the pages of history with these stones and sands – which was the Israel we found when we came here eighty years ago – then, surely, you would have challenged the whole of Judaism and said : "Where is the proof, where is the vindication ? After all, your masters said, thousands of years ago, that this would be the proof."

'But since the proof is there,' I said to him, 'without accepting our faith, even without accepting any faith, surely you must have a great audacity indeed to question, in pragmatic terms, a vision foretold thousands of years ago and fulfilled before your eyes, without parallel in the entire canvas of human experience.'

In the precincts of this room, I can say that we have had talks with Rome. There is no possibility of reaching an agreement with Rome on Jerusalem – certainly not at this stage – but we have reached a situation, I would say, of a *de facto* relationship, where they express appreciation, not in writing but only orally, of our attitude towards Christian holy places in Jerusalem, towards the Christian communities ; they are ready, pragmatically, to wait and to see what happens. But at least they agree that our position should not be assaulted internationally and that silence is prudence for Rome. That in itself, I would say, is of historic significance.

If we move on, we come ultimately to the crucial situation, the crucial dialogue, the crucial heading, and that is the Arab States and Israel. Where exactly do we stand ? Has the past year and a half deepened the bitterness, or has it raised the 'iron curtain' ? Is there any hope that the present situation will lead to peace, or is it merely a temporary respite as their re-armed forces prepare for another assault, probably with far more sophisticated weapons ? I would venture the thought, although this is probably a personal assessment that will not necessarily be agreed to by many of my colleagues, that historically – and I stress historically –

and not in the contemporary sense, for the first time the curtain has been raised. Historically, for the first time, there is communication between Arab and Jew. The sealing-off of minds, in the total sense for over twenty years, has changed. Even if, God forbid, war comes, it will be a different type of war : fought, maybe, with more sophisticated weapons, but fought against a background of thought totally different to what existed previously.

For the first time, the Arabs, in a very innermost sense, are beginning to grasp – and I stress beginning – that the nature of the Jewish link with this land is not what they convinced themselves during twenty years of self-propaganda and illusion. It is not only a gathering of flotsam and jetsam of refugees, cast in here by Nazism and by other forms of perse-cution across the world, gaining their roots with Jewish money and the forces of imperialism across the world, a beach-head for imperialism intruding into the Arab lands and seeking to disrupt their independence, their soul, their sovereignty, their ultimate destiny. For the first time – and I say this not only in speculation – they are beginning to ponder this phenomenon of an ingathering of a people after 2,000 years. They are beginning to understand that this is something deeper, and I see in this the ultimate seed of a new perspective that I believe will flourish, come what may, in the next months or maybe years.

This communication you can witness in the practical sense on the West Bank. They have not given up their identity or their inner animo-sity to Israel, but they have decided – in their Arab fatalism – that they will live in peace with us for the time being. But once you decide *de facto*, you often get very dangerously close to a *de jure* situation after a time. And meanwhile they are becoming interlocked with our economy. Meanwhile, thousands and thousands go back and forth from other Arab lands – from Kuwait, Jordan and Saudi Arabia – to the West Bank. The monster image of Israel, the frightening image of an overall bestial imperialism that hung down on the Middle East, is being changed. They are seeing our humanity ; they are seeing paratroopers – who have the capacity to do very far-reaching things, as they have learned – walking round in peace and harmony with them ; they have seen our troops keeping away from their towns and villages – and the fact is that among the civilians there have been hardly any casualties over this past year and a half, as indeed there were not any during the war in the entire range of the West Bank and the Gaza Strip. With all the Arab oriental imagery, with all the self-illusion, with all this frustration of thought that links itself, ultimately, with the lack of clear destiny, with all that, there are sparks of understanding. This dialogue develops on the West Bank, in the Gaza Strip, through people who travel back and forth, with feelers from various countries, in Europe, in universities. For the first time each side sees the other.

But having said that, I would warn that the balance of development is still in a very crucial stage. The Arab armies are re-arming – particularly

Egypt – on a large scale. As far as we understand, it is Nasser's assessment that the end of 1969 and the beginning of 1970 might mark the date when he will be able to mount an offensive that would, at least as he terms it, be able to wrest the Sinai from Israel. He does not talk in his inner councils of destroying Israel any more, at least not in the immediate sense. He talks publicly of Palestinian rights. His foreign advisers warn him that his army will not be ready for three to five years. His officers claim that the army is already ready, not only to defend the heart of Egypt from any attack or movement across the Canal, but even to undertake limited, but considerable, action across the Canal.

So you have a balance of pressures in Cairo that is echoed in the fanaticism of phobic Damascus and that is not looked on with favour in Amman, for the King of Jordan wants peace – of that we are quite convinced. He wants peace, but there is Cairo. Cairo gives him the green light for meetings in New York with Dr Jarring, if we will accept the Security Council resolution for implementation, but Cairo is not, as far as we can judge, giving him any green light for peace. Secondly, King Hussein has, within his country, vast Fatah groups, which are determined, come what may, to turn back the clock of history. As far as we can judge, he will overcome the present wave of dissension in Jordan, but we doubt very much if he can crush it totally, so that you have there an Arab leader who wishes peace, but who faces enormous blocks on any movement towards peace.

This, I would say, is more or less a brief summary of where we stand. If you ask us – as everybody asks us, and everybody asks himself – so where on earth are you people going ? How do you see the future ? Essentially, if I were to be quite frank, I would say that the essence of Israel, as the essence of Judaism throughout the ages, has been the capacity to live for the unknown. People who live abroad in the Western countries, in affluent societies, who live on clear balance sheets, who have a measure of certainty as to the future, cannot understand this capacity to live in the unknown. When they come here, as you have come here, they link with us in the unknown. It is a most remarkable thing : I have spoken to Jews in Jerusalem and given them an assessment of a situation that is the unknown, and they have understood it and said : we are with you because there is no alternative. But when I have flown back with the same Jews on an El Al plane and they have talked to me of the same assessments, they have raised much graver doubts than in Jerusalem – and if you travel on a BOAC flight, or Pan-American, the doubts are even deeper. Now, there is a reason for that. The reason is the origin, the circumstance and the dynamism of the society in which they live ; whereas in this entire spiritual venture into which is Israel reborn, nothing has been achieved without jumping into the unknown. In no case, under no circumstances, at no period, has the future been clear.

Well, we all remember those stark years of 1946–8 when we suddenly realized the loss of one-third of our people ; when we realized that we were an orphan people. We faced an empire, in decline but still capable of delivering heavy blows, and within the Yishuv there was always the danger of a clash, of a civil war between our brethren.

Looking back over that past, we look to the future with faith. You cannot play stakes with cosmic elements. You cannot be involved in an issue that affects people all over the world, the balance of power, the future of oil and the Persian Gulf, the dialogue between Rome and Jerusalem for 2,000 years ; you cannot communicate with half of the southern part of the globe, which looks upon you with animosity, whether Arabs or Islam, and with another half of the globe that looks upon you with doubt, and expect in such a situation to sit down and say – as though you were running a factory – now here is my balance sheet : this will take three or six months, two or three years.

It doesn't work that way. If we love the capacity for faith in the unknown, the ability to march forward with a sense of providential assurance that this is a turning-point in Jewish history, we cannot plan realistically. I know that one cannot confuse mysticism with reality, but if you try entirely to separate them in this venture, then your reality may become very stark and oppressive indeed. But having established the basis of the assumption that all Jews carry in some inner point in their souls, I would say that we look ahead on various lines of thought.

We feel, number one, as the Prime Minister said yesterday, that the Arabs have failed in their three major objectives. They have failed to turn Israel and the territories into a second Algeria ; they have failed to budge us after a year and a half, with their thousands of Soviet advisers, from the cease-fire lines, and from there we will not move without peace ; they have failed internationally to damage, in a basic sense, Israel's image and to get through resolutions on withdrawal without any basic element of progress towards peace.

On balance, it is not so bad. Let us not only think of our problems. Let us think of the unknowns in the Arab world ; let us think of the dialogue between Nasser and his officers. How long can he survive with Egypt in such economic difficulties, its international prestige at such a low, and at the nadir of its position in the Arab world ? How long can he survive and keep his soldiers on the Suez Canal ? How long can Hussein survive, when the Fatah say to him : either a political solution involving a total withdrawal, or else we take over your kingdom ? How long can Feisal speak in vague terms of Jerusalem, when he knows the Soviet threat is deepening in the area ? In other words, the dilemma of the Arab capitals is, for the first time in twenty years, even more incisive than ours. We believe that, if we hold on, and, above all, if we maintain these crucial bridge-heads of support in Washington and London, in Canada and in various countries of Latin America and Scandinavia – let us call it understanding, not support – some change will take place in the area.

Who can prophesy what will happen in Cairo in six months to a year ? Who, a year ago, would have said that India and Yugoslavia – because of

Czechoslovakia – would not speak up with decisive force in the United Nations in favour of Egypt, as they, in fact, did not just two weeks ago ? In other words, the entire neutralist bloc is falling apart. Who could have foretold that Moscow, after this fantastic build-up about eight months ago towards the threat of a new war, would suddenly yield and move towards a search for a *rapprochement* with the United States ? All this is shrouded in dark. But we return to this feeling with faith that, if we stand firm, maybe this turning-point will take place in the Middle East, and as we go back over the assessments of the past year, we see that they have not proved correct – if I take the Washington assessments that we heard in June and July, in January with the President of the United States in Texas, here with Ambassador Ball and now at the United Nations.

They spoke, firstly – and this is the President himself – of Soviet intervention since last July. This, as I said, may happen – nobody can foresee the future – but where we stand today we may find consolation in the fact that there is no indication that it is necessarily closer today than it was six months ago. Secondly, the State Department officials spoke of the collapse of Arab societies into Communism – that, by standing where we are, we are handing over the area to Communism. This has been proven not to be the case. The swing of the government in Baghdad has been to the right and not to the left ; in Damascus last week, again it was a change with the expulsion of the only Communist Minister in the Cabinet. Even in Cairo – and I have spoken to American experts like Bundy and Yost – we asked them what would happen if Nasser falls tomorrow, and their answer is probably a right-wing takeover. Certainly Muhi ed-Din's chances are stronger than those of Ali Sabry. They have spoken to us for an entire year of the sudden collapse of Hussein and the invasion of Amman by Soviet and Egyptian experts.

Again, this is still a precarious situation, but their prophecy so far – and let us be thankful to Providence for it – has not been fulfilled. They have spoken of Security Council pressures, of the Russians asking for sanctions, of the United States being faced with the crucial alternative of either letting the sanctions go through or casting a veto despite her traditional policy. They have spoken of a dozen other fears – of Israel becoming a second Algeria, of incapacity to hold the Fatah, of an economic collapse because of the burden of the occupied territories. All of these so far have not proved correct.

So, finally, I would say that, as always, as we face up to these problems and march into the unknown, let us recall the final and ultimate dialogue that gives us strength. That is the faith linked with the unity of the Jewish people, with this phenomenal new communication of Jews – of which this meeting is one expression alone, but a very important one – with this sense of the new epoch, with this phenomenal upsurge of Jewish identification, and all that is rooted in faith and unity.

Part Two : Jewish Destiny

Israel and the Diaspora : Dichotomy and Unity

Address to the Canadian Jewish Congress in Montreal,
14 November 1971

My subject this evening is, indeed, the story of Jewish history : Israel and the Diaspora from the perspective of the twentieth century and, more tangibly, from the perspective of the past four and a half years, since the unification of Jerusalem. The subject, Israel and the Diaspora, is a dichotomy yet a unity. The one is diffusion and disperson, the other is coherence, entrenchment, ultimate destiny.

This dialogue, which has been part of the essence of the Jew from earliest times, has been a practical fact of history. At every stage of Jewish history, it has remained an ever-deepening metaphysical concept. As our sages tell us, *Shechinta begaluta*, it is as if the Divine Presence itself went into exile with Israel after the destruction of the Temple. The idea of exile is at one and the same time an innermost concept of the Jewish people and a subject for universal inquiry and study by great thinkers throughout the ages. In essence, then, in discussing this subject, in following its evolution, in seeing where it stands today, after the various ages that have passed over the Jewish people, we are studying the story of the Jewish people, the story that enshrines the temporary versus the permanent.

At a symposium with the *Life Magazine* editorial board four and a half years ago, we discussed the criteria of what would be considered a turning-point in world history. In other words, if the great historians of the world could conceivably meet, how would they attempt to establish and define those events without with the nature of man and the overall experience of the human kin would be different. During that debate I was asked about the Jewish people. What were the events in the history of the Jewish people that have assumed a universal character, without which the human being today, in whatever part of the world, would be different from what we know. I answered that there were four such events. All of them accepted three ; on the fourth they withheld judgement. They accepted the Exodus from Egypt as a matter of universal import ; for whether interpreted in traditional Jewish fashion, or in any other fashion, the whole concept of liberation under Providence from slavery, from totalitarianism, from bondage, dates back in human consciousness to the Exodus from Egypt. The second was the Sinai dispensation. The third I counted as the phenomenon of prophecy. The concept of penetrating the veil of immortality across time and foreseeing the nature of a people, its development, and how it would link up with the entire harmonization and ultimate uplift of the human race is a phenomenon without which neither philosophy nor literature nor, indeed, the quality of the human race can be properly analyzed.

Finally, I included the destruction of the Temple. Here they claimed that I was exaggerating, that I was being subjective. After all, when the Jewish Temple was destroyed, it is true that four Roman legions had to be called in to destroy it, it is true that the Roman commander could not report back to the Senate that all was well with his troops ; but, during that same period, China was passing from its second to its third millennium, India was filled with vast motley tribes, sacred places of worship were destroyed by the thousands, Greece was at its zenith, Rome was ruling the world. What then does the destruction of the Jewish Temple mean in terms of world culture and in terms of the impact on the human mind ?

I explained that from then on the concept of exile was born in the universal mind. Before that, the idea of a man or of a nation being in exile – in the sense that he seeks fulfilment, that he has been cut off from his sources, that he is somehow searching for his path – did not exist until the destruction of the Temple and until the Jew was uprooted from his land.

Down through the ages, stage by stage, the dichotomy and debate have continued. When our forefathers were expelled to Babylon by Nebuchadnezzer, they wept by the rivers of Babylon and said : 'When the Lord shall return the captivity of Zion, we shall be as dreamers' (Psalms 126 : 1). And the question is posed : if the return is a reality, it will not be a dream, but if it is a dream, then why is it not reality ? Today we understand the word as never before, for we have returned and yet all is as a dream, constantly unfolding. The metaphysical and the real, the material and the spiritual, the sense of being and belonging and the sense of going through some exercise of historical destiny are all so intermingled that a man, while knowing he is in reality, feels he is dreaming.

Indeed, the captain of, I believe, Apollo 10, while circling the moon, was consulted by his priest by radio as to what Psalms he wished to read that Sunday in his church in Texas. He suggested a few Psalms that related to creation – that is understandable – but he also gave the Psalm : 'Jerusalem which has been reunited' (Psalms 122 : 3). What relevance has that, why did this strike his mind as he encircled the moon ? The answer, I believe, is very simple. Being where he was, he had lost his anchor. He did not recognize his surroundings. He lived in a world that he could not pin down or define. And the first thing to come to his mind, which was an analogy of a kind, was Jerusalem. There you can walk the streets as in any of the thousands of cities of the world ; you can travel there by plane ; you can pay for a hotel – are overcharged in the hotel – exactly as anywhere else, and, yet, people from across the world, including the greatest cynics and sceptics, come to you and say : we are seized by a higher sense ; *Atzal aleinu haruah*, 'There is something higher which uplifts us.' And so that moment, in trying to pin down his feelings, to define himself, the captain looked for a place that involved matter, that could give him the anchorage of being linked to some earthly structure, while, at the same time, reflect his feeling of uplift in endless spirit – and he chose Jerusalem.

The Jew can live in a contemporary society only if he is touched by the eternity of his destiny ; even as the Prophet of Destruction said : *'Avad nitzhi vetohalti mehashem'*, my eternity has been lost, and therefore my hope (Lamentations 3 : 18). That idea seemed old-fashioned and anachronistic 100 years ago. No longer was the Messiah of the House of David awaited in Jerusalem, across Europe, in various countries and groupings, age-old faith was questioned, established thought was challenged, and the question was raised : why cannot one build a totally exclusive Jewry in the Diaspora ? Why, as Geiger applied it to Germany, do Jews in this land of the highest culture have to cast their spiritual anchor to the tiny and not-so-attractive village of Jerusalem ? What is this link ? How can we build a future on that basis ? And he was not alone. We may recall that the 'protest rabbis' in Germany about the time of the First Zionist Congress and the Central Conference of American Rabbis spoke out on the same issue. Even the Orthodox British Chief Rabbi, in 1878, wrote that, after all, Jews in Britain, like every other group, were divided on purely religious grounds – as if he could deny the uniqueness of the Jewish people without falsifying history, without confusing the very nature of the Jew in the eyes of his neighbours.

But the paradox of it all is that at the moment when the atomization of the Jewish people seemed to be bringing it to an end, at the moment when the name of Jerusalem was excised from prayer-books, when new messiahs arose from the social movements of reform and liberalism the return to Zion began.

One of the participants in this debate was the second President of Israel, Isaac Ben-Zvi, of blessed memory, in 1905, in the small town of Poltava in Russia. In 1905, there was an abortive revolution aimed at overthrowing the Czar. At that time it took some days and weeks before it became known across the vast expenses of Russia that that revolution had failed. When the report came to the small town of Poltava – where the late Ben-Zvi then lived as a young man – that the revolution had succeeded, all the workers and revolutionaries gathered in the square of the city. From a balcony overlooking the square, three representatives were called upon to speak : one from the extreme group, which later was to become the Communists ; the other of the more moderate group ; and Ben-Zvi, the representative of the Jewish workers of Poltava.

A year earlier, Ben-Zvi had been in Jerusalem as a student, sent by his father. He wrote in a letter that, as he stood on the balcony and began to proclaim to the workers of Russia that redemption had come, that the Czarist power had been overthrown, that a new era was opening for all Russians – Jew and non-Jew alike – 'Suddenly the memory of Jerusalem, the scene of Jerusalem, flashed before my eyes, and I asked myself :

what exactly am I doing here ? After all, I am a stranger ; my soul has been captured by Jerusalem ; I no longer belong.' Only with difficulty was he able to finish his speech.

One of those to grasp this debate was Winston Churchill, who wrote in the *Morning Post* of 1920 that, in the struggle between the Zionist-identified Jew and the Communist-diffused Jew, we are facing no less a problem than the destiny of the Jewish people. Balfour also grasped – almost in Talmudic terms – the nature of the Jewish Diaspora. When the Balfour Declaration was challenged in 1921 by Lord Rothermere, Lord Balfour replied in the House of Lords that he was well aware of the number of Arabs in Palestine when he proposed the Balfour Declaration. I accept self-determination for all countries of the world in general and the Middle East in particular, Balfour said, but I cannot accept it for Palestine, because Palestine is unique. Every Jew throughout the world has his portion in Palestine, and, therefore, if I take all the Jews throughout the world, surely in strict numbers they overcome the Arabs present. This was Balfour's concept of the Jewish Diaspora, on which the sages, 2,000 years before him, said : *'Ehad hanolad bah ve'ehad hametzapeh lir'ot'*, 'He who lives in the land and he who waits to see it are both part of the patrimony of the Jewish heritage and its destiny.'

But Churchill's grasp of the conflict between the Jews themselves was played out by Trotsky himself, who said : I have the deepest respect for Judaism, but the time has come for it to dissolve into a universal system of world redemption. Fifty years later, his disciples – emaciated bodies from the vast icy wastes of the Siberian slavelands – stir with another message : the Messiah lies in Jerusalem.

So there is a turn, a swing round, from the Jewish people on the verge of dissolution and from the debate being on the supremacy of the Diaspora or of Israel to the acceptance of the distinction of Israel as the cardinal point, the corner-stone, of the entire system of Jewish thought. Indeed, millions of Jews in the Diaspora have concluded : only in Jerusalem can we find our fulfilment.

Even across the Western world, with all the assimilation and inter-marriage, with all the hippie-ism and anarchism, there is a new coherence, a new search, a new probing of sources among Jewish youth, particularly since 1967. And where there is a search for identity, a new radiation, a new communication, develops between the Jew and his fellows, and across the world we all say together, *Leshanah haba'ah biyrushalayim,* next year in Jerusalem !

Indeed, speaking as one coming only a few days ago from Israel, this sense of the overall unity of the Jewish people and this unprecedented acceptance of Israel by the Diaspora, as well as the end to the sterile debates and a separate Diaspora trend and the complex-ridden myths of dual allegiance combine to produce one of the major forces in strengthening our soldiers and in strengthening the fibre of nationhood as it faces vast military and political challenges.

And, indeed, this is the crucial debate with our neighbours : are we permanent, or are we temporary ? Their caravans have marched across the desert without instruments of distance or time ; they feel the area and they know the shifting sand. And they have been asking themselves whether the Jewish people is rooted in this area or, like the seventeen foreign conquests that have come and gone, are merely passing strangers. Our question is whether they understand the continuity of the Jew, whether they realize his uniqueness and grasp his historical memory. I believe that, as we grow closer, this understanding is penetrating their minds. They cannot have fought three wars with a tiny people of two and one-half million - outnumbered by 100 million - and not ask themselves whether this is purely a temporary phenomenon, to be washed away by the sands of time. As long as this understanding penetrates - and it will penetrate - we are on the path to peace. It is interlocked in a peculiar way with the inner, subjective feelings of the Jew. As he asserts his identification with the past, so other will recognize his rights as being linked to the past, as being rooted in the past ; and together we will move on to a higher future.

Explaining Ourselves to the World

*From an Address to a Bnei Akivah Conference in Jerusalem,
9 January 1970*

The Jewish people has been trying to explain itself for the past 4,000 years. I have no intention, at the moment, of going into the question of the great argument about Israel's right to its homeland. I am not going to touch on the balance of forces in the Middle East, nor on the question of whether time works in favour of Israel, or, heaven forbid, of the Arabs. I am not going into all the areas of dialogue between Israel and the various elements of world public opinion – our dialogue with Catholic Rome, with Islam, with the West headed by the United States, with the Soviet Union and its satellites. I am referring here to the dialogue, or the debate, within the Jewish people itself in the world in which you live, a world of the university campuses in the Western world.

The problem is not so much the non-Jews, though there is no doubt that they can do us much harm. The problem, first and foremost – and much to our surprise – is the Jewish intellectual, or at least some of the Jewish intellectuals. I am speaking primarily about those who are slipping away from the basic concept of the nature of Israel's return to its land. They are once again deceiving themselves and repudiating at one and the same time their Jewish identity and the State of Israel, which they rightly regard as embodying Jewish identity at this time in history.

What is the central argument we hear from this circle of Jewish intellectuals on the campuses ? First of all, they have received no Jewish education and therefore lack the elements of the Jewish outlook ; they wander in a spiritual desert. They have no attachment to Jewish distinctiveness ; they believe that there are no grounds for any such distinctiveness either in logical thinking or in solid historical experience. Everything that has passed over the Jewish people is a chain of accidents – a result of sociological and economic circumstances and political vicissitudes – with no distinguishing element that can be pointed to as a permanent thread in the annals of humanity. They repudiate any idea such as 'a people that dwells alone' as being egocentric, a rejection of progress, an abnormality, a self-imposed ghetto – in short, something that twentieth-century civilization cannot tolerate.

They say, more or less, the same as Trotsky said in 1917 to the man who had been his Talmud Torah teacher when he was a young boy called Leibele Bronstein. (Churchill tells the story in a famous essay in his book on outstanding world personalities.) The teacher, a simple old rabbi, came one day in 1917 to the Bolshevik Minister of Defence, leader of the revolutionary army in Russia. He had heard that the Yevsektsiya, the Jewish section of the Communist party, was trying to crush every spark of Jewish feeling and Jewish devotion, to suppress synagogues, rabbis and Jewish communities ; and he was told that this campaign was led by Leibele Bronstein, alias Lev Trotsky. The old rabbi could not believe his ears and he said : 'Is this possible ? Is it really true that you are the leader of such a movement to suppress the Jewish people in Russia ?' Trotsky replied that it was not true, that he had no part in it. But, he continued, his view was that, while Judaism was once a universal movement, now that world messianism was becoming a reality through communism in the Soviet Union, it was no longer a Russian national matter, but a universal development that would flood the entire world, and the time had come for Judaism to merge into this universal movement for the redemption of humanity, which was called the Communist Revolution. And indeed, there was a period in Russia, lasting about three years, when many people, not only in Russia, were convinced that the messianic era, in the universal sense, had arrived, that social and economic regeneration would sweep the whole world.

I doubt if there is any parallel in history to this immediate expectation, this belief that redemption was at hand, followed by such bitter disappointment. So today if anyone said that world redemption was near, even the Communists themselves would smile. They would still claim that this is a movement that has rectified wrongs, that strives for a more just world, but I doubt whether even the most devoted Communist would claim today that the Communist Revolution is going to regenerate the world.

But this was Trotsky's outlook, and not only Trotsky's, but that of a large part of the Jewish people, especially during the past 100 years. The Jew has believed that the gates of the world are open before him on condition that he improve his image, his Jewishness, reduce his distinctive character to that of a universal mission and become an integral part of the other nations. Some believed in some kind of attachment to Judaism, in the sense of 'Germans of the Mosaic persuasion', but on the central point of Jewish distinctiveness, the point at which we part company with the other nations, where our history diverges onto a separate path, there was a glaring incomprehension, a failure to understand. And this was the central mistake in Jewish experience during the past century and a half.

I remember talking to a Jewish delegation from the United States a few years ago ; they were discussing the question : what is the criterion of a Jew in America ? Is it a question of learning, piety, Jewish identity, Jewish devotion ? They did not exactly know. They also wanted to know when a Jew could claim that he belonged to the totality of the separate history of the Jewish people even when he was an American. I replied that, in my opinion, it did not depend in any way on his social standing : he could sit in the White House, or be a general in the American Army, or a member of the Senate, and still be a Jew in the full sense of the word. The question was whether he was prepared to recognize that at a certain point his spiritual mission did not begin with American culture and would not end with the realization of America's aspirations, that the Messiah was not in Washington but in Jerusalem.

In the campuses the world over there are some 400,000 Jewish students, and they are being tossed about in a world of spiritual anarchy, in a world of revolt against conventions, in a world in which the great dogmas have been plunged into a tremendous melting-pot of intellectual quest and perplexity, with no apparent way out. Perhaps there never has been such a period in the history of the world, when the revolutionaries themselves, in trying to define the goal of the revolution, can find no goal except the shattering of existing institutions. The minds and souls of hundreds of thousands of Jewish students are now immersed in this process. And as they seek to define themselves, they are attracted, on the one hand, to this tremendous debate, to this universal perplexity of the revolt against conventions ; yet they are also gripped by reunited Jerusalem, the city that, in the words of the sages, makes all Israel comrades. Till the Six Day War, the Jew on the world's campuses could escape the State of Israel. Israel, for him, was an important event, an asylum for Jewish refugees, but it did not affect his essential being. Donations – certainly ; assistance – willingly ; but there was no connection with his individual purpose in life. After all, this was a small country dependent on the mercies of great powers. And, as an American or an Englishman, he was quite prepared to help his brethren who sought refuge, but it did not affect him personally.

My impression is that the assimilated sections of the Jewish people were subjected to a shock since the Six Day War. The assimilated Jew could run away from the synagogue or choose to take no part in any Jewish activity, but he could not avoid the BBC, the London *Times,* or the *New York Times,* or television, which he watched daily. And these powerful information media confront him with a challenge : what about Jerusalem, what about the Jewish State, what about the Middle East ? In whose favour is time working ? What about the balance of forces ? So long as there is any spark of Jewishness within him — and, after all, there is such a spark in at least ninety per cent of Jews – he cannot completely ignore this challenge. It penetrates his soul.

It is very easy for a Jew to abandon his people, but it is very, very difficult, if at all possible, for him to join other people. Churchill, in his essay on Disraeli, sums up : 'Despite all this Disraeli never fully assimilated to the British people.' I remember Ben-Gurion asking me once about this passage. How was it possible that Churchill, a great Englishman, could have written this about one of his three or four great predecessors, one of the builders of the British Empire and founders of the philosophy of conservatism, the man who led England and gave India to his Queen, who bought control over the Suez Canal, who personified British romanticism during the century before World War One, a man of culture, a fertile author with a tremendous imagination and whose tomb is still a place of pilgrimage. I replied that the same concept was expressed by the Midrash nearly 2,000 years ago : a Jew can be cut off from his people, but this does not mean that he becomes an integral part of another people. In his heart, in his feelings, he remains suspended in a world of limbo. He will always continue to seek himself, perhaps even more when he abandons his people than when he remains a Jew.

This is the crisis that is sweeping the campuses all over the world. Many try to escape their Jewish identity, but they are incapable of becoming part of another identity, despite all the superficial resemblances, despite all the attempts to convince themselves that they have really forgotten their father's house. There is a certain barrier, and it has become more perceptible in recent years than ever before in modern times. Jerusalem gives them no rest. And when this Jew tries to run away from himself, he finds himself facing the challenge of Jerusalem ; he finds himself involved in the central question that Rashi, the great interpreter of the Scriptures, posed in his commentary on the very first verse of Genesis. For what is the central argument of the New Left the world over, of those circles who oppose Israel and try to attack it ? They charge, as Rashi put it : 'Ye are robbers, because ye have conquered the Land of Canaan.' But our defence is : 'In the beginning God created the Heavens and the Earth,' and the same God who created the Heavens and the Earth gave the Land of Israel to the Jewish people.

Now, the modernity of the Bible is an extraordinary thing. There are hundreds of Midrashic comments on the ideas of creation and Jewishness, and, out of them all, Rashi chose this one to start his commentary on the Bible. I have no doubt that millions of Jews in the past, upon opening their Bible to the first verse of the first book, could not understand what Rashi was driving at, why he introduced this question at this particular point, what it all had to do with the creation of the world. But today, looking back on Jewish history, we can understand it very well, because we are faced with the conflict between historic rights and the concepts of the twentieth century, and it is all concentrated in this question. With his prophetic spirit Rashi foresaw that, when we returned to this land, we would again be confronted with this challenge : 'Ye are robbers !'

This is the problem of our rights, this is the struggle between the uniqueness of the Jewish people and the twentieth-century concept of self-determination. It is this that troubles human thought today, for there is no problem that has stirred the conscience of humanity so much during the past fifty years as the problem of Israel in its land. There is no problem that can compare to it in scope and persistence, in the extraordinary combination of economic, strategic and political interests, religious faith, social outlook, historical conceptions and international principles. They are all intimately intertwined in a struggle that encompasses the entire world in the course of these fifty years and gives it no rest.

I have no intention, at this time, of going into the problem of propaganda images and passing feelings ; in the nature of things these are transitory. Let us not live in a world of mistaken evaluations. Today, world public opinion looks on Israel in a certain way because Israeli soldiers carried out a successful raid in the Gulf of Suez and carried off a radar station ; tomorrow it will take a different view because the Fatah will claim that it threw a bomb here or did not throw a bomb there. But that does not affect the fundamentals, the foundation of the problem. The problem, in the last analysis, is the problem of our right to this land. And the debate will move more and more onto the plane of rights when the Arabs say – and they are joined by Toynbee and others – how can a nation come back and claim its country after 2,000 years ?

Toynbee put this question to me himself in London a few months ago. 'After all,' he said, 'how can I explain to Nasser that here comes a nation, after 2,000 years, and claims the right to this country ? And what shall I tell him if he asks me : what about the Vikings in Norway, who settled in England 1,000 years ago ? What if they want to go back to London, and the Indians want to take back Montreal, where they used to live ?'

I replied : 'Logically, you are right, but there is one small flaw in your argument : there are no Indians who claim Montreal, or Vikings who claim England. There is only one case of a people that claims it cannot live without its land, and, for 2,000 years, it did not live there and was physically distant from it, in some abstract spiritual sense, beyond time and human grasp, was part of its land. How can you apply to this case the ordinary laws of history when, as you yourself have written, over a score of empires and cultures have risen and disappeared from the horizons of civilization during the same period in which this little people has continued to exist ? This, then, is the crucial question. So long as the world agrees that there is something unique about the Jews in the history of mankind, it cannot deny the right of the Jews to this land. No doubt it is a complex question ; undoubtedly it is unique, and let us not imagine that it is easy for the Arabs to grasp it. Even the founders of Zionism, with all due respect and honour to them, did not grasp the dimensions of the great edifice they were building. When you re-read their writings and speeches, when you examine their political ideas, you see that they did not understand the Arabs and the Arab peoples. Their concepts of Jewish history, too, were, in my opinion, hardly adequate on the spiritual plane. It is only recently that Jews themselves have begun to understand the roots of the question, and they are arguing about it on the campuses.

In this argument on the character and position of the Jews in the Land of Israel, the Jews themselves are a decisive factor ; a great deal depends on them. If they appear to be cut off from their Jewish heritage, they cannot defend our right to the Land of Israel. If one discards the idea of Jewish uniqueness in human history, it is very difficult to counter the argument of the intellectual. But if, on the other hand, the idea of Jewish uniqueness is accepted, then there is a reply, which is not only the religious Jewish reply, but which has a place in the world outlook of the twentieth century - no less than in any previous century.

Three thousand years ago, Balaam the Prophet described the Children of Israel as 'a people that dwells alone'. This is a very strange concept, one that cannot be explained in terms of any mythology of the ancient world. And today, in the twentieth century, when you analyse it objectively and scientifically - not from the point of view of faith and feeling - there cannot be any doubt that this is how most of the world sees us : a people that dwells alone. The problem is whether this concept denotes a privilege - not an escape from society as a whole, but a unique role within it - or whether it is an anomaly, which must be denied and discarded. This is *the* question of Jewish history.

The Quest for Jewish Identity

At the President of Israel's Circle for the Study of Diaspora Jewry, 24 November 1969

It seems to me that the Six Day War, the reunification of Jerusalem and everything connected with these events have transformed the Jew's conception of himself to take into account the background of the new image of the State of Israel with united and liberated Jerusalem at its centre. The question is not the image of the State of Israel as it appears to the Jew, but how the Jew sees himself. I think that fundamental changes have taken place among the Jews in the world. First of all, they now have an understanding of the return to Zion as a spiritual concept, something they did not have before. Secondly, they have an understanding of the concept of the Jewish people as a people that dwells alone and of Jewish history in the context of the history of mankind. Thirdly, I believe that, for the first time in 150 years, they have entered an era marked by the quest for their own identity, in contrast to the flight from Judaism that was characteristic of the previous period.

All this is something new in the Jewish soul, with far-reaching implications for the future. The crises in Christendom, in the affluent world, in the Communist bloc, in humanism, in the socialist movement have combined to create a cultural vacuum within which the Jew feels even more isolated than in years gone by. On the one hand, there is the powerful lodestone of resurgent and victorious Israel, which has succeeded in overcoming the appalling perils of the period before the Six Day War and has established herself as a permanent factor in the Middle East, inspiring the Jew with a sense of his own identity. On the other hand, the counter-forces – the world of assimilation and spiritual extinction, the world that tends to obliterate Jewish identity – is itself immersed in a painful crisis of the quest for its own identity. Thus, when the Jew looks around him, he sees those trends in the civilization of mankind in which – so he tries to persuade himself – he could, of his own free will, find self-oblivion through assimilation and spiritual extinction overwhelmed by a volcanic eruption throughout the world, as humanity seeks itself.

These crises affect us daily and it is not difficult to enumerate them, but I would add one paradoxical factor. It was generally accepted in the past century that, as national frameworks were shattered and some kind of cosmopolitanism spread over the entire civilization of mankind, it would be easier for the Jew to be swallowed up and forgotten. The Jews in the affluent countries have made every effort to recover their equilibrium after the Holocaust, to explain it away in logical terms as the consequence of economic crises, social ferments, the affront to the self-respect of the German people after World War One and their quest for self-identity. And yet, despite all these explanations, Jews in those countries cannot escape a sense of uneasiness, a kind of insecurity. This is an extraordinary development which has become more and more obvious during the past four years. Previously, it was believed that anti-Semitism could no longer exist in a civilized human society, that the stronger civilization became, the more secure would be the position of the Jew. And now, suddenly, this confidence has been undermined, and the developments I have enumerated are closing in upon the Jew and pressing him to seek his own identity.

Thus, against the background of the status of independent Israel in the Middle East and the reunification of Jerusalem, with all its profound religious and historic significance for the Jewish soul, the world crisis of civilization and anti-Semitic manifestations – although many still hesitate to call them by that name – are keenly felt by the Jew. There are even some thinkers in the Western world who compare the position of the Jews in the United States and Western Europe with that of German Jewry in the 1920s. That seems to me to be a highly exaggerated view. But the very fact that Jews who do not hold the prophetic concept of Israel, of the dialogue between Jews and gentiles, that Jews with a universalist concept of world civilization, can admit such a possibility – and opinions to this effect have been published recently – shows how far the uneasiness has reached, if only in the subconscious of the Jew in the Western world.

All this applies to the majority of Jews, those have some kind of bond – religious, historic, or even undefined – with Judaism. But I find in my contacts with what I might call 'assimilated Jewry' – which comprises millions in the Western world, especially in the universities and among the intellectuals – that even they have not succeeded in escaping that inner, spiritual shock that has struck Jewry as a whole.

This group may be divided into two sections. The one, which is seeking a way back, has joined in the quest for Jewish identity, though in its own way ; the other – perhaps resenting the demand for identity – has found its place, in many quarters, at the head of the anarchistic 'protest' movements. Jews of the latter type are influenced by propaganda hostile to Israel. They want to suppress their spiritual shock, and so they go to extremes in the direction of cosmopolitanism ; they seem to be trying to justify themselves by extravagant criticism of Israel without any objective basis. Criticism is legitimate in a world of freedom of thought, and it is our duty to criticize ourselves, but they are going too far. The shock among these Jews is so profound that a man like George Steiner of Cambridge, who regards Israel as an imperialist monster, a nation that conquers and oppresses another nation, is nevertheless able to declare that if Israel's survival were in danger, he would be prepared to come and risk his life in her defence. This is a most extraordinary paradox ; it is inconceivable that such a Jew could have spoken in these terms before 1967.

As we have seen, this shock is expressed mainly in the quest for identity. It gives rise to the idea of the return to Zion as a spiritual concept ; it is expressed in the almost complete acceptance of the moral authority of the State of Israel ; it is expressed in *aliyah*. On this last there are still various difficulties, but no one now objects to *aliyah*. Even among those who insist on the independence of the Diaspora or on the existence of a separate Diaspora stream in Jewish history, it is now permissible to talk about *aliyah*, or even to decide on *aliyah*. Finally, it is also expressed in a readiness to strike deeper roots in Jewish education and expand the Jewish educational system in Diaspora countries. If what has been done in this sphere is still inadequate, that is largely our fault. But above all, there is the recognition of the validity of the return to Zion and the supremacy and centrality of Israel in the Jewish consciousness of our generation.

At the Conference of Leaders of Jewish Organizations, which met in Jerusalem at the beginning of the year, at the invitation of the late Prime Minister Levi Eshkol, we heard a leader of Reform Jewry in the United States get up and proclaim : 'We are in exile !' This was a revolutionary admission, the outcome of deep heart-searching, profound spiritual crisis, constant quest and perplexity, the effort to adapt historic concepts to the twentieth century. This is also true of the attempts of the better elements in the New Left to wrestle with the problem of the Land of Israel and the bond between the land and the Jewish people for over 2,000 years as a historical concept, to view the claim of a Jewish right to the land against the twentieth-century concept of self-determination. Jews are no longer so shaken by the criticism levelled against us abroad as they were before 1967. Instinctively, as it were, they make common cause with us against this propaganda. They do not come to us and complain : 'What are you doing in the occupied areas ? The whole world is shocked. You are blackening our name in the eyes of the world.' Perhaps they feel this, but they suppress their criticism. And this is not because of their admiration for us, but because they feel that they share with us a common fate ; they feel that without us their lives would be meaningless.

These are fundamental changes that have taken place within the Jewish people. How this intellectual quest, this new spiritual direction, will find concrete expression against the background of world changes, it is difficult to foresee. But, as history has shown, developments of this kind have an impetus of their own, and they are not necessarily halted by changes in one direction or the other in this world of perpetual motion. There is not the slightest doubt, it seems to me, that a cycle of 150 years of Jewish history, marked by self-deprecation and assimilation – which includes the Zionist aspiration 'to be like all the nations' – has come to an end. The entire picture has been altered, a new chapter has been opened, and the Jewish people – and I believe this is the supreme manifestation of the change – is prepared to march forward with us into the unknown and, despite all its growing perils, into the future.

Theodor Herzl

At a Convention of the Zionist Organization of Canada on the Centenary of Herzl's birth, November 1960

The Third Commonwealth of Israel is now a fact of contemporary history. After a gap of close to 2,000 years, Jewish statehood has resumed continuity. In reviewing this span of time in the course of the nation's history, one defines in the broad sense two distinctive epochs. The one stretches over some seventeen and a half centuries, from the extinction of the Revolt of Bar Kokhba, the last resistance against the Romans, till the turn of this century. This was the period of Diaspora. It was also the period of preparation. The other epoch is much shorter – in all sixty-three years.

The State of Israel was born as a viable entity, nationally and internationally, twelve and a half years ago. The world then recognized it. But the Jewish people recognized it sixty-three years ago at the First Zionist Congress in Basle. In Jewish consciousness it was then that the epoch of renewal, statehood and political independence began. In inaugurating this second epoch, in stirring Jewish consciousness to a recognition of its reality and destiny, in fashioning the tools whereby this destiny was to be fulfilled, Theodor Herzl made the oustanding contribution. If, as [Thomas] Carlyle claims, the history of the world is the biography of its great men, Herzl is part of the essential fabric of this epoch. Architect and leader, statesman and visionary, his memory and his testament are lastingly enshrined in the foundations of renewed statehood.

Although in physical terms Israel's statehood in exile was ethereal, the destruction of the Second Commonwealth did not result in the extinction of independence. The Jewish communities of the Diaspora not only maintained an integrity of spirit and unity within themselves and with each other, but also enjoyed in varying terms and degrees some of the aspects of statehood : a judicial system, organs of public representation and control, communal taxation, a system of organized philanthropy, and an internal national discipline arising from a voluntary acceptance of spiritual authority. Evolving patterns of society, religious movements, philosophic analysis, the search after human destiny, political developments, economic and social upheaval, the changes in the balance of world power nearly all had an impact – direct or indirect, positive or negative – on the spiritual, political or economic fortunes of Jewry.

In essence, the story was that of the struggle to harmonize two apparently conflicting trends : the maintenance inviolate of the sanctuary of the spirit, on the one hand, and involvement with extraneous trends, on the other. The continuity of Jewish tradition was preserved ; external religious faith and the essential unity of a people diffused to every corner of the globe were upheld and fostered ; generation after generation defied the erosion of time, physical oppression and assimilationist pressures. Great communities of the Jewish spirit arose successively, each adding its contribution to learning and philosophy, to the analysis of destiny, to the contemplation of the significance of the Diaspora in the prophetic interpretation of Jewish history ; each adding its layer to the edifice of Jewish heritage.

But all this experience was seen in a temporary perspective. The Diaspora was only an inn for the night, where the rise of the new dawn was awaited. The expectancy and yearning for renewed statehood was a measure of identification with the prophet's message. For if the attribute of continuing prophecy was withheld, the heirloom of the past was preserved intact. But this independent survival, in both its conscious and subconscious aspects, was hardly noticed by historians. Certainly its impulse and goal were overlooked.

When Herzl inaugurated political Zionism in the last decade of the nineteenth century, he found difficulty in convincing the world of its contemporary reality, of its ultimate validity and of its being an expression of the will of the Jewish people. On the other hand, the masses of Jewry rallied automatically to his summons. What was for the international community a novel idea was for them not only an elementary truth, but the natural sequel to an uninterrupted process of self-preparation.

Within three years after Herzl conceived his concept of political Zionism, the First Zionist Congress met in Basle and formulated the Basle Programme. In those three years, Herzl set his idea within the framework of conventional political thought and conceived practical instruments for its implementation. But the groundwork of the transition from the one epoch to the other, in terms of a people's consciousness, had already been laid. The movement of a practical and early return to Zion was already stirring great communities of Russia and Eastern Europe. Herzl's work on the Jewish State was preceded by the works of Rabbi Alkalai, Rabbi Kalischer and Leon Pinsker. An American Jew, Mordecai Noah Moses, had also spoken and written of national restoration. Herzl arrived at the concept of political Zionism in an attempt to find a rational solution to the dilemma of Jewish survival as it appeared to him in Europe at the end of the last century. Denying the validity of the process of emancipation, he spoke and wrote of the Jewish people attaining a normal status among the nations of the world. But for the masses, who were gripped by his message and acknowledged his leadership, the goal was not normalcy. It was redemption : that indefinable feeling and urge that had remained inviolate in their innermost souls down the ages.

Herzl's dialogue with them was therefore uneven. He spoke of liberation, independence and normal status in terms of conventional political parlance. They answered him in terms of immortal prophecy, undying faith and historic destiny. In the unity evolving out of this dialogue – a dialogue never spoken or written but implicit in Herzl's acceptance by the masses of his brethren – the link of continuity was forged between the outgoing and incoming epochs. It was Herzl who accepted the thesis of the masses. In this context, the gap in time, of close on two millennia, between the Second and the Third commonwealths of Israel was bridged. The timeless nature of the experience and vision were reaffirmed ; the reunion was but an affirmation of a permanence and a common destiny that had been dictated from the dawn of history. This interlocking of the two epochs is inherent in the harmony of continuity between them.

This is relevant not only to historical analysis. It touches the very roots of another dialogue between Israel reborn and the nations of the world. Those who deny the validity of the Third Commonwealth as a historical process in moral terms, those who seek to stab at the vitals of the link between faith, people and land, seek first of all to separate the epochs and deny them the aspect of continuity.

Herzl knocked on the gateway of Jewish destiny. The masses of Jewry, who were its guardians, opened wide the gates to him. Indeed, he felt instinctively that they would open the portals. In his letter to Baron Hirsch in 1895, just after he had been fired by his vision, he writes, 'For the sake of speed, I wanted to win you, Baron Hirsch, as a well-known power. But you would have been only the power with which I would have begun. There are ultimately and above all the Jewish masses to whom I will lean to find the way.'

I remember my late grandfather, of blessed memory, telling of the scene that he had witnessed when Herzl was acclaimed by the Jews of Vilna. This was in 1897, on his way back from Petersburg to Paris. Tens of thousands greeted him, led by their rabbis carrying Torah scrolls. What a meeting ! Vilna, the sanctuary of Jewish law and *halakhic* thought and practice ; its rabbis, the heirs of the Gaon of Vilna, acknowledging a Western Jew, a journalist from Vienna, a man suffused with West European culture. It was a paradox only for those ignorant of the essential theme of Jewish unity and the undercurrents of Jewish destiny. At that meeting we see the link symbolically forged between the epochs. Not all were present there. But even those who had never heard of Herzl and his work were affected, and they accepted the new epoch. Even the Jews from the remote deserts of Yemen, who had never heard of Herzl, or of Basle, or of the Congress, were there – unknowingly – for, although they had been cut off for millennia from Jewish communities elsewhere, upon the proclamation of the State of Israel, the entire community made the trek to Aden and from there were flown to Israel.

In an atmosphere of emancipation, Herzl spoke with foreboding and in awesome terms of the oncoming fate of Europe Jewry.

Indeed, as one recalls his picture, above all his eyes, one seems to sense a foreboding. His picture, which I recall from early boyhood, seems to convey something distinctive, set apart, even remote, in its dignity. There is the aspect of the natural leader, the 'first citizen', instinctively recognized and accepted by the people, as described by Thucydides in his eulogy on Pericles : the leader not by force or intrigue or personal ambition, but by gentle persuasion and sense of mission. There is also that sense of mystique, which, according to the great French philosopher, is the aspect of true leadership ; in his words, 'the feeling of having made a movement out of something which by definition is a halt'. There is tranquillity of achievement as he seemed to have reached the sabbath of his life. There is a nearness and immediacy combined with something far off and visionary. There is the aspect of nobility and there is contemplation.

But all seemed bathed in pathos. What was this pathos ? When one is uprooted even for a moment from the press and rush of daily experience, when you stand on a ship's deck and contemplate the endless expanse of ocean and the distant horizon, when the melody of great music stirs you to the depths, when a deep spiritual experience shakes you, there is a stirring of the soul, the beginnings of insight – and then the loneliness in the presence of the unknown. Men with great ideas are so seized ; theirs is the pathos of vision. But perhaps with him it was the pathos of an ominous feeling, a sense of oncoming tragedy : if the new epoch were beginning, would its march be rapid enough to avert the catastrophe that seemed imminent in the outgoing one.

Four decades after his passing, and before the realization of his dream, a tragedy of hitherto unknown dimensions was to overtake the Jewish people. The Jewish State was too late to avert this tragedy. It could only save the remnants. It became the providential consolation in the mourning of an entire people. Never before had homelessness and statehood, agony and fulfilment been intertwined in the tapestry of the nation's experience in such dimensions and in such proximity. Six years after the European Holocaust, after the one epoch ended in blood and tears, the validity of the second epoch, already in existence nearly half a century, was affirmed. The Jewish State became a fact. This phenomenal transition from the pit of despair to the uplands of fulfilment is the central experience of the transition from the one epoch to the other. The manner of transition, the paradox of circumstance, was alive in Jewish consciousness thousands of years ago. An ancient Midrash says : 'If you see a graveyard by the way, know that redemption is at hand.'

In retrospect, then, Herzl's message may be described as an appeal for action in time, a call for a race against time. The sands of the first epoch were running out ; the dykes were giving way. And if we look back to the crucial years of the 1940s, we indeed see that the race against time was in full momentum. I will not speculate here on what might have happened to Herzl's dream had the sense of the new epoch not braced the Jewish people to a supreme effort in the years 1947–8.

I have spoken of two epochs in successive terms, the one expiring and being overtaken by the other, as if we had before us two distinctive experiences of Jewish history that could tolerate a parallel existence. As the new experience rose, the earlier one had to subside – a memory of the past, an inspiration for the future, but lifeless in terms of contemporary achievement. This was Herzl's understanding. This was the impression of the pioneers and successive generations who implemented the ideal. I think it is correct to say that this is an instinctive impression of modern Israeli youth.

But there is yet another interpretation of the relationship between the two epochs. Herzl's environment was that of emancipation. In his education, his profession, his social behaviour, his manner of definition and the clothing of his vision, he was a Western Jew from the lands of evolving freedom and equality. His inner sense was that of Jewish history, but his external expression was that of the Western world of his time. He was instinctively accepted by the masses of Eastern Europe, who translated his message into the context of their belief, prayer and yearning. But Herzl also spoke with those of his own surroundings.

Here, again, we find a paradox that has to be solved in terms of Jewish destiny and unity. For the communities that had already achieved, or were about to achieve, their freedom did not immediately accept his analysis that emancipation had no lasting validity, that their freedom in the Diaspora was a hollow concept, which would not be vindicated in the long run. And yet they lent him their support. Nordau and Zangwill were with him at the first Congress in Basle ; Lord Rothschild, who at first refused to receive him, called on him in London in 1902. Zangwill's masterly description of the majesty of his personality appears in the context of the 'Dreamers of the Ghetto'. Did all these leaders and Jewish communities of the West accept Herzl's thesis of the expiry of one epoch and the beginning of another ? Do they today ?

In reviewing this enigma, we can go back to a somewhat similar situation 2,500 years ago. Few indeed of the Jewish community of Babylon, who had been exiled there only seventy years earlier, returned to reconstitute the Second Commonwealth. Babylon continued as a great Jewish centre, with academies of learning, which produced the Babylonian Talmud. And there ensued a bitter debate : the dialogue between Jerusalem and Babylon. Heated though it was, however, the dialogue did not disrupt the basic unity of Jewry. Babylon did not deny the spiritual primacy of Jerusalem ; it remained constant in its faith in the fulfilment of prophecy on the return and restoration. It sustained the fabric of unity.

There is a parallel between the dialogue today and that of thousands of years ago. Yet one cannot but feel that there is a different aspect today.

The Jewries of the lands of freedom in our time encouraged Herzl in his mission ; in the years of crisis preceding the implementation of his dream they were not found failing. Indeed their assistance to European Jewry in its travail, their support for Israel on the threshold of its independence, their unqualified support since then for the onward march of the state towards stability and peace indicates more than a mere philanthropic gesture of Jewish brotherhood, more indeed than an external identification. The second epoch has not left them unaffected, they do not deny its validity even though the definition may remain ambiguous in certain respects. Against the background of the European calamity they have become partners in Jewish destiny and in the preservation of Jewish continuity side by side with Israel. If homecoming has not been the common theme, Jewish unity has been all-embracing. Its message and dynamics has penetrated and uplifted every Jewish community in the Diaspora. There is a debate. This cannot be denied. But underlining it is an acceptance by all of the theme of redemption. The Jewish destiny unfolding is greater than the debate which accompanies it.

The relationship of the two epochs need not remain in conflict within the heart of Diaspora Jewry. The resolution of this conflict and its harmonization, the acceptance of the new epoch and the transmission of its impact to a new generation, the fashioning of lasting spiritual links with Israel and the deepening of the common identification, the acceptance of the theme and its translation into practice is the subject of Zionism today. Herzl meant this when he said that even after the establishment of the state, the Congress would remain. Zionism's function is not finished.

The Spiritual Dimension

From an address to the Federation of Welfare Funds in Chicago, 18 November 1958

The spiritual unity of the Jewish people has maintained its vigour unimpaired throughout the trials of millennia, and in our time it has attained unprecedented heights. This expression received its first impetus in the depths of tragedy. It has found continuity in the framework of redemption. It has kept pace with phenomenal transformations from despair to hope, from anguish to triumph. It has been a fitting expression of the renaissance of the Jewish spirit that has taken place in our time.

The European Holocaust swept away, in limitless tragedy, a commonwealth of the spirit that embraced one of the most glorious epochs of Jewish history. The Nazi onslaught did not only physically exterminate one-third of our people, it sealed an epoch in Judaism – the great communities of Europe, the power-houses of Jewish learning, the centres of *halakhah*, of mysticism, of Hasidism, of Jewish philosophy. An orphaned people surveyed the scene of Europe at the end of World War Two. The sources of centuries-old faith and inspiration had dried up, the soul of the nation had been ravaged, its spiritual continuity was threatened and its very life hung in precarious balance. The cup of misery was filled to the brim. The poignancy of our tragedy was without parallel in the annals of mankind. The tide had reached its lowest ebb. In the words of the author of Lamentations, we cried out : 'Is there any pain equal to our pain ?'

There have been other periods of calamity in Jewish history, but none was followed by immediate recompense and revival. Seventy years elapsed from the exile to Babylon, after the destruction of the First Temple, till the return to the Land of Israel under the 'mandate' of the Emperor Cyrus of Persia. From the destruction of the Second Temple till the beginning of the restoration of the Third Commonwealth, there was a lapse of over 1,800 years. In our day and before our very eyes the revival and restoration came immediately in the wake of destruction. Only six years after the greatest crime in history had been perpetrated against our people, the international community recognized Israel's right to exist as an independent national entity in the land of its fathers. The scar of exile was healed ; the continuity of Jewish statehood was restored ; Jewish dignity was rescued and uplifted. A nation regained the sources of its eternal inspiration, and immortal prophecy was vindicated before its very eyes. A new and glorious epoch was opened to our people. The valley of death suddenly issued in the broad uplands of hope. Hope and dignity were vouchsafed.

The light of redemption has also cast its shafts on the Jewish Diaspora. The new epoch is not only one of physical regeneration but, no less, of spiritual revival. And this revival relates not only to Israel but also to the Jewish Diaspora. The ash-heaps of Europe have been a prelude not only to Jewish renaissance in the Land of Israel but also to a phenomenal upsurge of Jewish faith and consciousness throughout the Diaspora and, in particular, in the United States. This revival finds expression in many forms – in Jewish education, in synagogue and communal activities, in an interest of third-generation American Jews in their age-old faith and tradition, in Jewish thought and experience and in the significance of the revival of Jewish statehood.

As a representative of Israel to this great land I cannot discuss Israel's immediate political problems without paying tribute to the status of the relations between our country and the United States, which plays so central a part in our foreign policy. There have been differences of a temporary nature between our two governments on various questions, but, broadly speaking, the political and material aid we have received from the US has been constant and far outweighs any difficulties that may have come up in the broad texture of diplomatic relations. This sympathy and interest on the part of a broad segment of American public opinion arise, so it seems to us, from the deepest sources of American civilization. The founding fathers of America did not conceive the message of liberty and democracy as one of only national application. They viewed it as a goal and destiny that, while carried forward within a national framework, would be likewise linked in a close and mutual relationship with other forces throughout the world that aspired to its fulfilment.

This concept is rooted deep in biblical thought and morality. Its lasting significance is the spiritual responsibility of the individual. The measure of biblical impact on nascent American thought can be seen in Jefferson's proposal that the seal of the American Union bear the recollection of the exodus of our forefathers from Egyptian bondage. A corollary of this thought is the right of every nation, in liberty and international equality, to achieve full self-expression of its spiritual credo, thus able to make its unique contribution to the sum total of moral experience. The reverence for the Bible naturally aroused interest in the restoration of the people of the Bible to its ancient homeland. As early as the last century, the second President of the United States, President Adams, expressed his hope that Judea would be reconstituted as a Jewish State.

Thus our many friends in this country are not only expressing goodwill to a sister democracy in the Middle East. They are at the same time paying homage to the biblical heritage that inspired the architects of their own tradition. They are lending continuity to a trend of interest, sympathy and goodwill that has been constant in American history. A nation of overwhelming material capacity and resource, a nation fore-most in the leadership of the Western world, chooses to associate itself in an intimate relationship with a small people of minimal technical re-sources, thousands of miles away, situated in an area no greater than that of the State of New Jersey.

A paradoxical relationship ! In material terms perhaps, not so in terms of eternal verities. Not so, indeed, when it is recognized that if mankind is to survive the momentum of its own physical progress it must recog-nize the supremacy of the spirit. For in this generation of ideological confusion, of erratic thought, in the press and rush of a civilization haunted by doubt, fear and spiritual inadequacy, the still small voice of Israel reborn has a significance overreaching the criterion of material capacity, extending beyond the boundaries of geographical dimension and the gradation of international status. For Israel represents a vindi-cation of faith and prayer through the ages ; it is a symbol of revival, a message of hope, indeed a lasting evidence of the integrity of the spirit. Even as in our religious belief the particular redemption of Israel is linked irrevocably with that of the human race, so has support for the process of our statehood come to be an index of the rule of law and morality in international affairs. If of our own redemption it was foretold 'even though it tarry it shall surely come,' this assurance has similar reference to the vista of world progress. Here lies the core of the rela-tionship between the United States and Israel.

A great American writer posed the question of our immortality in incisive expression : 'Other peoples have sprung up and held their torch light for a time, but it burned out and they sit in twilight now, or have vanished. The Jew saw them all come and go and is now what he always was, exhibiting no decadence, no infirmities of age, no weakening of his parts, no slowing of his energies, no dulling of his alert and aggressive mind . . . What is the secret of his immortality ?' The answer, we know, cannot be found in the regular means of historical analysis. It is rooted in the depths of intuitive faith.

The Jerusalem Talmud tells us of two great masters who were walk-ing on the plain of Arbel as the first dawn broke. They contemplated the shafts of light penetrating the gloom, at once disappearing into darkness and rekindling themselves, until the morning set in. In prophetic vision one turned to the other and said : 'Thus shall be Israel's redemption, slowly as the dawn arises, even as the light grows, so it will be.'

When the gloom seemed overwhelming, when the very survival of our people lay in question, the new dawn broke.

The Continuity of Jewish Destiny

From an Address at Yeshiva University, New York, 12 June 1963

We are gathered to honour an outstanding institution of knowledge and general learning, which has developed, over seventy-five years, into a Jewish and academic landmark on this great continent of freedom. Yeshiva University – with its constant search for a synthesis between the timeless message of Judaism and the cumulative wisdom of human thought, with its manifold colleges of learning, with its tens of thousands of graduates across the length and breadth of this continent in almost every area of life, with its growing academic stature – no longer needs commendation. Its commendation is writ large, day in and day out, on the tablets of Jewish consciousness and of academic excellence. We are gathered to render tribute not only to its distinguished president, teachers, trustees and supporters who have succeeded in sustaining and expanding this vast complex, whose imposing external architecture mingles with inner content to establish it as an enduring monument into the future ; above all, against the canvas of Jewish experience in our time, we are gathered to render homage to a great ideal of which Yeshiva University signifies fulfilment, to note the answer to the challenge of Jewish survival within freedom and equality, to define its crucial significance in the new epoch of Jewish history now unfolding.

In Jewish tradition, edifices of study are not merely physical structures serving a spiritual function. A distinctive sanctity attaches itself to the building – a sanctity that continues even if the building is physically destroyed or dismantled, or if it ceases to fulfil its designated function. The building becomes part of the continuity of Judaism ; its heritage and destiny belong to the future.

The house of learning established in Yavneh by Rabbi Johanan Ben Zakkai after the destruction of Jewish independence by the legions of Imperial Rome close to 2,000 years ago, Sura and Pumbedita of Abbaye and Rava in Babylon, the great houses of study of the Spanish school of Halakhah, Rashi's synagogue in Worms, the house of study of the Gaon of Vilna, Volozhin and other great *yeshivot* of Eastern Europe in the modern era physically belong to the ashes of the past, some expiring in the natural course of history, those of Eastern Europe wiped out in the Holocaust. But in Jewish consciousness these are not merely signposts of learning in the past, not merely repositories of thought, not even merely sources of inspiration. Time has placed them in their proper proportions in the overall pattern of Jewish thought, defining the significance and contribution of each distinctive strand ; but they remain ever-present and undimmed. The thesis of their thought – its tenor and direction, as well as the spiritual fabric underlying it – is still being discussed today in the houses of learning as if it were uttered only yesterday. Today, as we gather to pay tribute to Yeshiva University, the sense of continuity is with us. This great institution, taking its place in the fabric of our history, is the momentum of continuity.

The rise of Israel is at the centre of a new epoch : the renewal of independence, meaning not only a haven of refuge for the body but the basis for the resurgence of the spirit, an affirmation of faith and prayer down the ages, a vindication of the supremacy of the spiritual over the material in human history, a providential consolation after the climax of torment. Great as the difficulties attending its onward progress have been, great as they remain, achievement far outweighs setback ; and the nation moves ahead in confidence of ultimate fulfilment. 'God hath not wrought a miracle in vain.'

I am, however, here today not as an official representative of Israel but as a member of one party to a dialogue meeting with those of the other party, an onlooker at an occasion touching vitally on the other aspect of this epoch. Israel is not the patrimony alone of those who live there and those who escape oppression and insecurity to pass through its gates of redemption. Israel is no less the spiritual patrimony of the Jewish communities of the great lands of freedom. In this new epoch, whether in rescuing the remnants of the European Holocaust, in sustaining the struggle for independence, in unqualified support for the onward march of the state towards stability and fulfilment, there is more than a mere philanthropic gesture of Jewish brotherhood, more indeed than solely an external identification.

It is a relationship that may defy precise definition. In considering it, there is a historical analogy to the period of the 'mandate' of Emperor Cyrus of Persia, 2,500 years ago. Few indeed of the Jewish community of Babylon returned to reconstitute the Second Commonwealth of Israel. Babylon continued as a great Jewish centre, with academies of learning that produced the Babylonian Talmud. There consequently ensued a bitter debate between the masters in Jerusalem and those in Babylon, of which scant record has remained. But the feeling in Jerusalem was summed up in the Midrash : 'And the dove could find no rest for the sole of her foot and she returned to Noah to the Ark. Had she found rest, she would not have returned. So it is with Israel in the Diaspora.'

Heated though it was, the dialogue did not disrupt the basic unity of Jewry, although it most definitely held in it potential seeds of schism and disintegration. Babylon did not deny the spiritual primacy of Jerusalem : it remained constant in its faith in the fulfilment of the prophecy on return and restoration and thus sustained the fabric of unity. Moreover, when the Second Commonwealth was locked in crucial, and what proved to be mortal, struggle against the might of Rome, the Jewish communities of the Diaspora rallied to its side. The unity was not shattered. If you seek proof 2,000 years later, you can find it. Had the unity been disrupted, there would be no debate today between leaders in Israel and the Zionist movement.

Moreover, in our time, against the background of historical experience, with the consciousness of the enigma of Jewish survival as successive eras have unfolded, in the shadow of the endless tragedy that inaugurated the present epoch and with the uplift of the renewal of independence, Israel and the free communities of the Diaspora have acknowledged their partnership in Jewish destiny and in the preservation of Jewish continuity. If homecoming has not been the common theme, the sense of redemption and of unity have been all-embracing. Its message and dynamism have penetrated and uplifted every Jewish community in this great land of freedom and throughout the Diaspora. This is a debate ; this cannot be denied. But underlying it is an acceptance by all of the theme of redemption. Against the canvas of this epoch, what unites is far greater than the points of division. Let us then address ourselves to the theme of continuity - continuity in revival, continuity in renaissance - by which this epoch is and will be measured, by which the leadership of Diaspora, and primarily American, Jewry, will be judged no less than the leadership of the other partner, Israel.

If Jewish independence in the Land of Israel is the primary mark of the new epoch, surely its other outstanding aspect is the status that Judaism has achieved in the lands of freedom, and primarily in the United States. I refer to a public status in terms of the recognition of Judaism's place and contribution to the fabric of national life. Only two decades ago, American Jewry, as Israel, could draw perennial inspiration from the commonwealth of the spirit in Eastern Europe that bore the main burden of Jewish spiritual survival. There has probably never been a period in Jewish history when this burden has passed to a community living in freedom. An outside observer cannot help but note how, in so short a time, American Jewry has matured in its distinctive responsibility, a responsibility shared with Israel to ensure Jewish continuity.

It is told of Baron Nathaniel Rothschild that, after winning his battle of many years to have the disabilities to members of the Jewish faith removed from the House of Lords, he slipped away from the hierarchy of Britain congratulating him on the achievement and was to be found prostrate in prayer in a small synagogue in the Whitechapel ghetto of East London, his lips murmuring, 'Would that this freedom shall not mean the diminution of our faith.' One has the impression that in this great land, where freedom coincided with national independence, this fateful question is more and more penetrating the consciousness of American Jewry.

Pluralism, it was said, does not mean that minority components lose their identity ; freedom, it was said, has no meaning if it is to signify the loss of distinctiveness. And indeed the pluralist civilization itself would destroy its very foundation if its components were to lose the capacity for distinctive contribution to its general fabric. Was there ever a time when mankind, overwhelmed by the nature of its own progress, was groping for spiritual uplift, was turning to sources for a sense of guidance and stability. Can this period be marked by the self-abnegation of Jewishness by withdrawal from the circumstances of freedom, from the challenge of freedom. Yeshiva University, one feels, is symbolic of the answer. In it are interwoven the strands of the past, the challenge of the present and the hope of the future.

The Uniqueness of the Jew

At Bar-Ilan University, Ramat Gan, December 1967

We who live in Israel live in a totally Jewish atmosphere and share basically one culture. We cannot understand the nature of the Jew in the Western world. The entire population of Israel, with very few exceptions, is drawn from strata of Jews who either had no other culture or were thrown out or expelled from another culture. On the other hand, the Jew of the Western world, particularly on the American continent, finds, for the first time in Jewish history, that Judaism is accepted. More so, it is considered to be one of the three religious foundations of American and Canadian civilization. The Jew therefore feels, with considerable right, a sense of equality ; being a Jew means to voluntarily maintain the Jewish heritage in the deepest sense, to establish a harmony between Judaism and external influence. It is a constant struggle to find oneself ; many try and many fail, but those who succeed achieve a harmony of the deepest historical Jewish sense.

Actually, the Scriptural portion of the week, which we read this Sabbath, clearly indicates this ambivalence and search, which dates from the first exile of the Jews, the exile to Egypt. Joseph, in naming his two sons, referred to this dichotomy. Of Menashe, the older one, he said : *'Ki nashani Elokim et kol amali ve'et kol beit avi'* (Genesis 41 : 51), 'the Almighty has made me forget . . .' *Nashani* is not forgetfulness in the familiar sense ; it refers to being 'pushed aside', hence '[He] hath made me forget all my toil, and all my father's house.' And of the second son he said : *'Ki hifrani Elokim be'eretz onyi'* (Genesis 41 : 52), 'For God hath caused me to be fruitful in the land of my affliction.' However, the Aramaic version translates *'onyi'* as *'be'eretz sha'budi'*, in the land of my bondage.

It is understandable that Joseph should have said of Menashe *'Ki nashani mikol amali'* : he had forgotten his labour, the affliction of his home in Canaan, the slave boy brought to Egypt and tormented in the Egyptian prison ; but is it conceivable that he should say : God has made me forget *kol beit avi*, all my father's house? It was indeed very conceivable. Here you have a reflection of the inner struggle of the Jew in every Diaspora down the ages. In the first stage, he lives in the illusion that he is fully accepted into the surrounding society, that he can forget his background, his sources, his origin, his father's home, the entire civilization from which he sprang. But no matter how powerful, how central a figure he is in that society, there must come a point, there must come a day, when he feels that ultimately it is *eretz sha'budi*, the land of bondage. No material gain, no sense of status or influence, no feeling of power can remove this central fact.

These two stages were likewise part of Joseph's experience. As he recalled the phenomenal transition from the depths of bondage to the heights of princely power in Egypt, he felt that he was accepted by the Egyptians and was able to forget his father's home. He said : I will be a new type of Jew, I will be an Egyptian of Jewish origin, and this withdrawal, this separateness from another society, will not be mine ; I have left my brethren in Canaan. But very rapidly he realized the truth, and by the time his second son was born, he thanked the Almighty for his providence. *Hifrani Elokim*, God has made me fruitful, in the land of my bondage. He accepted that he too was a slave of a deeper sense, that if he were to lose his Jewish spirit he would lose his balance. If he were to lose his Judaism, his sense of Jewish history, he would lose not only his essential core but even his capacity to contribute to the external society.

This I believe is the story of Jewish history down the ages, of the endless exiles through which we have traversed as we have sought to return to the Land of Israel in hope and prayer, and finally, with God's help, in our generation, in fact and in rebuilding. It is found in the Midrashic commentaries and the dicta of the sages at every point, from the concept of our father Abraham as *ger vetoshav* 'a stranger and a sojourner', or, as the Midrash explains the term *Avraham ha'ivri*, 'Abraham the Hebrew' : *'Avraham me'ever mizeh vechol ha'olam me'ever mizeh'*, 'Abraham is on one side and all the rest of the world is on the other side.' It is inherent in the concept expressed in the Midrashic comment on the verse *'Viyeshavtem lavetah be'artzechem'* (Leviticus 26 : 5), 'And ye shall . . . dwell in your land safely' : *'be'artzechem lavetah velo be'eretz aheret'*, 'safely in your own land, but not in any other land'. It is not the concept of physical security, but that of inner security, which the Jew can have only if he lives in the Land of Israel.

This is the essence of that remarkable Midrash that notes that Moses said : *'Uvagoyim hahem lo targia'* (Deuteronomy 28 : 65), 'And among these nations shalt thou find no ease,' while Jeremiah seems to contradict Moses by saying of Israel in the wilderness : '. . . when I went to cause him to rest' (Jeremiah 31 : 2). Thus, it appears that Jeremiah said there could be tranquillity in exile. The fact is that there are two aspects to tranquillity : there is a sense of physical tranquillity – and not all Jews in all ages have been under threat of extermination – but that sense of inner tranquillity, a sense of *bitahon*, safety, or security, that feeling of wholeness, a sense of belonging, of a totality of existence and experience is rooted only in the Land of Israel.

So, as we survey wave after wave of Jewish history, as we traverse every course and every age, we find this experience constantly repeated. We have seen it in our own time. We saw it seven months ago, when just before the Six Day War the Jews were suddenly isolated. Even the most assimilated Jews felt the isolation, and they lived in Jerusalem with us.

This was a sudden trauma, a fear, a sense of exultation – analyse it as you wish.

But there are the few who are the core of Jewry throughout the Diaspora : they live year in, year out, day in, day out, in Jerusalem, they have attained that inner harmony, they are wholesome Jews in every sense. They feel the distinctiveness of the Jew and yet they are part of society. This surely is a phenomenal aspect of the Jew through the ages.

Only a year ago I was host to fifteen non-Jewish heads of theological faculties from the United States. They wanted to discuss with me the spiritual nature of Israel reborn. They entered into the area of Christian theology in terms of the status of the Jew throughout history. I asked them if they were familiar with the passage 'the people shall dwell alone' (Numbers 23 : 9). They were, and I said that in traditional Jewish belief this was said 3,300 years ago. I asked if there were Bible critics among them, and one replied. I asked him what date he would give as the earliest and he approximated 2,700 years. 'But you too say at least 2,700 years ?' I asked. He nodded in affirmation. I continued and told them that Balaam was the greatest prophet of the nations of the world, of whom the sages said : 'In Israel there arose none like Moses, but among the nations of the world there arose such a one and he was Balaam.' It would seem remarkable that the sages should say such a thing, and I explained to them my interpretation of it. All prophecy relates to events as they will unfold, but Balaam's prophecy was even higher in that it related to the nature of a people until the end of time, which lies beyond any possible human concept. A human being with wisdom, with insight, with intuition may see ahead a year or two, or perhaps ten or twenty, and conceive of the unfolding of events in some form. If this reaches a perception over thousands of years, it is clearly Divine Providence that has been given to the man. But totally beyond our concept is the idea of a person being able to foretell the nature of a society's development. If we were to ask how a child from Israel would react to being transferred to Peking – what will be his behaviour, his attitude, his psychology five years hence – it is beyond us to imagine anybody foretelling such a matter. Yet we see in the case of Balaam that he indeed foretold the nature of the Jewish people over thousands of years. Therefore his prophecy was put above all other prophecy except that of Moses.

As we analysed further, I asked them whether they accept that this was said of the Jewish people thousands of years ago ? All the theologians said, 'That we accept.' And I said, 'Is there any other people of whom a prophecy has been said thousands of years ago in any form, in any part of the ancient world ?' They said no. 'Now,' I said to them, 'has this prophecy remained true to the present day ? Has it been fulfilled in the realities of history ? Has the prophecy "a people set apart" stood the test of time ?'

Of the State of Israel, I told them, there is no question that this is so. Israel is alone – contrary to what the original theoreticians of Zionism assumed, that we could become like all nations and become a normal people. Now, 17/18 years later, we are still alone ; we have friends across the world and yet we are isolated. We belong neither to East nor West, neither to NATO nor the Warsaw Pact, neither to the neutralist bloc nor the Arab League, neither to the Afro-Asian bloc nor the underdeveloped countries. We belong to no framework except our own. We are totally isolated in the inner sense of family.

There is but one people in the world that has one religion, and one religion in the world that has but one people. Israel alone, of all the nations of the world, could not survive without her Diaspora. If all the Irishmen in the world were to cease to exist tomorrow, there would be no question that Ireland would continue to exist. If, God forbid, the Jews of the Diaspora were to disappear, it is very, very doubtful if Israel would continue to exist ; and as we need the Jews of the Diaspora, so they need us.

I then asked my guests, 'Now don't be afraid of sounding anti-Semitic. Tell me the truth. In your universities is the Jewish student "a people set apart" or not ? Is he totally part of American society or is he separate ?' A Catholic nun who was present – a very brilliant woman, head of a university faculty – answered me with a very, very wise definition. 'The Jew in our university who is proud of his Judaism is distinctive. The Jew who hides his heritage is even more different.' A very incisive definition indeed of the nature of the Jew in the Western world.

The vast masses of our brethren across the Western world seek themselves and are seeking themselves more and more deeply as the months elapse since the Six Day War. As the nature of this trauma defines itself in their souls, they ask 'Who am I ? To what world do I belong ?' They suddenly realize they are something more than Americans of the Jewish faith. They belong to a distinctive course in history, which marches parallel to and interlocked with the general course of human history. As they seek this definition, as they turn to their sources, they turn back to those Jews who have maintained the embers of Judaism over the decades, who refused to yield to an external society, who have sought the harmony, who have developed educational processes across the American continent ; but who, above all, claim this uniqueness, that while they live in another society, while they are part of that other society, ultimately they live in Jerusalem. They are part of its eternity and immortality and they live in Jerusalem in expectation, in prayer and in faith, but, even beyond that, in the totality of the civilization.

Exodus and Redemption

From an Address in New York at a 'Third' Seder (Passover Celebration) under the Auspices of the Histadrut Campaign, 24 April 1959

Eleven years ago the Third Commonwealth of Israel became a fact of contemporary history. It was a product of the twentieth century : modern methods had been employed in the struggle for its establishment – in diplomacy, in public relations, in resettlement and in self-defence. Israel's statehood is cast in a modern mould ; her emergence has been part of a process through which many nations have achieved independence. But her inner truth and lasting significance can only be defined in terms of a continuous national and religious experience through the ages.

Immortal prophecy foretold that the agony of exile would usher in restoration. The reunion of land and people was but an affirmation of the bond forged when the sons of those who had been redeemed from Egyptian slavery entered the Promised Land. The impulse for freedom and independence was born some 3,500 years ago in challenge to Egyptian bondage. In the span of Jewish experience in our time, torment and fulfilment, homelessness and statehood have been interwoven in a unique tapestry of faith and poignancy. In terms of the nation's subjective experience, the threads of the pattern lead back to the emergence of nationhood under providential dispensation in the Egypt of the Pharaohs. But even the outsider can find analogy and continuity between the first redemption and that which has unfolded in our time.

Jewish bondage in Egypt took place at an early stage of the first recorded cycle of civilization. Planned agriculture, the harnessing and canalization of water, the rudiments of medicine, mathematics, economics and trade, hand-propelled machinery, writing, plastic arts and architecture all were proof of systematic intellectual enquiry and discovery. Social and national structures bore evidence of state cohesion and organization. Elaborate internal networks guarded the persons and régimes of the ruling orders. Organized armies defended national and territorial integrity from assault and, at the same time, engaged in imperialistic expansion. The map of the area we now call the Middle East showed broad lines of geopolitical units. Egypt in the south and Mesopotamia in the north were the great powers, and between them were sandwiched many smaller units and tribal frameworks. International rivalries, plots, alliances, tensions, wars and conquests were the ingredients of the power struggle relentlessly pursued across the area.

Technological development had found its direction ; internal national and social structures showed lines of definition ; relations between nations had begun to assume an orderly pattern of alternative – peace or war.

There were social and political reasons for the antagonism of the royal house of Egypt towards the Hebrew community. Their separatism aroused suspicions ; their distinctive tradition was a challenge to the homogeneous framework of thought and conduct ; they refused to be absorbed into the slave structure that was the dominant social framework of the day. But a careful reading of the dialogue between Pharaoh and Moses will show that the final rift took place on the spiritual issue. The Hebrews challenged the combination of mortal divinity and human debasement. They rejected the underlying concept of human experience as a chaos of events without moral direction and destiny. They gambled their life and survival on the belief in providential guidance over the individual and the nation. They proclaimed the supremacy of spirit over matter. Their message was that Egyptian civilization, with all its progress, carried within it the seeds of its own destruction.

They could not convey to their oppressors the source of their subjective faith in redemption. This faith was to be translated into a discipline at the foot of Mount Sinai, receiving there the stamp of eternity. In the world of those days it was obscure and enigmatic ; it involved a phenomenal challenge to basic concepts ; it fashioned the spiritual basis for the material development that, till then, was the central story of human progress. Well over 3,000 years later, contemplating in retrospect the significance of this event, an outstanding architect of freedom in our time, Winston Churchill, described it as a decisive leap forward in human history. In objective historical appraisal the exodus of the Jews snatched them from imminent extinction.

Although the movement of national revival in our time at first found difficulty in developing the posture, terminology and method of a movement for sovereign independence and international status, the masses of Jewry were not unprepared for redemption : the central experience of exile had been the refusal to recognize its permanence. But what was for the masses of Jewry a natural sequence, a continuous process of self-preparation, was for the outside world a novel and revolutionary idea. Redemption as the theme and promise of survival, as a concept that defied the logic of time and the circumstances of historical development, as a bridge that united past, present and future was exclusive to the innermost sanctuary of the nation's spirit.

But two aspects did not fail to draw the attention of the objective onlooker. Within the decade preceding the rise of statehood, the very existence of Jewry lay in a crucial balance ; destruction, torment and despair, without precedent in the annals of Jewry, assaulted its integrity and survival. Secondly, the State of Israel has come into being at a time when scientific discovery and technological development have reached a point where mankind faces the alternative between universal destruction and the acknowledgement of the supremacy of the spiritual factor in human affairs. As international consciousness becomes aware of the dilemma of survival, many eminent thinkers point to the providential transition of Israel from the valley of death to the upland of destiny as a theme for reflection and encouragement for the broad gamut of human experience.

In the modern era, as in Egypt of old, the threat of extinction was the preamble to redemption. In the first cycle of recorded civilization, Israel's redemption revealed the spiritual factor in human destiny. At the present time, Israel reborn affirms anew the lasting truth of spiritual values and the prophetic interpretation of the human story. Jewish statehood as the fulfilment of an historical process is now a subject for the historian, theologian, sociologist and political scientist. For the Jew it is not only a vindication of faith and an affirmation of national revival. It is above all a living drama. In exile, redemption meant survival and the hope of a new dawn ; with its realization, it casts up a constant challenge.

In modern times, the dictionaries of political, spiritual and economic terms have become very confused. In the general confusion, our people, too, have not always agreed on a common definition for certain concepts. But the idea of redemption has not suffered distortion. It has been preserved inviolate in the innermost recesses of the nation's soul. Geography and time did not confuse its meaning nor weaken its summons. In the struggle for statehood, particularly in the years before 1948 and in the years immediately after the rise of the state, it embraced every part of Jewry. But the redemption is not yet consummated : Israel is still threatened on many fronts ; the Middle East is seething throughout, as the intra-Arab conflict and East-West dispute develop in intensity. Israel enjoys at present comparative security and quiet, but none can tell how long this situation will prevail.

In celebrating the festival of Passover, may the sense of continuous redemption strengthen your resolve to fortify the state against danger. In the race against time, much more can be done to advance the ingathering of the exiles, to broaden the economic framework and to buttress defence. Active support means direct participation in the process of redemption. This effort requires unity and partnership of all the components of Jewry - in Israel and the Diaspora. Philanthropy is not enough. What is required is partnership, flowing from a sense of common destiny.

Of all the ancient empires and cultures that swayed the fate and mind of mankind when our forefathers went forth from Egypt, the Jewish people alone resides anew in the area. In dedicating ourselves to the task of furthering redemption, let us contemplate the meaning of this spiritual phenomenon. The Third Commonwealth of Israel has its roots in the first redemption from Egypt. Somewhere, somehow, the thread runs through our distinctive march across history under providential guid-

ance. This is the enigma of the spirit that we are privileged to behold.
May we be worthy of the destiny it enshrines.

Chanukah and the Rebirth of Israel

From an Address under the Auspices of the Israel Bond Drive in Boston, 13 December 1959

I bring you greetings from Israel reborn. After an exile of long and dark centuries, a people has come home ; after captivity and desolation for close to 2,000 years, a land has been renewed with life. The reunited people and land salute their kinfolk and men of goodwill across the world. The message is a message of achievement and redemption and, above all, of faith. In a generation haunted by doubt, fear and ideological confusion, the revival of Israel has a significance beyond its material dimensions. Land and people throb in vitality and homecoming. For common nationhood has been reaffirmed among the immigrants from many lands. The Negev Desert is being watered ; the Hulah swamps have become fertile land ; the city of Jerusalem, Israel's capital and fountain-head of lasting inspiration, is being rebuilt ; the hills and valleys are covered with hundreds and hundreds of settlements ; great academies of learning – religious, secular and scientific – are flourishing. There has evolved a democratic society that has withstood the test of external threats, economic difficulties and all attempts at communal diffusion. Israel feels her central responsibility for Jewish survival. She realizes that she is the repository of the Jewish dignity that has been restored to our people. She is well aware that she enshrines the hope of her kinsfolk throughout the world.

The key-note of her message is that of Chanukah [the Festival of Dedication, commemorating the victory of the Maccabees]. You have gathered to celebrate the advent of Chanukah in the year 5708 (according to the Hebrew calendar), 2,100 years since the Maccabees wrested Jewish independence from their Greek oppressors, the Temple in Jerusalem was reconsecrated and the eternal light rekindled.

Chanukah comprehends Judaism to mean Jewish independence – in the physical and political sense – in that small land on the eastern coast of the Mediterranean where the threefold bond of land, people and faith was forged for all time. Chanukah also enshrines the dialogue between Israel and the nations of the world from earliest times. The central theme is of the few against the many, of a people – its soul kindled by immortal dispensation – pursuing its distinctive course through the ages against all odds ; a people confident in its faith that no mortal force, whether active or passive, whether of oppression or hatred, whether of discrimination or assimilation, could in the final analysis deny it the fulfilment of its spiritual and national destiny, both for itself and in the broader context of human progress.

Over 2,000 years of human history you will find the Jewish people and its faith, in relation to the majority of temporal and spiritual forces, affected directly or indirectly by most developments. No period during this time has been without the struggle of the few to survive against the oppression or against the spiritual influence of the many. Moreover, the effort of survival has lent resilience to the fact of survival. Indeed, if one were required to characterize Jewish history in a single word, that word would be 'Chanukah'.

The Maccabees of old were not only members of the priestly house and, as such, guardians of Judaism; they were also leaders of their people – generals and statesmen. In summing up political and military prospects, the criteria were the same in ancient times as today. The Maccabees could not have ignored them, and yet they embarked on a revolt against Greek oppression that, in light of what we know today about the balance of forces in those days, must have seemed remote indeed from any chance of success. They acted as they did because failure to act would have meant total physical destruction and spiritual eclipse. But an inner voice told them that if the tragedy of Jewish destiny is a precarious existence on the brink, its triumph is achieved by total commitment to faith through which peril can be challenged and overcome. In our time, over 2,000 years later, the sons of the Maccabees faced a situation that, in poignancy and despair, recalled the circumstances in which their forefathers had likewise found themselves.

In 1947/48, a few years after one-third of the Jewish people had been annihilated in the Nazi Holocaust, the Jewish community of Palestine was thrust into the final stage of a fateful and decisive struggle for the renewal of Jewish independence in the land of our fathers. It was the story of the few against the many in a climactic form. The prospects of success seemed remote at best. Seven Arab governments gave notice that they would strangle the state at birth and proceeded to perfect their military machine for this purpose. Bitterness and suspicion marked relations with Great Britain on the expiry of the British Mandate. Beyond the Arab complex in the Middle East and in Asia, the attitude was one of hostility or indifference. The future of Jerusalem aroused concern and sentiment across the Christian world. In the capitals of the world the prospect of the unfolding drama was the subject of extensive political and military analysis. Nearly every appraisal of which we know prophesied defeat – partial or total – of the new state in the first days or weeks of its existence. Indeed, there was even talk in certain Mediterranean countries of preparing homes for Jewish refugees who would have to flee from the Land of Israel.

But the passage of time had not obliterated the spirit of the Maccabees: their resolve, their faith, and the message of their experience bridged the gap of time and guided their heirs in the twentieth century. If archaeology will one day uncover the political and military estimates of those who sent Greek forces to crush the Hasmonean Revolt, we might assume that their analysis of the Jewish prospects would not be far different from the assessments that were prevalent in 1948. Redemption flashed anew, when every mortal assessment would seem to have denied its validity. The few vindicated their cause against the force of the many. As Chanukah is celebrated throughout Israel today, its true significance and innermost spirit can be grasped for the first time since the festival was initiated thousands of years ago.

With the establishment of the State of Israel and the defeat of the Arab attempt to destroy it, Israel's troubles were not settled. Eleven years after her establishment, Israel is still threatened with destruction by her neighbours. Boycott, blockade, intrigue, aggressive intent and armed threats still exemplify the Arab posture towards Israel. Israel's effort to secure full and unqualified recognition of her equality and international rights still continues. The struggle of the few against the many persists, but it is of a different nature. Today it is the struggle of an independent people living in its homeland in freedom.

Today we face our Arab neighbours with more calm and confidence than heretofore. We say to them : your threats do not frighten us, but they do distress us, for they indicate that you are still lacking that sense of rational fulfilment that brings peaceful intent and the urge for international cooperation. We have neither land nor water nor any other resource that you need for your survival or advancement. We have not exploited to our advantage any of the stresses and tensions that have convulsed your lands in the past two years. If you attack us, we shall defend our land and liberty with a capacity born of experience. If you wish neither war nor peace, let it be so. If you are ready for peace, we are ready to meet forthwith and to discuss any problem disturbing our relationship. We are as much a part of the Middle East as you are. We seek its welfare no less than you. How long will you perpetuate fear and tension in our area, for it is harmful to you no less than to us. To the dictator of the Nile we say : we know you and by now you should know us. We view with sympathy legitimate Arab nationalism. Our quarrel is only with a doctrine whose tenets breed intrigue, subversion and hostility across the Middle East.

World statesmen will not help solve the Arab-Israel deadlock by compromising with Arab boycott and blockade. They cannot, in the broad international sphere, espouse direct contact, disarmament and relaxation of tension and leave the Middle East to fester endlessly in tension and hostility. They cannot continue to agree to keep the masses of Arab refugees in misery and despair, just because the Arab governments can find no better pawn in their campaign of hate against Israel. There are positive trends among the people of the Middle East, including the Arab peoples. Surely the time has come for world statesmanship to foster them, for they – not hate – represent the true trend of history.

On Chanukah we proclaim our confidence that peace will come. It may take time, but it will come. In the measure that Israel's security will be buttressed, her economy broadened and her international status enhanced, the impact of her progress, coupled with peaceful intent, will make its lasting mark on the Arab mind.

The dialogue of a redeemed people with the world has but begun. The testament of the Maccabees will be vindicated. On Chanukah let us clasp hands in spiritual fraternity and historical involvement. Let us recall the testament of the Mattathias, father of the Maccabees : privileged indeed are we to live in this generation. May we be worthy of the destiny that summons us forward.

State and Religion in Israel

A statement prepared for the guidance of Israeli diplomatic missions abroad, 20 March 1951

I

During the past few months, a number of articles have appeared in journals abroad that are of one theme, although they vary in the measure of their criticism. In short, they depict the State of Israel as having forfeited its title-deeds of democracy and freedom of thought. Political manoeuvring is described as having imposed a primitive theocracy involving coercion of conscience upon an unwilling population. The outstanding example of this unbridled virulance is William Zuckerman's latest article in *Harper's Magazine* (November 1950), which goes so far as to interpret the present immigration of the Jewish communities of North Africa and the Near East – who are largely Orthodox – as part of the plan for implementing theocratic rule in the country at large. A further passage in the article details the *halakhic* laws [Jewish rabbinical law] of Sabbath observance, followed by meaningful ellipses that are clearly designed to intimate that all citizens of Israel are obliged to observe these laws in their every detail and with utmost rigour. Of a similar nature are other articles that appeared last year, notably that of Professor Konvitz, who, as an expert on constitutional law and history, would wish the State of Israel to conform to the American Constitution far more than is the case in the United States itself.

A second category of critics is constituted by a number of Reform rabbis who naturally feel irked at what they term the refusal of the government to acknowledge their rabbinical status in Israel. Finally, there are some non-Jewish genuine liberals who have been assured by members of the above two categories that the State of Israel, instead of being the promised bastion of democracy for this backward area, is retrogressing into the general pattern of Middle Eastern countries. The coalition tension on religious issues and debates on religious questions in the Knesset, instead of being interpreted in their natural context, are distorted to represent the last convulsions of democracy in the new state.

These allegations are so remote from the truth that, apparently, adequate retort has hardly been considered necessary. This is, however, not the case. Malignant hostility to the State of Israel as such clearly has its subconscious place in the minds of many of these critics. For them any aspect of historical continuity in the life and spirit of the state is a recollection of a Jewish distinctiveness that they would prefer to forget ;

if Israel were to make a total break with the past, the last shreds of their Jewish conscience would be appeased, as a bolt from a vacuum is infinitely more acceptable than from a living content. These critics are hardly likely to be silenced by refutation. On the other hand, experience has shown that reasoned exposition will be understood and accepted by constructive people, whatever their personal convictions. Paul Blanchard of *The Nation,* who came to Jerusalem last year to follow up his book on Catholic influence in the United States with an analysis of the Vatican's plan for Jerusalem, was given the additional assignment of revealing the alleged plan of the Jewish Elders of Zion to blot out freedom of conscience in the State of Israel. After studying the position at first hand, Blanchard found that the thesis he had been set on was hardly accurate and his subsequent articles in *The Nation* could in no way have satisfied those who sponsored his mission. Similarly, a number of American Reform Jews, after a visit here, wrote home withdrawing their previous criticism.

The first and obvious answer to this problem is that Israel, as an independent state, is not obliged to pay attention to the criticism of outsiders. As the Prime Minister has well said, opinions on the spiritual character of the state are welcome only from those who choose to shoulder its burdens by becoming its citizens. However, as the unity of Jewry everywhere is a primary principle of our nationhood, no good can come from widespread dissatisfaction in the Diaspora with regard to the spiritual affairs of the state, particularly when this is contrary to the truth. The average Diaspora Jew who sees in the state a test of the vitality of Jewry is prepared to grant Israel a lease of inner spiritual peace in the decisive years of *kibbutz galuyot* [the ingathering of exiles], economic reconstruction and security stabilization. But the spiritual integrity of Israel may depend on the working out of a satisfactory status quo on religious matters in the decisive epoch of nation-building, and the outcome of this controversy may well determine whether an essentially united nation is to dedicate itself to the Third Rebuilding, or diverse groups, rent asunder in frustrated assimilation, are to repeat the fatalism of self-disaster that marked the end of the last Jewish Commonwealth and the external corrosion of exile.

Kabbalistic tradition perceives the age of redemption as the spiritual melting-pot for the national soul, which, heretofore lacked fulfilment in the vicissitudes of our history. The striking similarity of the inner conflict of our day with that in other periods of our ancient statehood lends a frighteningly literal sense to this tradition. Those Jews of the Diaspora – to the right as well as to the left – who sincerely wish us to defy ominous precedent this time must be asked not to exacerbate the tension that naturally accompanies this unprecedented experiment : the unification of diffusion, as entire communities relinquish the heritage of dispersion for their integration – social and spiritual – into a common nationhood. The following few points may be of use to those who are required to defend the State of Israel from accusations of this sort.

II

The attitude of Orthodox Jews in modern times to their fellow-Jews of non-Orthodox convictions has been defined at length by the late Chief Rabbi Kook, of blessed memory, whose decisions on this matter have been acknowledged by the present Chief Rabbinate of Israel and even by the outstanding religious authority of the extreme wings of Orthodox Jewry. At the source of this approach lies the injunction that 'the paths of the Torah are the paths of harmony and all its ways are peace.' The social relationship between religious and non-religious groups in Jewry is to be conducted in a spirit of moderation and understanding, and every effort should be made to preserve the essential unity of Israel in the belief (laid down by Maimonides as an axiom of faith) that 'as the nation regains the sources of its native inspiration, those who have fallen victim to the corrosion of assimilationist doctrines shall, of their own volition, return.'

1   As recorded in the new *Talmudic Encyclopaedia* (which enjoys the sanction of the greatest contemporary authorities on the *halakhah*), the punitive measures mentioned in Jewish law as applicable to Jewish non-believers are not relevant to modern times and can only be revived after the appearance of the Messiah. At that time, the Divine manifestation foretold by the prophets will 'rekindle anew the absolute belief' that, as a result of the trials of tragic destruction and dispersion, has become dimmed in the souls of vast groups of Jewry. This authoritative thesis acknowledges that the gaps of history cannot be bridged in a day and that the unity of the nation has in itself become a religious precept.

2   The application of the punishment for offenders against certain precepts could only be applied if the great Sanhedrin be reconstituted in the Temple enclave. Such reconstitution must be preceded by a supernatural revelation.

3   The suggestion that religious Jews in this country constitute no more than twelve per cent of the population is without actual basis. At least twenty-five per cent of the Jews of Israel attend synagogue on the Sabbath (if the new immigration is taken into account, the percentage would probably be forty to fifty); thirty per cent of the children in the country go to religious schools; an overwhelming majority of the population purchase kosher meat; and there are an estimated 100,000 practising Jews in the Histadrut and very considerable numbers in the General Zionist and Herut parties. These people practise their religion and send their children to religious schools absolutely of their own volition. Only a small percentage is organized in the religious political parties constituting the Religious Bloc; this does not mean, however, that the greater number, who belong to other political groupings or are altogether without party affiliation, are not interested in a positive public attitude

towards religious questions. What's more, of that part of the population that is termed 'non-religious' the majority is by no means anti-religious.
4   Even the most extreme faction in the Religious Bloc has declared more than once that its religious demands relate solely to government and municipalities and by no means to the citizen's personal life. They have asked that public policy in the state should give expression to Jewish tradition, so that the country as such would preserve a distinctive Israeli character. They see in this an affirmation of our historic continuity, an emphasis on the distinctiveness of our nationhood and a tribute to a heritage without which, they believe, the nation is liable to lose its native bearings and the link between Israel and the Diaspora would be weakened beyond any tangible identification. Most people who are not religious quite naturally differ from this viewpoint, but the critics who abuse those irreligious Jews who have indeed made concessions to the religious groups fail to appreciate that this has not merely been done as cheap political manoeuvring. The history of religious faith in the Redemption through the return to Zion can hardly be summarily brushed aside even by those who do not share in this belief. There is, therefore, a genuine desire to go far in giving to that substantial section of Jewry that sees in the establishment of the State of Israel the fulfilment of immortal prophecy and the beginnings of an all-embracing spiritual redemption a true feeling of a homeland in the wider sense. The process of renewed nationhood requires concessions from all sides, and deep intuition, making for national unity, lies at the root of this process.
5   The Prime Minister, when first presenting the present government to the Knesset, declared that even if the Religious Bloc had not entered the government his party would not have instituted civil marriage and divorce. Such a step, he explained, would mean 'rending asunder the soul of a nation at a time when its basic unity must be the prime objective'. Civil marriage and divorce would result in the creation of two Jewish communities in Israel, the one unable to intermarry with the other. Apart from the consequent disruption among the veteran population, the new immigrants from Arab countries would be altogether cut off from a large section of the former.
6   For non-believing Jews, the Jewish marriage and divorce ceremonies involve no denial whatsoever of their non-religious convictions. The participants in these ceremonies are not required to make any declaration of religious faith, nor is such belief considered necessary for the validity of the act in question. The non-believing Jew may choose to see in these ceremonies a national form rather than a religious prescription, and in subscribing to this form he had the satisfaction of knowing that he is sustaining the essential spiritual unity of the nation.
7   On the question of *kashrut* in the army (and this applies equally to *kashrut* in government or municipal-maintained institutions), the Prime Minister explained that a non-religious Jew does not undergo any infringement on his conscience by eating kosher meat, but that a

religious Jew required to eat non-kosher meat would most certainly experience an infraction on his convictions.

8   The argument that Sabbath public observance laws is tantamount to theocracy may equally be levelled against Britain. In Britain there is no final separation of church and state : the bishops are appointed by the Prime Minister, and the religious schools of all communities, including those of Catholic and Jewish communities, are fully maintained by the state. Some months ago, Parliament by an overwhelming majority, even prohibited the opening of amusement centres on Sundays during the Festival of Britain. It is a fact that in New York – the home of most of the critics – there is no lawful possibility of divorce unless adultery is proven. [Ed. Note : In 1951 this was the case ; the laws have since been made more lenient.] This restriction is more severe than anything even remotely thought of by the extreme sections of the Religious Bloc. A well-known figure on the American Jewish scene, who was outspoken in his criticism of the alleged theocracy in Israel, was asked how he could reconcile his conscience with the divorce laws of New York. His answer was that to upset this system would mean creating a rift in the American people. Apparently he had not yet agreed to recognize us as being in the same category of nationhood! These examples are not an index to the behaviour of a nation that has endured by virtue of its spiritual distinctiveness ; they can, however, be quoted to illustrate that Israel is not the sole democracy that must compromise on religious questions.

9   The critics wax fierce that the Government as such has a religious budget. On this, remarkably enough, they will not find support even in Mapam [the left-wing United Workers' Party], which has twice declared its non-opposition in principle to the government's religious budget. In the Scandinavian countries – whose democracy is assumedly unquestioned – the governments also have religious budgets, and even in certain areas of France the French Ministry for Religious Affairs pays the salaries of the clergy. M. Jules Moch, when here last year, told government officials that, as Minister of the Interior in the French Government, he consulted the Vatican and the Chief Rabbinate in Paris on the appointments of Catholic and Jewish clergy in certain areas of France, although the appointments were officially made by him. In America, admittedly, things are different. But the American practice has specific roots in American history and in the contemporary fear of Catholic political domination ; to translate this practice indiscriminately to a totally different climate would be as unscientific as it would be un-Jewish.

10   There is no prohibition in the State of Israel against any sect – Jewish or non-Jewish – worshipping in accordance with its faith. Reform Jews may maintain their synagogues with no less freedom than other Jews. However, to grant them the right to perform marriage and divorce ceremonies without their compliance with Jewish law would mean, in fact, the institution of civil marriage and divorce. If the

government, on national grounds, has refused to accede to this demand from a substantial section of its own population, how can it be expected to grant this for the sake of critics from abroad? As far as Reform Jews here are concerned, there are no more than a few hundred ; and one of their rabbis, Rabbi Wilhelm, who agreed to conform to Jewish traditional law, was in fact permitted to conduct marriages. It should further be explained that in Israel rabbis are also religious judges. No Reform rabbi to date has suggested that his knowledge of Jewish law is such as to equip him for exposition on the religious judicial bench. The practice in Israel in this regard is similar to that prevailing in the British Jewish community, despite the fact that in the latter there is a considerable number of Reform congregations.

If people of devout secularist belief are prepared to compromise for national unity, surely Reform Jews in America can appreciate that the state must not be required, particularly at the present time, to engage in an inner spiritual conflict for what is for them merely an academic principle with hardly any relationship to practical needs. The majority of Reform Jews in America will agree that the Reform movement is the result of a distinctive environment and that an Orthodox Jew cannot be considered to be of less religious faith than a Reform Jew. They surely will not suggest that the religious convictions of a Reform couple would be upset by their marriage being performed by an Orthodox rabbi.

Israel and the American Jew

Address to the Convention of the Union of Hebrew Congregations of America in Miami, Florida, 18 November 1959

Of the vast range of questions – political, economic, religious and social – that have been discussed by the government and parliament of Israel over the past eleven years, the question of the relationship between Israel and the American Jew has never been the subject of substantive discussion. It has been touched on in various articles and in public debate, but opinions have differed, and it is difficult to find a consensus that one could say would reflect the final view of the people of Israel. All I can attempt to do is to delineate certain trends in approaching the question. What I say, of course, is not an official statement of policy, but merely my personal observations.

Great thinkers of other faiths have interpreted the rise of Israel as an index of the supremacy of the spiritual factor in human history. After close to 2,000 years of separation, people and land have been reunited. Geography and time are obliterated, as communities from the far-flung deserts of Yemen, India, Iran and Morocco mingle in a common nationhood with Jews from Eastern and Western Europe.

The Middle East has but archaelogical recollections of those empires and doctrines that swayed the mind and controlled the fate of the ancient people of the area. One people alone resides anew in the Middle East with its continuity unimpaired, practising the same religious faith, speaking the same language, tilling the same soil, reaping the same fields as did their forefathers thousands of years ago. Call it what you will – immortality, revival – continuity remains its central theme. It is this sense of continuity, coupled with an undying religious faith, that preserved our people through the ages and that formed the spiritual foundation of the Jewish renaissance in the land of our fathers. Moreover, it is this continuity that has engaged the sympathetic attention of men of goodwill throughout the world.

The longing for restoration to Zion was deep and persistent ; it was part of the spiritual ego of the Jewish People. But even in ancient times there was a conflicting trend. From the first exile in Babylon, some five centuries BCE, we have tangible evidence of this. Only a small sector of the Jewish community of Babylon returned to help in the establishment of the Second Commonwealth of Israel. The same was true also of Jewish communities in other lands. Over the centuries great academies of Jewish learning grew up in Babylon. Their contribution and experience in the theory and practical application of the *halakhah,* in *aggadah* [the corpus of rabbinical ethical teaching, scriptural commentary and legendary lore], and in the Jewish relationship with the prevailing civilizations of their era are all enshrined for perpetuity in what is known as the Babylonian Talmud. The products of the great academies and masters in Israel were incorporated in what is known as the Jerusalem Talmud.

Throughout the period of the Second Commonwealth, Babylonian Jewry recognized the spiritual authority of the Land of Israel. After the Jewish communities in Israel were uprooted and exiled, the two Talmuds vied for authority in Jewry. Till the tenth or eleventh centuries CE the Jerusalem Talmud enjoyed primary status in certain communities in Italy and in the Eastern Mediterranean area. Later, it was largely ignored, and the Babylonian Talmud reigned supreme. It was the Gaon of Vilna, some two centuries ago, who again opened up the Jerusalem Talmud for study. His disciples made the pilgrimage to the Holy Land and settled there.

We know little of the debate that took place between Babylon and Jerusalem in the period of the Second Commonwealth. We know that the link between the Jewish people and the Land of Israel was never challenged. Ultimate restoration was accepted as a tenet of religious faith. And yet there were more Jews at that time in other lands than there were in the Land of Israel. The debate between Babylon and Jerusalem, which began some 2,500 years ago, remained quiescent till the latter part of the last century, when the theory of political Zionism was formulated by Theodor Herzl and gave this issue renewed significance.

Zionism met with heavy opposition within Jewry. The opposition came from many quarters and on various grounds : it was denounced as a dream incapable of realization ; it was challenged on religious grounds as being contrary to messianic belief and concept ; it was argued that it ran counter to Jewish destiny in terms of a spiritual example to the nations of the world. The question was raised as to whether it would imperil the political and social status of Jewry achieved under emancipation. The ancient debate was resumed, with its lines of argument receiving clear definitions. But this debate did not block the road to fulfilment. The international community recognized the right of the Jewish people to independence in the land of its fathers. While the debate continued within Jewry, statesmen and thinkers of the Western world saw no contradiction between an independent Israel and the existence of Jewish communities throughout the world possessing an equal and integral part in the countries and societies of their residence.

Events blurred the debate, for the embryonic Jewish State became the focal point of rescue for European Jewry assaulted by the Nazi Holocaust. Jewish statehood became the answer to the extermination of one-third of the Jewish people. Jews throughout the world – Zionists and non-Zionists alike – stunned by a calamity almost without precedent in human annals, rallied to the support of the Jewish community in the land of Israel in its supreme effort to achieve independent statehood.

There are one and three-quarter million Jews in Israel today. Since the establishment of the state over one million Jews from some fifty countries have immigrated to Israel and developed a base of common nationhood. The overwhelming majority of Jewry lives in other lands. The debate is no longer on whether there should be a Jewish state, but on the relationship between the state in existence and Jewish communities throughout the world. If I dwelt on the historical background, it is because this lives in the consciousness of the people of Israel and is a primary factor in their attitude to Jews elsewhere. Add to that the fact that the overwhelming majority of the people of Israel has been directly affected, indeed, has participated, in the epic of Jewish experience in our time, in which agony and fulfilment have been intertwined in a unique tapestry of faith and poignancy. In the consciousness of the people of Israel there is intermingled the devotion to biblical prophecy, the belief in providential guidance, the pride of renewed independence, the feeling of homecoming and the memory of the circumstances under which the major part of the population came to our shores.

Throughout its existence Israel's efforts have been almost wholly confined to the struggle for survival and to facing up to the great problems of immigrant absorption and economic development. In these efforts she has looked to Jewish communities throughout the world, especially to American Jewry, for assistance. At the same time she has not had the possibility to contemplate the nature of her long-term spiritual relationship with American Jewry. In the adverse sense it might be said that she has taken American Jewry for granted. In the positive sense it might be said that she assumed the relationship to be self-understood and automatic. Certainly she instinctively feels that the theme of continuity and unity have not been limited to Jews in Israel alone but are the common inheritance of Jews everywhere.

In the throb and vitality of homecoming, Israelis could not understand why their kinsfolk in the land of freedom did not join them in the great adventure of the spirit in which they are engaged. This approach was based on the assessment that the totality of Jewish life can only be experienced within the framework of an independent Israel, where every aspect of the national existence is linked in one form or another to Jewish tradition. Moreover, as a basic principle, political Zionism denied the permanence of Jewish life outside Israel. The assumption was that inexorable doom or decline would eventually engulf those Jewish communities. And the past experience of the majority of Jews in Israel underlined this approach.

All this led – certainly in the first years of our statehood – to a popular attitude that was not kindly received by American Jews. Israeli Jews were not acquainted with the plural nature of American civilization and, above all, with the fact that Judaism has achieved here a state of equality and public recognition without precedent in Jewish history. They could not grasp the subjective feeling of the American Jew in terms of his assertion that he can maintain his Jewish heritage and ensure Jewish continuity within the framework of American society. The dialogue has been uneven ; the one party talks to the other in premises that the other claims to be irrelevant.

Over the past few years I believe that a new trend has developed in Israeli thought. Paradoxically enough, as Israel develops in stability and its permanence on the Middle Eastern scene becomes more apparent, its youth, far from relinquishing its interest in and link with American Jewry, is approaching this great community with much deeper understanding and objectivity. If American Jewry has refused to accept emigration to Israel as the path for its Jewish survival, it does acknowledge Israel as a focal point for Jewish survival as a whole. It has acknowledged redemption in Israel as the central theme of Jewish experience in our time. On the other hand, in Israel there is the growing realization that the problem of the spiritual relationship with American Jewry will not be solved by futile recrimination and debate on Zionism and non-Zionism or by prophecies of extinction or assimilation. The road is being cleared for this age-old debate to take place in an atmosphere of dignity and mutual respect. Time will tell how it will evolve.

If Israel's approach to American Jewry is marked by a greater perception than heretofore, American Jewry is developing a growing intimacy with the Jewish experience in Israel reborn. And this applies to groups for whom only a short time ago the idea of Jewish statehood in Israel was anathema. There is a basis for a covenant of trust. Even as historians have failed to unravel the enigma of Jewish survival down the ages, so the spiritual bond uniting American Jewry with Israel defies precise definition. Events have outstripped formulation. Through objective debate misunderstandings will dissolve and the way will be opened to a lasting relationship of Jewish destiny and historical involvement.

The constant flow of visitors in both directions, the increasing studies in Israel on contemporary Jewry generally and American Jewry in particular, and the studies on Israel being undertaken by American Jewry all lead to a process of interchange that solidifies the relationship. Intemperate public statements on either side can hardly be helpful. Israel must look – and will look – on American Jewry as its greatest partner in Jewish destiny in this age of Jewish renaissance. It cannot yield on certain fundamentals – such as on the Jewish life experienced in Israel in contrast to elsewhere or on its appeal to American Jews to come to settle in Israel – but it can explain its viewpoint within a framework of support and growing interest for the Jewish revival in this great land of freedom. And in its appraisal, American Jewry might take greater account of conditions and circumstances arising from the central effort to create a common nationhood in the land of our fathers.

The debate will intensify, but it will encourage cooperation and understanding rather than weaken it. The relationship will move from the area of crisis and mere survival towards a permanent framework of partnership in perpetuating immortal Judaism and the newly won consciousness arising from the phenomenal experience that Jewry has been vouchsafed in our time.

The Bar Kokhba Letters – A Backward Glance

From an Independence Day Address, May 1961

Only a few weeks ago an Israeli army unit together with archaeological experts discovered in a cave near the Dead Sea eleven letters of Bar Kokhba, commander of the last rebellion against the Romans approximately 1,800 years ago. They were letters to his deputy on defence and a requisition of soldiers for the last desperate attempt to assert their independence against the legions of Rome. The rebellion was overwhelmed. The remnants hid in the caves of Judea till they too met their heroic end. Ponder for a moment the thoughts that must have passed through the mind of Bar Kokhba and his associates as they put away these letters. Judea had been laid waste, the last ember of Jewish independence was extinguished. The night of exile enveloped the Jewish people. In his last moments, Bar Kokhba must have thought of Rabbi Akiva, saint and master, who had encouraged him in the effort of rebellion : My master and spiritual mentor, where are your assurances that Judea would be restored? Did you not carry my sword and shield in public to attest to the spiritual authenticity of my rebellion? When, indeed, shall the promises of the prophets be fulfilled: Is not all at an end?

And in Rome, capital of the ancient world, the generals and statesmen must have crossed off the story of Jewish resistance. What folly, they must have thought, that a small people on the eastern coast of the Mediterranean had tried to challenge the powers of Rome! Had this puny nation really felt it could successfully assert its political independence from Rome and its spiritual independence from the prevailing doctrines?

But if Bar Kokhba would rise from his grave he would be saluted by the soldiers of modern Judea. He would survey the landscape that he had sought to defend and would see that which he had left desolate was now springing to life. He could relate the saga of Jewish nationhood and of the vision of independence that had inspired his soldiers as they went into battle. He would be welcomed today as a brother in Jewish redemption. He would be told that his same inspiration for independence had fired the soul of the modern soldiers of Judea as they went into battle twelve years ago. But if the Roman commander, whose soldiers had scaled the cliffs to feret out Bar Kokhba and his men, came to life, what would he find? He would find that the empire he had served had since been washed away in the tide of history and its records existed only in textbooks.

Soldiers and Kabbalists

From an Address in Capetown, South Africa, May 1971

This world of dialogues, which we follow day in, day out, as the pendulum swings back and forth, came home to me very vividly on 8 June 1967, the day after we took Jerusalem, reunited for all time. I went to the Old City. I heard the muezzins proclaiming prayer from the minarets. I closed my eyes for a moment and hoped that it was no longer the call for jihad, holy war. Surely the time had come for the call for peace.

I saw our soldiers as they handled their machine guns in the deserted city, as their eyes met the Arabs behind the lattices of their homes, as they began to weave a new dialogue. No longer, as depicted in Arab propaganda, was this Israel the monster, no longer Israel the conqueror. This was Israel coming home. And, as I moved up towards the Mount of Olives, I saw a great stir as the soldiers moved toward the Western Wall. I inquired what was happening, and they said : a great Kabbalist in Jerusalem has asked to see the Western Wall. He fears he may pass on before he sees it with his living eyes. And so they took him by jeep, for the roads were torn up, so they brought him to the Wall.

I recalled how, twenty years earlier, in 1948, on that Sabbath when the labour of exile came to an end and Jewish independence was proclaimed, I saw the Kabbalists in Jerusalem, in the city under siege, as they eyed the young soldiers, and the one said to the other. 'These methods of the twentieth century will not bring us Redemption.' The other seemed to answer with his eyes : 'But how long can we wait? We have waited long enough.' Their eyes met at first in suspicion, but later in harmony. And the Kabbalists were with the soldiers as they reached the Wall.

Part Three : Evocations of History

Yaacov Herzog had it in mind to write a History of Israel in the Middle East, assigning a central place in his discussion to the unfolding of the Israel-Arab confrontation over the last two generations. He opened the major work with an extensive introduction that is inspired by wide knowledge and that sought to give the background and the historical setting of each of the issues that led up to the heart of his theme. The plan of it he had conceived and worked out in great detail. Fate, to our bitter grief, decreed that he should not live to complete the task. But the introduction, which he did finish, is a treatise in itself, well worth the study by the intelligent reader, student and scholar alike.

The greater part is devoted to the period of World War One, and he did not profess to write it on the basis of research into primary sources alone. He was helped by new findings that dealt with many of the subjects which it was necessary for him to expound, and he was at pains to examine, also, basic archival documents. But his intellectual powers and his political experience lent him the wisdom to reach the very roots of the motivations of policy-makers, and he succeeded in charting the salient features of the policies that were determined by the decisions of statesmen and the events on the battlefield. And on everything that he penned, there is the imprint of his personality – of the Jew and the Zionist, imbued with a profound faith in the righteousness of Zionism, not merely as the one and only honourable solution of the painful and humiliating 'Jewish Question', but, no less, as the high road, throughout the age-old annals of Israel, along the way 'unto the land that I will shew thee'.

The qualities of this essay, written in fluent and lucid style, make it an indispensable foreword to the modern history of the Middle East, and of Palestine. Lest the reader be burdened by distracting footnotes, references are not given to the origin of quotations that bear on matters whereon historical research has thrown no fresh light in recent years. More detailed bibliographical references can be found in *Introduction to Israel in the Middle East,* Jerusalem Papers, published by the Leonard Davis Institute for International Relations of the Hebrew University of Jerusalem, 1975.

M. Vereté

Israel in the Middle East

I Introduction

By the outbreak of the First World War, the first chapter of modern political Zionism had reached an abortive close. In the cataclysm, the second chapter opened. Within less than four decades, it was consummated with the sovereign reunion of land and people in independent Israel.

The prelude covered close to two millennia, from the exile of the Jews at the hands of Imperial Rome in the second and third centuries. In the interim, the dispersed people were stirred by the memory of their tragic past to the hope of future redemption ; the present was but a meaningless transitory phase. Throughout the long gap, the land of Israel passed from one foreign conqueror to another and was denied indigenous identity and character ; its continuing desolation remained a reminder of past vitality and glory.

The nineteenth century, in which modern Zionism was born, was a period of the atomization of the Jewish people. For the first time in Jewish history, the traditional concepts of exile and return, which formed the essence of Jewish belief, seemed to be on the road to dissipation. Enlightenment, emancipation, liberalism, romanticism, social and economic revolution seemed to mark the end of the traditional epoch of Jewish history. In Western Europe and in the Austro-Hungarian Empire, society after society, with varying degrees of reluctance, accorded rights to the Jew. Simultaneously, within the Jewish communities, age-old beliefs and traditions were questioned in the general context of nineteenth-century enquiry. The distinctiveness of Jewish nationhood across recorded history – the dual Abrahamic title of stranger and resident – seemed at once to pose a barrier to full integration, into the external society and to be an anachronism in the atmosphere of self-enlightment. The Messiah need no longer be awaited in the restoration of the House of David in Jerusalem. In the age of reason and emancipation, the messianic period seemed at hand in the movements of liberalism and nationalism, of social and economic progress and in the erosion of religious barriers. At the opening of the century, seventy-one wise men, summoned by Napoleon and patterned on the ancient Sanhedrin, formally abandoned the concept of a distinctive Jewish nationhood. In Germany, the bridging of Jewish and Christian culture, undertaken by Moses Mendelssohn, set in motion for many the process of assimilation. The German Reform movement exorcized Zion from the prayer-book and proclaimed that Israel's existence among the nations was no longer the punishment of exile, but the means to a prophetic mission for mankind. Even in westernized Orthodox Jewry, which asserted the eternal survival of the Torah unaffected by the integration of its adherents in an alien society, stress was laid on the religious distinctiveness of the Jew, and the element of separate nationhood was either relegated to a remote messianic context or totally denied. In 1878 the British Chief Rabbi declared that 'Ever since the conquest of Palestine by the Romans we have ceased to be a body politic . . . We are simply Englishmen . . . in the same relation to our countrymen as any other religious sect.'

In the second half of the nineteenth century, in most Western countries outside the Russian sphere, the legal issue of emancipation seemed to be decided. But this very consummation was caught up in the vortex of the violent ideological clashes that shook the foundations of European society ; the forces of liberalism and social reform were pitted against those of the conservative or aristocratic status quo, those of progressive versus reactionary nationalism.

As the emancipated Jew deepened his identification with the general society, he was paradoxically accused of being more alien than his ghetto forefather. A new and pernicious concept of the isolation of the Jew began to be fomented, particularly in France and Germany. The age-old doctrine of his accursedness as a result of his refusal to embrace Christianity was augmented or replaced by the theory of his racial impurity.

The unusual rapidity of Jewish economic and professional advancement aroused at once the wrath and envy of the aristocratic classes, which were under challenge from the emerging bourgeoisie, and of the masses, inflamed ideologically, yet frustrated socially and economically. Simultaneously, the Jewish merchant-capitalist was represented as the symbol of unholy avarice, the Jewish liberal-revolutionary as the paradigm of the anarchy threatening the foundations of society. Theories indeed are not wanting for the origins of the racial doctrine. Bearing in mind all the prevalent circumstances, including the paucity of Jews in the countries of emancipation, these theories drawn from a contemporary reading of society's action and counteraction, merely deepen the enigma and irrationality of anti-Semitism, rather than lend it a basis in rational thought. These theories stand the test of rational historical analysis as much as the description of the Jewish people 'as a people set apart' made by Balaam, the prophet of Moab, thousands of years ago. The undeniable fact remains that the racial doctrine was born immediately in the wake of emancipation, the new barriers of consciousness blocking what seemed to be an inevitable process of the erosion of the Jewish people from within. Within little more than a half-century these poisonous seeds sprouted into a monstrous Holocaust, without parallel in human history : the planned extermination of the Jewish people, executed with fiendish cruelty on that third of its members who were caught in the clutches of the executioner.

In the throes of the new anti-Semitism the vision of Theodor Herzl was born. Herzl was a fully emancipated Jew, of broad general culture and subtle thought, but of minimal Jewish training, background and involvement. With all his formal integration into European society, he sensed from his student days the invisible yet tangible walls of the new ghetto growing up around the emancipated Jew. His highly sensitive nature was bruised by the ambiguity of the relationship ; the affront was even more despairing because he had little, if any, Jewish religious or historical sense on which to fall back. The formative turning-point in the development of his Zionist consciousness was, in his own words, the spectacle of the mob outside the École Militaire in Paris in 1894, crying 'death to the Jews', as the French Jewish officer Dreyfus was stripped of his rank after he had been falsely sentenced on a charge of transmitting French military secrets to the German General Staff. Herzl wrote :

> . . . the Dreyfus case contains more than a miscarriage of justice, it contains the wish of the vast majority in France to damn one Jew and through him all Jews . . . in Republican, modern, civilized France, one hundred years after the Declaration of the Rights of Man . . .

In 1896 Herzl published *Der Judenstaat,* The Jewish State, in which he described an independent Jewish entity on its own soil (he did not specify Palestine) as the only solution to the Jewish problem. The idea of Jewish statehood in independent territory had already appeared – hardly arousing attention – in the writings of such diverse Jewish thinkers as Rabbi Zevi Hirsch Kalischer (as a fulfilment of biblical prophecy), Moses Hess (as a source of ethical regeneration of Jewry and the world) and Leon Pinsker (against the background of the anti-Semitic regression in Russia). In practical terms, Herzl created the framework for modern political Zionism. Ideologically, the novelty of his approach lay in the fact that he was the first emancipated Jew to reach the conclusion that the grant to the Jew of formal citizenship would not mean his inherent acceptance.

In the emancipated Jewries, Herzl's appeal faced derision, indifference or hostility. There were exceptions, among them some leading Western Jews ; however, they supported Zionism as a positive idea rather than as a corollary to Herzl's analysis of external forces blocking full Jewish emancipation. It is difficult to conceive of any of the Western Jewish delegates to the First Zionist Congress in Basle in 1897 subscribing to Herzl's statement to Baron Hirsch three years earlier :

> To the German Emperor I shall say : let us depart. We are strangers. We are not allowed to merge in the people, and what is more, we cannot. Let us depart.

Western Jews looked on the new creeping anti-Semitism as a temporary aberration, a relapse to be cured as the forces of progress accelerated their onward march. After successive crises, which racked the soul of

France, Dreyfus was exonerated in 1906. Those Western Jews who supported Herzl's initiative looked on the regeneration of Jewish independence as a means for Jewish renaissance against the forces eroding the integrity of Jewish peoplehood. Above all, they were concerned with the plight of vast Jewish communities under Czarist rule and in Eastern Europe – that great commonwealth of Judaism and Jewish consciousness, containing three-quarters of the Jewish people and embracing the ferment of its thought and spirit. In recent decades, those communities had come under ever-increasing repression as a result of the Czarist régime's extinction of liberalizing trends in the wake of the assassination of Alexander II.

In the Pale of Settlement, in which millions of Jews were cooped up, as throughout Eastern Europe, Herzl's call had an electrifying impact. Had the Russian-Jewish dream of emancipation in a reformed Russian society been moving to realization towards the end of the nineteenth century, had the Czarist paranoiac and repressive rule been ended a few decades before this finally took place, Herzl's call might well have taken place amongst those of the many 'dreamers' who dot Jewish history. The historical paradox was that when, in the aftermath of World War Two, international recognition was granted to the Jewish right to the Land of Israel, Russian Jewry was cut off from participation in the rebuilding whose early momentum it had generated close to two decades before the first Zionist Congress. It was to remain sealed off for fifty years.

Herzl died in 1904, six years after the First Zionist Congress, under his leadership, had set up the Zionist Organization for 'the creation in Palestine of a home for the Jewish people secured by public law'. He died broken-hearted and disappointed. During his brief tenure of leadership, the heights of his vision, the majesty and nobility of his personality, the total self-sacrifice with which he poured out his life talents and personal means, etched an indelible impact on Jewish consciousness. His deep eyes peering from photographs in Jewish homes and assembly halls lent their vision to an entire people. As in later years, his forebodings about European Jewry found cruel vindication ; the pathos in his eyes seemed in retrospect to signal the oncoming tragedy.

At the Basle Congress he felt that he had established the Jewish State, setting possibly five, probably fifty, years as a definite date for the fulfilment of his prophecy. The second date proved as uncannily correct as the first was unrealistic. With the ebbing away of his life, the hope of achieving an international charter for the return of the Jewish people to its homeland seemed to be rapidly receding. The three prongs of his political endeavour had been successively frustrated. Despite Herzl's initial expectations, the German Emperor had not agreed to use his good offices with the Sultan of Turkey for the setting up in Palestine of a Jewish Chartered Company under German protection. Herzl subsequently offered directly to the Sultan a loan of four million Turkish pounds to relieve Ottoman financial stress as part of an overall scheme involving the establishment of 'Jewish-Ottoman Land Company', with autonomous control over a designated area in Palestine and Syria, with authority to purchase lands in that area and to bring Jewish immigrants freely into it. The Sultan wished to see the money first. The bankers Herzl approached wished first to see the Sultan's agreement. Until close to his death, Herzl maintained his abortive negotiations with the Sultan, at the same time pursuing his efforts in Russia, with the Vatican and in Italy to gain support for Zionism and influence in its favour in Constantinople.

Finally, Herzl's negotiations with the British Foreign Office on the settlement of Jews in El Arish, in the vicinity of the southern frontier of Palestine, foundered on the rocks of the opposition of both the Egyptian and Turkish governments.

What was mistakenly termed the 'Uganda proposal' darkened the last years of Herzl's life. It was actually a proposal for the settlement of Jews within the colony of Kenya in East Africa. It came from Britain's Colonial Secretary, Joseph Chamberlain. He had been involved in the El Arish negotiations and felt that Jewish settlement in East Africa could achieve the triple purpose of strengthening Britain's position in the area, of contributing to the alleviation of the plight of East European Jewry and of relieving the pressure of immigration of Jews from Eastern Europe to Britain, which was arousing anti-Semitic reactions. Herzl favoured the consideration of the proposal as a stepping-stone to the ultimate fulfilment of territorial independence in Zion. However, the great majority of the Zionist delegates from Russia, towards whose constituents the proposal was aimed, rose in protest against the idea of setting aside, even temporarily, the return to Zion as the immediate and sole objective of Zionism. The nascent Zionist Organization seemed in danger of falling asunder.

Inner peace was restored before Herzl's death, and a year afterwards the Zionist Congress formally rejected the Uganda proposal. In any event, the British Government, in face of the indignant protests of British settlers in East Africa, likewise cooled towards its own proposal. A little more than a half-century later, when Prime Minister Levi Eshkol of Israel visited the independent African state of Uganda, he referred in public to the Uganda proposal as a curious historical episode. The private retort of President Obote of Uganda was that if the proposal had been implemented, the Ugandan Africans, on attaining independence, would have expelled the Jewish settlers.

Even had Herzl procured the necessary financial backing for Sultan Abdul Hamid, the latter's official acquiescence in an alien element gaining a foothold in the heart of Turkey's Asiatic empire would have been most improbable. The Ottoman Empire was in the process of dissolution, with internal unrest deepening in the Balkans, with the Powers pressing their rival penetrations into the heart of the Empire, on the one hand, and cutting away at the Empire and its authority in Africa and the Balkans, on the other. With the rise of the Young Turks in 1908, and, in its wake, the upsurge of feeling against external interference and the programme of Ottomanization of the subject peoples, the concept of the charter was not only even more impractical than hitherto, it was positively dangerous. At the Ninth Zionist Congress, in 1909, Max Nordau proposed that Herzl's charter idea, on which Wolffsohn, Herzl's successor, was still negotiating with the Turks in 1907, be assigned to 'the archives of modern political Zionism'. He summed up the attitude in Constantinople as : 'We will not admit you into Palestine, you may not live as a Jewish nationality, Turkey is ready to receive you only if you give up Zionism.' The answer to this was no longer to ask Turkey or the Powers for a Charter. It was also not to abandon the Basle programme for 'a home for the Jewish people secured by public law'. Nordau advised to wait until 'elucidations, the effect of time, political developments, and greater maturity will have changed the attitudes of authoritative Turkish circles.' The elucidations took place through the Zionist Office that had been established in Constantinople in 1908. They were accompanied by repeated statements by Zionist leaders at the Congresses till the 1914–18 war of loyalty to Turkey. At the Tenth Congress Nordau declared that 'it is our duty to convince [the Turks] that . . . they possess in the whole world no more generous and self-sacrificing friends than the Zionists.' The Jewish community in Palestine sought in vain to gain representation in the parliament in Constantinople. Young Jews from the community, among them David Ben-Gurion, made their way to Constantinople to study and to explain Zionist aspirations. All this activity made no impact whatsoever on the Young Turks whose xenophobia was fed by Turkish losses in North Africa and in the Balkan Wars, the latter being the curtain-raiser to World War One. Jewish immigration into Palestine enjoyed no more favour from the Young Turks than from the Sultan. It was illegal in the sense that legality and illegality were measured through the chaotic and venal perspective of the Turkish régime in the provinces of the Empire. Zionist activity did have the result of arousing suspicions, in both British and Arab circles, that the Zionist Agency in Constantinople was deeply interlocked with the Young Turk régime, through Jewish influence in Salonika, where the foundation for the Young Turks movement had originally been laid. It was also suspected of a pro-German bias. The Turks gave no sign as to the validity of the first allegation, and the Germans in no way acknowledged the second.

In the years immediately preceding World War One, the Arabs, for the first time, entered the focus of Zionist attention. On the one hand, the 'Ottomanization' programme of the Young Turks stirred up the first embers of Arab nationalism ; on the other hand, there were signs of Arab disaffection with incipient Jewish settlement both in Palestine itself and outside, including statements by Arab members in the Turkish Parliament. Victor Jacobson, head of the Zionist Agency in Constantinople, established contacts with Arab politicians and journalists. Nahum Sokolow, in the spring of 1914, met with Arab representatives in Syria. They were the pioneers in the Sisyphean effort, which has continued for sixty years, of convincing the Arabs that the renascence of both nationalisms would benefit from mutual cooperation. The Arabs remained unconvinced. In any event, they themselves had not yet found a clear course between two conflicting directions : planning to sunder themselves in thought and action from the Turks, or continuing to try to gain partial status for their distinctive nationhood by cooperation with them. The Zionists were careful not to show too deep an interest in nascent Arab nationalism for fear of antagonizing the Turks. In September 1912, the *Times* correspondent in Constantinople warned that 'indirect manifestations of sympathy with Zionism on the part of any important section of the British public might conceivably cost us the confidence of the best elements in the Arab world.'

By 1914 the Zionist political effort, in the words of Dr Weizmann, reached a 'blank wall'. At the Zionist Congress in 1913, he had declared that 'the greatest of the Great Powers we have to deal with is the Jewish people. From this Power we expect everything, from the other Powers very little.' In 1955, when the perennial isolation of what by then was the seven-year-old Jewish State had entered a peculiarly acute state, David Ben-Gurion declared : 'What is important is not what the nations say, but what we do.' Both statements, in their relative contexts, contained only one kernel of the overall truth. Without Turkey entering the war, a year after Weizmann spoke, leading to the break-up of the Ottoman Empire, without the Pax Britannica that superseded it, it is difficult to imagine how the Jews could have beaten the Arabs in the first lap of the race for fulfilment of the destiny of Palestine. In the period in which Ben-Gurion spoke, the Jewish State's hope of survival against the crucial threat bearing on it was strengthened by the aid it received from the outside in 1956. The two speakers were successively in the forefront of the struggle for Jewish independence : the first during World War One and in its immediate aftermath, the second in the period 1946–8 and throughout the fifties. The statements they made, respectively, in 1913 and in 1955 were the products of momentary frustration. In the period of their respective leadership both laid stress on independent Jewish action. At the same time, they sought increased support from the outside and, above all, to avoid isolation. They ultimately parted ways more on assessments and tactics, in the aftermath of World War Two, than on the substance of policy.

Dr Weizmann's reference in 1913 to the response of the Jewish people reflected the growing dissemination of the Zionist idea throughout Jewry. It was also an expression of the disaffection of what was termed the school of practical Zionists with the almost exclusive concentration of the Zionist effort, since the Basle Congress, to attempt to achieve a charter for the return, while paying scant attention to the strengthening of the process of Jewish settlement in Palestine. At Basle in 1897, the latter objective took fourth place in the objectives of the new Zionist Organization – the first objective being to secure 'governmental acts of approval' for the securing of the national home under public law. In 1908, without formally changing the priority of its objectives, the Zionist Congress in fact upgraded Zionist involvement in the expanding Jewish settlement in Palestine. In contrast to the failure and frustration of the political effort, this settlement was a growing tangible reality.

The process of modern settlement had begun some three decades earlier. Intermittently, across the centuries, Jews had asserted the precepts of *aliyah* and settlement. From the end of the eighteenth century a steady flow of immigrants had come largely from the disciples of the Gaon of Vilna and various Hasidic sects. Like their predecessors in earlier centuries, they sought religious fulfilment in mystic union with the land on which 'God's eyes rest from one end of the year to the other'. They also intuitively felt the need for spiritual equilibrium in face of the forces that had begun to threaten the spiritual integrity of Jewry. Their initial vocation was prayer and study in Jerusalem, Tiberias and Safad. Sir Moses Montefiore made successive efforts to move them to menial and agricultural vocations. In the second half of the nineteenth century small groups moved to constructive work. This change coincided with the arrival in Palestine in the early 1880s of the first of the Bilu'im, groups of Jews from Russia and Rumania who were the 'pilgrim fathers' of modern Zionism.

In Russia the story of medieval pogrom and repression had come to life again for the Russian Jew. For him the clock of history seemed to grind to a halt. Cooped up in the Pale of Settlement, Russian Jews cast about for their release ; and their plight became a central concern for their Western brethren. Having tasted emancipation at least in expectation, Russian Jews spurned the passivity that had traditionally marked Jewish reaction to persecution. Emigration to the West, and particularly across the Atlantic to the New World, provided an outlet for some two million from 1880 to 1914, till legal restrictions on entry began to limit it. This vast immigration engendered anti-Semitic tendencies in certain circles in the countries of absorption (Herzl described the immigrants as carrying anti-Semitism 'in their baggage, wherever they went'), with the possible effects on their own position not lost on Western Jews. Amongst Russian Jews there were also those who felt that the regression would yield to the healing process of time and that they would ultimately enter the fabric of a reformed Russian society, like their brethren in the West. Large numbers of the youth progressively became part of the revolutionary thrust, seeking the panacea for Jewish plight in a general overthrow of the existing Russian order, some believing that within the new society a distinctive revolutionary Jewish identity could be maintained and fostered.

The Bilu'im were a handful. They believed not only that the answer to the Jewish problem lay in the Jewish people becoming master of its own destiny in Zion ; intuitively they felt that only there could that Jewish regeneration take place which would halt the inner erosion of Jewish identity. They tried to get approval from Constantinople for their settlement in Palestine, supported by an English Christian Zionist, Laurence Oliphant. They failed, but went ahead nonetheless. (The name Bilu they took unto themselves was based on the biblical passage, 'House of Jacob, go and let us go.') After further pogroms at the beginning of the twentieth century, after the failure of the 1905 revolution, a further wave of immigrants came from Russia and Poland to the shores of Palestine. Touched by social revolutionary enthusiasm, they aimed at resurrecting Zion with a combination of prophetic justice and modern socialist doctrine. They wished not only to change the face of the land, but to alter the social and economic character of the Jewish people. For them the dignity of labour was intertwined with that of auto-emancipation. These young idealists, known as the Second *Aliyah*, felt that even in the revolutionary movement in Czarist Russia the Jew would ultimately remain an outsider, that the law of non-absorption would yield to no ideology, however expansive and universal. The truth of their perception was tragically vindicated in the aftermath of the Russian revolution. Side by side with the immigration from Russia, the indigenous Sephardic community was augmented by immigration from Yemen at the turn of the century. The pattern of the ingathering of the exiles was laid ; this was to be the central theme of the return then and in succeeding decades, at once the symbol of Zionism and its formative force.

In 1880 there were some 25,000 Jews in Palestine ; by 1914 the Jewish population reached approximately 85,000. During these three decades, Jewish 'colonies' and kibbutzim – some of whose economic survival owed much to the generosity of Baron Edmund Rothschild of Paris – were established on the coastal plain and in the Galilee, and the Jewish presence in Jerusalem and other cities was strengthened. Tel Aviv was founded, a social and economic revolution began in the character and vocation of the Jew, the Hebrew language became again a living tongue of parlance ; the infra-structure of an autonomous community, of the rudiments of self-defence, were laid. Pioneering became the challenge ; the restoration of a people to normalcy, free from the ills and aberrations of exile was the keynote. Visionaries stalked the land, projecting new dimensions for Jewry : Rabbi Kook proclaiming the beginnings of the messianic period, Achad Ha'am searching for a centre for a secular Jewish culture, Berl Katznelson proclaiming the vision of an egalitarian Jewish society, A.D. Gordon calling for personal redemption through manual labour. Ideological divergencies were not lacking. The various groupings – small Jewish landowners and extreme socialists, Ashkenazi and Sephardi, the adherents of the religion of eternity and those of the religion of labour – subsisted in hostile coexistence. They retained an essential unity not only because of external threat. They were linked – each in its own version – by the sense of being emissaries of the whole of Jewry, affirming the continuity of Jewish uniqueness in the twentieth century, elevated by the fulfilment of the return, constantly refreshed by the unfolding of historical memory. In the succeeding seventy years the numbers increased twenty-five fold and more : the foundations of the society that evolved in the early part of the century remained undiscarded.

'Your beginnings will be small and your growth will be great indeed.' The beginnings were a leap into the unknown, an act of faith and self-sacrifice, a proof of the mystic assertion that, under the layers of centuries of desolation, Zion retained its link with the eternal life of Jewry, that exile had not quenched the capacity for self-regeneration. The nascent community became for itself and for Jews everywhere the mirror of a new Jew restored to health, invested with dignity, self-reliance and constructive purpose. Elsewhere, diffusion and anarchy threatened Jewry. The embryonic community of Zion demonstrated the vitality springing from homecoming. It appeared at the twelfth hour. The turning-points in the record of the Jewish rebirth have always seemed to come at the last moment, beyond which historical opportunities would have been lost, never to be retrieved.

From the beginning of the nineteenth century, at various stages of crisis in the 'Eastern question' – Napoleon's expedition to Egypt and to Palestine, Muhammad Ali's conquest of Palestine and Syria, the Crimean War, the Congress of Berlin – the idea of restoring the Jews to Palestine had been floated in the international atmosphere. In Britain, particularly, Christian proto-Zionists joined their religious conviction to what was a latent strand of imperial thought. In 1840 Britain's Foreign Secretary Palmerston recommended to the Sultan the settlement of Jews in Palestine as a means of strengthening the fragile fibres of the Ottoman Empire. Palmerston wrote of a 'strong notion' [amongst the dispersed Jews] that 'the time is approaching when their nation is to return to Palestine'. His source of information is not clear, unless he mistakenly considered the effort of Sir Moses Montefiore to achieve facilities for Jewish settlement in Palestine as enjoying a broad base of Jewish support. But the Jewish people, on the whole, then sought redemption in other paths. It was not till the 1880s, in face of renewed Russian repression of Jews, that the return to Zion became an important element in the search for the solution to the Jewish problem.

The modernist Zionist immigration in the 1880s coincided with Britain's gaining control of the Suez Canal and occupation of Egypt. Not recognized at the time, the seeds were thus sown for the inter-weaving of the Jewish state in Palestine with a British strategic interest. But by the 1880s Britain's capacity to influence Constantinople in favour of Jewish settlement declined. The 1880s also marked the first stirrings of modern Arab nationalism in Syria. Had the Jewish people acted to secure a firm foothold in Palestine earlier in the century, the whole history of the Middle East might well have been different. As it was, by 1914 the practical achievement, humble as it was, compensated for the failure of the political effort till then. The first shoots of Jewish revival – the existing microcosm enshrining the promise of a great future – lent reality to the claim raised in the throes of World War One for the international recognition of the link between a people and a land.

II   The Background : 1914–15

Palestine first entered British strategic calculations simultaneously as a northern defence buffer to Suez and as a point of issue for a strategic railway to Mesopotamia. Britain had long considered Mesopotamia as her sphere of interest in Ottoman Asia. In the event of a partitioning of the Ottoman Empire it seemed self-evident that its destiny would be controlled by Britain.

The day Turkey entered the war in November 1914, Britain took political and military action on the fringes of the Ottoman Empire in Asia : Cyprus was formally annexed to the British Crown. Under the Cyprus Convention of 1878, The Porte had assented to British occupation and administration of the island in return for British assurance of armed support against any attempt by Russia to broaden its territorial base in eastern Asia Minor beyond Kars, Ardahan and Batum, over which Russian control was acknowledged soon after the Congress of Berlin. Cyprus was Britain's first military base in the Middle East. It was also to be the last, surviving the final demise of British power in the area a century later. Forty miles south of Turkey, sixty miles west of Syria, 260 miles north of Egypt, the island interposed between the two narrow water arteries – the Straits of the Dardanelles and the Suez Canal – on which so much of world power turned. Cyprus constituted the eastern link of Mediterranean communications – starting with Gibraltar at the western point of entry and sustained by Malta in the centre : sentinels mounting a triple watch over the Mediterranean route to India. Little wonder that Britain decided not to leave its political fate open to any possible negotiations on the future of the Ottoman Empire. British military and administrative control over the island had lain under the umbrella of Ottoman suzerainty. British annexation of Cyprus put an end to three and a half centuries of Ottoman rule. It was Britain's first formal act in the dismemberment of the Ottoman Empire.

Constitutional change, but of a different character, was next made in

Egypt. Britain had taken over military control in 1882 in order to put down a nationalist revolt led by a young Egyptian officer, Urrabi Pasha, who aimed at freeing Egypt both from Turkish misrule and from the economic domination of the Powers. It was Gladstone's Liberal government that ordered the invasion of Egypt. Gladstone rejected as aberrations Disraeli's aggrandizement of empire, his injection of India into the life-stream of British consciousness. He had warned against the 'egg' of a new empire in Africa, coming on top of the Asiatic burden. In the period of dissolution of empire, Conservative governments would not be able to turn the clock back on the abdication fulfilled by their socialist predecessors. In the heyday of empire, Liberal governments could not shake off the expansion incurred by Conservatives. Gladstone acted not only to safeguard British interests in Egypt proper : he had to ensure the safety of the Suez Canal from the threat of an unfriendly government in Cairo. Only seven years earlier, in 1875, Britain had gained predominant financial control in the Suez Canal company, through Disraeli's purchase of the bankrupt Khedive's shares. The Canal, in Winston Churchill's words, drew Britain inexorably into Egyptian politics. Once order was restored in Egypt, Britain wished to withdraw its troops. But it sought agreement from the Sultan in Constantinople on its right to reoccupy the country in the event of renewed internal instability or external pressures. In 1887 the Sultan agreed. Under French and Russian pressures, however, he withheld ratification of his undertaking.

The more decrepit Constantinople looked, the more it resisted cures designed to block its diffusion : the closer it drew, from the end of the nineteenth century, to Germany, the greater grew the need for Britain's continued hold on Egypt. Suez was the artery uniting the British and Asiatic parts of the Empire, the connecting link of British presence and interests in four continents : through it flowed a significant measure of Empire trade, through it British troops were transported to India. At times there were almost as many soldiers in India as in the mother country. With the outbreak of the World War, Indian troops travelled through Suez on their way to the western front.

Three-quarters of a century after it occupied Egypt – in 1954 – Britain agreed to evacuate its base on the Suez Canal and thus finally to evacuate Egyptian territory. In return, the revolutionary régime of President Nasser acknowledged its right to return to the base in the event of external threat to the Canal. The thread of imperial thought had remained constant. In 1956 British troops returned to Egypt in reaction to Nasser's unilateral nationalization of the Suez Canal Company. It was the death-gasp of British power in the East.

By 1914 Britain had been in military control of Egypt for more than three decades. It had rapidly overcome the initial pains and embarrassment of occupation. From assurances of withdrawal as soon as internal stability could be ensured, it coined the conscience-palliative of modern imperialism : 'Our task is not to rule the Egyptians but as far as possible teach the Egyptians to rule themselves . . . ' Internally, British administration started on the assuredly slow process of preparing Egypt for self-government. On the strategic plane, areas contiguous to Egypt and the Canal were viewed as buffers for the consolidation of their defence. Diplomatically, international acknowledgement was sought for Britain's special status in Egypt. All three objectives were successfully attained. The reforms – administrative, economic and legal – brilliantly effected by Lord Cromer, consummated Egypt's entry into the modern period, a process initiated by Muhammad Ali and his son Ibrahim Pasha in the mid-twenties. The Sudanese provinces were brought under an Anglo-Egyptian condominium. Britain's sphere of influence in the Nile Basin was assured after the Anglo-French confrontation at Fashoda in 1898 ended with French withdrawal. By agreement with the Sultan in Constantinople in 1906, the northern Egyptian frontier was fixed on the line drawn from Rafah southwards to the proximity of Aqaba. The Canal was thus assured a defensive arc eastwards of 100 miles. The Sultan had yielded to something close to a British ultimatum. Had he had his way, it was certain that the frontier delineation, in Lord Cromer's words, would have carried 'the Turkish frontier and strategical railways to Suez on the banks of the Canal or, if the Ras Muhammad line were adopted, the Turkish frontier would be advanced to the neighbourhood of Nakhl, that is, within easy striking distance of Egypt, and . . . the Gulf of Aqaba . . . would practically become a *mare clausum* in the possession of Turkey and a standing menace to the security of the trade route to the East'. In the diplomatic wranglings between the Powers, Britain by 1904 achieved French recognition that Egypt fell within her sphere of interest. The particular British interest in Egypt was also recognized by Germany, Austria and Italy. With the entry of Turkey into the war, Britain forthwith dispatched reinforcements to her Canal base. A quarter-century later, the pattern was repeated : in 1940, troops were detached from the embattled British Isles for the defence of Suez.

At the time of the outbreak of the war with Turkey in November 1914, the government of Egypt was conducted on three levels : Britain held military and overall administrative control ; the suzerainty of Egypt was vested in the Khedive, representing the Sultan in Constantinople ; Egyptian self-expression was symbolized by a legislature, partly elected, partly appointed, whose competence was essentially consultative and advisory. The desire to emphasize the Anglo-Egyptian link, to annex Egypt outright for the British Crown, as had been done with Cyprus, might have exacerbated Egyptian nationalist sentiment beyond its perennial stirrings. The frail nexus with Constantinople had, however, to be irrevocably snapped. Egyptian nationalists were increasingly repressing the memories of Turkish misrule and recalling their Moslem bond with Constantinople, the home of the Khalifat. Britain took a middle course. By an announcement on 18 December 1914, Egypt was made into a British protectorate. The suzerainty of Turkey over Egypt was declared at an end. The following day, a further proclamation deposed the Khedive for adhering to the King's enemies. He had long been a mischievous burden. On the outbreak of war between Britain and Turkey, he was in Constantinople. He did not return. His place was taken by his uncle Husain Kamil. No longer a vassal of Turkey, the title Khedive was for him inappropriate. Kamil was given the title Sultan of Egypt, which evoked memories of pre-Ottoman rule and the spells of independence that had briefly upset it. Kamil was loyal to Britain. Egypt, from 2 November 1914, was under British martial law. The legislative assembly was suspended.

After Cyprus, Egypt represented Britain's second unilateral act of Ottoman dismemberment. This development was duly noted in Paris and Petrograd. Both sides were getting in line for Ottoman spoils. On the dispatch informing him of the British protectorate over Egypt, Czar Nicholas marked 'excellent'.

In Lower Mesopotamia – in the same class of significance for British interests as Egypt – Britain took instant military and political action. At the outbreak of war with Turkey, Lower Mesopotamia was the south-eastern edge of Ottoman dominion in Asia. From time immemorial it had been the last haul in the northern land routes from Europe to India. Goods landed on the Syrian coast were transported across the Syrian desert to Upper Mesopotamia, then by boats along the Euphrates to the Shatt-al-Arab outlet at the head of the Persian Gulf and from there to the Indian Ocean. In the late 1820s and early 1830s, long before work began on the Suez Canal, the idea was mooted in England of linking a port on the northern coast of Syria with the Persian Gulf by means of steam navigation on the Euphrates. Later, this idea gave way to several projects for a Euphrates Valley railway. The digging of the Suez Canal undercut the economic prospects of the northern project, water or rail.

In face of Russia's ongoing southward thrust, the railway idea assumed a strategic quality. For the British mind, Mesopotamia, alongside Persia and Afghanistan, constituted the outer frontier of India. According to a secret British Admiralty report of 1915, Lord Beaconsfield had a Mediterranean-Euphrates railway in mind when he ensured British occupation of Cyprus in 1878. Apart from the declared objective of checking Russia in Asia Minor, 'he regarded a Euphrates railway as the best means of checking a further movement of Russia southwards, Cyprus to serve as a *place d'armes* and naval station to cover the railhead . . .'

On 6 November 1914, two days after the declaration of war against Turkey, a brigade of the 6th Indian Division landed at the entrance to Shatt-al-Arab and moved up the coast towards Basra. This was not, however, the beginning of an invasion of Mesopotamia ; Britain's mind, men and energy were entrapped on the western front in Europe. But the

Anglo-Persian oil-fields in southern Persia and the refinery on Abadan Island required protection. The oil yield was already 25,000 tons per month. It was needed by the British Navy in the Persian Gulf and in the Indian Ocean. Oil was making its appearance in strategic and economic calculations in the Middle East. At the same time the landing force would affirm British protection of Arab sheikhdoms in the Persian Gulf, with whom Britain had established treaty relations in the nineteenth century.

By 21 November, the 6th Indian Division, under the command of Lt-General Sir Arthur Barrett, captured Basra. To the inhabitants, they carried a message from the Viceroy of India that 'the future would bring them a more benign rule' than that of the Turks. They probably had no difficulty in guessing which rule. An assurance that Basra would never again be subject to Turkish rule was also given to the Sheikhs of Kuwait and Mohammerah and to the Emir of Nejd. On 9 December, Barrett's forces reached Kurna on the Tigris, fifty miles upstream from Basra. In the spring of 1915, Lt-General Sir John Nixon took over the overall command from Barrett, whose slow-moving tactics were frowned upon by the Indian Government. The 6th Indian Division was reinforced by the 12th Indian Division. Turkish attacks having been repulsed, the 6th Indian Division, now commanded by General Sir Charles Townshend, took Amara, a further sixty miles up the Tigris, in June 1915. The following month the 12th Division took An-Nasiriya on the Euphrates. The entire Basra *vilayet* had been cleared of enemy forces. The oil-fields were safe.

The unqualified success of British arms had brought Nixon to set his sights higher. He received approval from the Indian Government to thrust further up the Tigris to the strategically placed town of Kut-al-Amara, where the Shatt-el-Hai river issues from the Tigris, meeting the Euphrates near An-Nasiriya. In two battles, on 15 and 23 September, the 6th Indian Division overwhelmed Turkish forces at the entrance to Kut. Moving beyond the city in pursuit of the Turks, British cavalry reached Al Aziziya, halfway to Baghdad. The lure of the ancient capital of the Abbassids, hub of Mesopotamian communications, was overwhelming. Nixon recommended an immediate advance on Baghdad with additional reinforcement. His military ambitions coincided with the acute need felt in London and Simla for a victory to offset the reverses in the Gallipoli Campaign, the final demise of which could not long be delayed. Townshend questioned the wisdom of thrusting further into enemy territory, with his communications extending back over 400 miles to the Persian Gulf, their defence resting, in all, on one other Indian division. He was proved to be right. But his objections were overruled.

In mid-November the attacking British force approached Ctesiphon, eighty miles up-river from Kut. There luck failed for the first time in the year-old Mesopotamian campaign. In a series of engagements in the latter part of the month, Townshend's forces, facing four Ottoman divisions, suffered grievous losses, and he felt obliged to retreat to Kut, arriving there on 3 December. Unsuccessful in frontal attack, the Turks proceeded to invest Kut. Thus began the famous siege. Townshend could have withdrawn down the river before the noose was tied, but he was ordered to stay, on the assumption that Indian reinforcements, dispatched from Europe and now approaching Shatt-al-Arab, would relieve him. In those very days the British Government was deciding on the evacuation of Gallipoli. Two retreats were too much.

It was a race between the dwindling rations of the 9,000 besieged soldiers and the movement up the river-coast of the relief force. Troops of the 7th and 3rd Indian divisions, transferred from France under the command of General Aylmer, forced the interposing Turkish force back from their outward lines of defence to Umm al Hanna, some twenty miles south of Kut, on the left side of the Tigris. The British force, suffering heavy casualties, could not make further headway. Nixon's health broke, and he was replaced by Sir P. Lake. A further division of reinforcements – the 13th division – was moved from Egypt to Mesopotamia. Another failure at breakthrough was repeated in March 1916 on the right bank of the river, a mere ten miles from the besieged garrison. Another month passed before the British forces were ready for a further assault. When it came, it was shattered by the lines of defence that the Turks had had ample time to fortify. All these months the gallantry of the surrounded force aroused widespread acclaim. But acclaim could not be eaten. On 29 April 1916, the exhausted and starved soldiers surrendered and were taken into Turkish captivity, where most of them subsequently perished. Twenty-four thousand casualties had been incurred in the abortive attempt to save them. Planned to recompense Gallipoli, the movement on Baghdad became its corollary in disaster.

The Turks, however, never regained Lower Mesopotamia. The attempt to avert disaster had brought a British Mesopotamian army into being. The avenging of the disaster became its objective. A year later, in March 1917, Baghdad fell to British arms, and, after it, in stages, the whole of Mesopotamia. The army of victory was headed by General Maude, who had commanded the last attempt to relieve Kut.

The landings at the head of the Persian Gulf in the early days of the war in 1914 were the first armed seizure of Ottoman territory by Britain. Moreover, these landings started a process whereby Mesopotamia came under British armed control at the end of the war. Parallel with the occupation of Mesopotamia in 1917 and 1918, British troops were to conquer Palestine and Syria.

This twin development had a far-reaching impact on the evolution of the new Middle East, which emerged on the ruins of Ottoman rule. As in the case of Mesopotamia, Britain slipped gradually into large-scale military action in the heart of the western part of the Ottoman Empire in

Asia. The genesis was a Turkish attack on the Suez Canal in February 1915. This was one of two military moves the Turks made in the beginning of the war, the other being in Transcaucasia. Before acting militarily, the Turks, in conjunction with the Germans, had identified the war against the *Entente* Powers as a war for Islam.

On 23 November 1914, the Sultan Khalif in Constantinople had proclaimed a jihad against the *Entente* Powers. Germany aspired to replace Britain in Moslem eyes as the ally of the faith. The Young Turk régime from its start had exhibited secularist tendencies. It was suspect and criticized on this score by the Arab guardians of Islam in Mecca. The new programme of Ottomanization had hardly gotten under way. It was divisive and repressive within, irrelevant and repulsive without. For centuries Islam had been an effective cement between the non-Turkish Moslem peoples within the Empire, at the same time inducing the reverence of Moslems everywhere towards the Khalifat in Constantinople. Religion was a traditional handmaid of empire : others had used it successfully as a wedge for penetration and incitement against Ottoman rule ; now it was to be called into service in Ottoman defence. The jihad, it was hoped, would ignite fires under British rule in Egypt, Sudan and India. Its repercussions might extend to the Moslem populations of North Africa and southern Russia. Britain responded by seeking to mount a counter-jihad. It turned to Mecca in search of a new Khalif. Race and geography would help to project him as religiously pure, untainted by political dross. The espousal of Arab in place of Turk, of Mecca for Constantinople, would underline Britain's reverence for the inner springs of Islamic tradition. It could lend a religious focus to initial Arab disaffection against Ottoman rule. In a written message, in November 1914, the British in London and Cairo laid bare their conscience before the Grand Sharif of Mecca :

> Till now we have defended and befriended Islam in the person of the Turks. Henceforth it shall be that of the noble Arab. It may be that an Arab of true race will assume the Khalifat at Mecca or Medina, and so good may come by the help of God out of all the evil which is now occurring.

Past omissions and present credentials both duly explained on religious grounds, the note proceeded to raise a practical suggestion for the future :

> It would be well if Your Highness could convey to your followers and devotees, who are found throughout the world, in every country, the good tidings of the freedom of the Arabs and the rising of the sun over Arabia.

The Ottoman jihad proved to be a whimper. It had no significant dissident impact throughout Britain's far-flung Moslem dominions.

Empires have, however, proved peculiarly prone to myths. Imperial sensitivity to religious antagonism first became acute with the Indian mutiny of 1857. Its traces can be discerned throughout the period of the Pax Britannica in the Middle East. Apologists for British policies in Palestine between the two world wars were to point not only to Britain's interests in the Arab world, but no less to the dangers of antagonizing the tens of millions of Moslems in India and elsewhere.

Britain's dialogue with Mecca brought, a year and a half later, the Arab Revolt. Side by side with its military and political strands, the war in the East possessed a religious element. It did not, however, produce a new Khalif. The lacuna was not due to lack of readiness on the part of the recipient of British encouragement, but because of internal Arab divisions. The idea was too tempting to fade, regardless of the practicality of implementation. It found impetus when shortly after the war the Ottoman Khalifat was discarded by the Turks themselves as part of the secularization of modern Turkey. The vacant religious throne titillated various Arab kings and leaders. It exacerbated the inter-Arab struggle for hegemony, pan-Arabism and pan-Islam, becoming enmeshed in the webs of intrigue and rivalry. In a peculiar, or maybe not so peculiar, way, dedication to the Arab cause in Palestine became an index not only of pan-Arab patriotism but also of the fitness of an Arab leader to assume the Khalifat. The invasion of Israel by Egypt in 1948 was related *inter alia* to Farouk's aspirations for the Khalifat, in rivalry with those of Abdullah of Transjordan, son of Sharif Husain, to whom the British had written in 1914. In the 1950s and 1960s the Arabs got a sort of secular Khalif : Nasser of Egypt. The Sisyphean fate of his effort to consolidate his power in the Arab world was due in no small measure to the antagonism of the successive guardians of Islam in Arabia : Ibn Saud and his son Feisal. Actions taken, alliances formed, maps drawn, ideas launched in the incipient period of 1914–22 have had their continuing impact for a half-century and more. One of the lesser known is the question of the Arab Khalifat.

In 1914 the idea of an attack on the Suez Canal stirred anticipation in both Berlin and Constantinople. The psychological significance for Africa and Asia of a strike at the symbol of British imperialism would be great. The immediate result of even a temporary disruption of passage through the Canal could be of advantage to the German forces on the major and decisive western front. It would delay the movement of British and Indian troops from Asia to Europe. The Suez Canal area was an assembly point and transit camp for these troops. At the very least, the assertion of a threat to the Canal would tie up heavy British forces for its defence. At the same time, a strike at the Canal would represent an Ottoman challenge to British usurpation of Egypt. The appearance of Turkish troops on the frontier of Egypt was expected to spark off revolt in the interior.

The units for the strike were drawn from the Ottoman Fourth Army, which covered the southern part of the Empire. Its headquarters were in Damascus ; its commander was Jamal Pasha, one of the inner group of the Turkish régime, who, till the outbreak of war, had been Minister of Marine. The plans for the offensive were drawn up by two German officers, Jamal's Chief of Staff, Von Frankenberg, and Von Kressenstein, Chief of Staff of the VIII Corps in the Ottoman Fourth Army.

British concern for the defence of the short sea route to India was as old as her control of that vital artery. Britain was in Egypt because of the Canal. On its account the Egyptian frontier had, in 1906, been extended eastwards across Sinai to the southern frontier of Palestine. From 1907 the problem of the defence of the Suez Canal against overland attack from the east came under leisurely review by the Committee of Imperial Defence and by various sub-committees. It was assumed that an invasion of force from the east could not be undertaken without railway construction across Sinai, or other preparations that would afford ample warning. The best way to meet this attack would not be by a defensive force in Egypt, but by the landing of at least four divisions in Haifa. Over a century earlier, a British force helped to block Napoleon at Acre. In 1840 Muhammad Ali had been denied the conquest of the whole of Syria by British intervention on the Syrian coast. Now Britain was in Egypt, her influence at Constantinople waning.

Palestine returned (see page 185) to British strategical calculations as the most plausible place at which to halt a large-scale Turkish hostile movement westwards. As already noted, a British hold on the eastern coast of the Mediterranean was also considered essential as a railhead for the defence of Mesopotamia. Here lay the twin key to the evolution of British positions on Palestine in the map-drawing of the Middle East during and after World War One.

As British military experts surveyed the Middle East in the years preceding the outbreak of war, they conceived of raids by small hostile forces on the Canal as the more likely development in the event of war. The Admiralty demurred at the suggestion that it tie down in advance ships for the defence of the Canal, thus restricting its full freedom of mobility in wartime. Moreover, it argued that for topographical reasons some sixteen miles of the Canal could not be adequately covered by ships. The Foreign Office objected, except in crucial emergency, to the use not only of naval but also of military power in the Canal area. Under the Constantinople Convention of 1888, the Turks seemed to retain the right to cross the Canal in force in order to put down unrest in vassal Egypt. Britain would be on safer ground if it claimed that it wished to block a Turkish offensive designed to upset the neutrality of the Canal. In that case, however, there would be the complication of the Convention's requirements for consultation with the other co-signatories. Quite apart from these political considerations, it was suggested that, strategically, the most effective line of defence for the Canal lay close to the new Egyptian frontier on the eastern side of Sinai. The oases of El Arish and Nakhl were the key : if occupied by British forces and if Nakhl were joined by a road to the Canal area, the possibility of blocking the Turks on the threshold would be enhanced. At any rate, foreknowledge of their movements would be assured, while the denial to them of the two oases would restrict the number of the attacking force. If not occupied in advance, the oases would be reached by the Turks coming from Rafah and Aqaba before British forces coming by sea and land from the Canal could outrace them.

All well and good, except that having first underlined the danger of building the defence around the Canal itself, the Foreign Office now pointed out the unfeasibility of making approaches to Constantinople on the road to Nakhl and the occupation of El Arish. Nothing was more illustrative of the tangle of the Anglo-Ottoman relationship. The Porte, under duress, had agreed that the southern frontier of Palestine be approximately the eastern frontier of Egypt. It still retained suzerainty over Egypt. It was hardly diplomatic to go back and ask for agreement for the stationing of British troops close to the new eastern frontier, particularly as the eventuality for which they were to be stationed was not unconnected with the Turks. Thus, after all the memoranda, the defence of the Canal remained with military forces mainly on its west bank, with warships passing through it by turns (not anchoring, so as not to blatantly offend the Constantinople Convention) and with the barrier of the water itself. Extensive reconnoitring of Sinai and the Negev, as of the Haifa area, had been successfully undertaken, British scholars and archaeologists displaying a sudden and intensive zeal to unlock the secrets of the desert. Kitchener, since 1911 Agent and Consul-General in Egypt (a gentle way of describing the imperial ruler of the country), was involved in these studies, just as he was in the entire scheme of British defence and interest in the Middle East. At the time of the outbreak of war with Germany, he was in England. When he embarked at Dover on his way back to Egypt, he was recalled to London and made Secretary of State for War. Far back in 1874, as a young officer, he had drawn maps of western Palestine for the Palestine Exploration Fund ; now he would shortly draw maps in the British Cabinet for the frontiers of British influence in the post-war Middle East.

As, in the early autumn of 1914, Turkey veered to the side of the Central Powers, the G O C in Egypt, General Maxwell, was in touch with Kitchener on the danger of an imminent Turkish attack on the land. According to Storrs, the Oriental Secretary at the British Residency in Cairo, Kitchener's first approach to Sharif Husain of Mecca, made on 24 September 1914, was designed to prevent Arab cooperation in providing camels for the expedition that the Turks had begun to organize for the crossing of Sinai to Suez. In the absence of a railway, camels alone were seaworthy in the desert. After much toting up of camels and other considerations, the British estimate was that an enemy force of some 5–6,000 could be expected. It was wrong.

In the first days of February 1915, a force of 12–15,000 reached the Canal. It had assembled at Beersheba a fortnight earlier. The Turks entered Sinai in the north through Rafah and El Arish, in the centre through El Auja and in the south on the route through Nakhl. The main force was deployed along the centre routes. Further forces in Palestine awaited the outcome of the initial attack, ready to cross the desert to buttress any bridge-head that might be established. The defensive arm of the Canal comprised over 30,000 troops. In addition, there were reserves in the interior. The warships were passing through the Canal on time. The fighting was brief. On the night of 2 February the Turks managed to get three platoons of soldiers across the Canal near Lake Timsah. They were rapidly overcome. Attacks by the Turks at El Kantara and near Suez on 3 February met a similar fate. The Turks retreated more rapidly than they had come. By 9 February the major part of their forces was back in Beersheba. They were not pursued. British strategy was entirely defensive. The attack had failed. Egypt had not risen in arms, but British defensive strategy had been shaken up. The passability of the desert by large forces had been proven. Moreover, in order to disrupt passage through the Canal it was sufficient for the enemy to operate on its east bank. British concern increased for the defence of the Canal. The final *débâcle* at Gallipoli at the end of 1915 and a further abortive Turkish action against the Canal in April 1916 turned concern into obsession. A great army was assembled. Suez pinned down considerable British forces from other fronts, just as the Transcaucasian front, despite Turkish failure there, kept large Russian forces occupied. First the west bank of the Canal was fortified, then, in order to assure its eastern flank, the British Army in Suez crossed Sinai to El Arish, making it, in early 1917, the front line of the defence of the Canal (as the General Staff had recommended it be made before the outbreak of war). It later moved to the offensive into Palestine and Syria. This process reached consummation in 1917 and 1918. Thus British influence became predominant in the post-war settlement in the Middle East, with Palestine falling within its exclusive patrimony.

Within days of the outbreak of war, the Caucasian, or to be more geographically precise, the Armenian, front was also activated. It was the natural scene for a Russo-Turkish confrontation. For close to two centuries, the scythe of the Russian southwards thrust had been slowly cutting through the area between the Caspian and the Black seas as well as through the area east of the Caspian. The Persian and Turkish frontiers had progressively shrunk ; British fears, more imaginary than real, for India had progressively grown. Caught in the vortex of advancing and retreating armies a *mêlée* of peoples and tribes – Circassians, Lesghians, Abkhasins, Tartars, Armenians – hovered in a twilight of semi-independence, subjugated by changing alliances with greater forces.

Under the treaty of San Stefano (March 1878) and, in this respect confirmed by the Congress of Berlin (July 1878), Russian control of

Kars, Batum and Ardahan in eastern Asia Minor had been acknowledged. Britain, as already noted, had guaranteed the shrunken Turkish frontier against further Russian encroachment. Now Britain and Russia were allies. The Turks had been forced out of territory but had retained, or believed they retained, the fierce loyalty of Tartars and Turkmans who had come under Russian rule but were Moslems and spoke a dialect close to Turkish. Russia planned to continue its encirclement east of the Black Sea and southwards to break through Mesopotamia towards the Persian Gulf. Turkey planned to reconquer Georgia, and possibly beyond, to recapture the ancient glories of empire through the interweaving into the fabric of a new and integrated Ottoman (Turanian) civilization millions of kinsfolk in religion and language.

The Russian defence rested on the imposing fortresses of Kars and Ardahan, while the Turks' was based on the no less imposing fortress of Erzerum some seventy miles distant. In winter, the terrain on both sides was itself a fortress – interlocked blade-like hills, wind-swept and snow-bound. The forward Russian positions were at Sarikamish, about fifteen miles from the Turkish frontier. The Turks knew that through this base an attack on Kars and Ardahan could be mounted.

On 8 November 1914, the Russians moved on Ottoman territory, but were stopped. Their failure encouraged the Ottoman Third Army, commanded personally by Enver Pasha, the Turkish Minister of War and the central figure in the Young Turkish régime, to attack Sarikamish. In the last week of December and the first week of January the battle surged around this key point. The Russian General, Yudenich, won the day. Sarikamish was saved. The Ottoman Third Army was shattered, losing over seventy per cent of its 100,000 strength. In Transcaucasia, dead and fallen were not synonymous : men remained standing after death, their bodies frozen against icy silhouette.

In the following months and throughout 1915, the orgy of killing terrorized an entire people. The Armenians were geographically sundered between Russia and Turkish Armenia, their menfolk divided up between the two warring armies. In the decades before the war, the massacre and oppression of Armenians – long suspect of pro-Russian sympathies – represented an assertion of Turkish virility in weakness. It was a burden on the conscience of those Powers, particularly Britain, that sustained the Ottomans in their decline. The Anglo-Turkish deal of 1878 on the British occupation of Cyprus in return for the promise to block further Russian expansion in eastern Asia Minor also included unfulfilled Turkish promises to mend their attitude to the Armenians. In Germany, Turkey found a Christian ally that showed scant interest in the plight of the remote Caucasian people. As in 1915, further armed initiatives were undertaken by both Russians and Turks, and the Turks decided to finalize their relationship with the Armenians with a clasp of total death. First in Turkish Armenia, then throughout Turkey, the genocide of a people was systematically planned and executed. It helped the Turks little. The Turkish haemorrhage on the Transcaucasian front continued unchecked. In 1916, the Russians conquered the key Turkish fortress of Erzerum and then reached the port of Trebizond on the Black Sea. Yet, after trying for two centuries, when Russian fingers were finally on Turkey's throat, they suddenly became paralysed. In 1917 the Russian armies in Europe began to disintegrate, and those in the Caucasus followed suit. At the end of the year Russia left the war. The Transcaucasian battles had no impact on the outcome of the war, except that the drainage of Turkish manpower facilitated the advance of British troops through Mesopotamia, Palestine and Syria. The first Russo-Turkish clash in January 1915 was, however, a lightening rod for the British Dardanelles expedition. This expedition was the outstanding event of the war in the Middle East in 1915. It set in motion in earnest, amongst the *Entente* Powers, the map-drawing of a new post-war Middle East. The failure first of the Dardanelles expedition and then of the offshoot Gallipoli Campaign left Turkey in the war for a further three years.

Various strands of thought and development combined to bring the Dardanelles expedition into being. Turkey's adhesion to the Central Powers frayed British reflexes in Suez and the Persian Gulf. It posed a threat to Russia in the Caucasus. But the immediate and most pregnant result was the snapping of the most effective sea lane between Russia and her Western allies. The only other approach was by the north to Archangel and Murmansk, ice-bound for many months in the year and served by indifferent rail communication to the interior. Russian trade was bottled up. Even more serious, military communication between the *Entente* Powers was undercut. The significance of this development, as seen from the German side, can be gauged from the assessment of the German Chief of Staff Falkenhayn that 'if the Straits between the Mediterranean and the Black Sea were not permanently closed to *Entente* traffic, all hopes of a successful course of the war would be very considerably diminished'. In German eyes, the closed Straits could contribute to the crippling of Russia and the general weakening of the *Entente*. For the *Entente* Powers, the opening of the narrows between the Aegean and Marmara seas would not only establish an effective munitions line to Russia, it could alter the whole strategic balance : Suez would be freed from threat ; Turkey, sundered in half, would be knocked out of the war ; the Balkans could be saved for the *Entente* ; the eastern flank of the Alliance in Europe would be exposed to attack from a new quarter.

The opening of the Straits might thus provide a key to the deadlock that had set in on both the western and eastern fronts. By the time Turkey joined the war in November 1914, the trench stalemate formed a line from Switzerland to the English Channel, a seemingly immovable swathe of blood and suffering. On the other side of Europe, mobility was less restricted. There, too, decision seemed no less remote. Some six million men on both sides were entrapped in the morass of indecisive battlefields. Their leaders foundered in the morass of war plans – drawn up over years, proven abortive within months.

For Britain, a reversal to traditional strategy offered an outlet. Naval superiority and mobility could carry the war to sensitive points on enemy coasts. Fisher, First Lord of the Admiralty, advocated a landing at Schleswig on the German coast. Kitchener set his eye on Alexandretta on the Syrian coast. Its occupation could impair communications in the heart of the Ottoman Empire and assure the defence of Suez. Lloyd George also urged the involvement of British troops on a large scale in the Balkan fighting. One version of the approach was that troops landed at Salonika should first capture Constantinople by land, after which they could turn around for action in the Balkans. From the start Lloyd George grasped the possibilities, immediate and long-term, inherent in the war in the East. In 1917 and 1918, as Prime Minister, he was to exploit these possibilities to the full inside Ottoman territory.

The War Council in London finally decided on 'a naval expedition in February to . . . take the Gallipoli Peninsula, with Constantinople as its objective'. Winston Churchill, now First Lord of the Admiralty, had his way. He had intermittently been taken with the idea from the beginning of the war. The decision fell on 13 January 1915. Some two weeks earlier, Grand Duke Nicholas, Commander-in-Chief of the Russian armies, had appealed to Kitchener for some immediate action to counter-balance the Turkish thrust in Transcaucasia. Before long the Russians gained the upper hand, but Britain clung to the original invitation. The fighting in Transcaucasia could not decide the war, the forcing of the Straits could. At any rate, it would ensure that Russia, reeling under German hammer-blows in Europe, would not defect to a separate peace. British conquest of Constantinople would, moreover, not be unhelpful when the contours of the post-war settlement were to be drawn. In the Dardanelles, decision could seemingly be reached without diverting large forces from the western theatre. Thus both those laying exclusive stress on the western front, known as the 'Western' school, and those favouring far-flung diversionary action, the 'Eastern' school, could be satisfied. Churchill, who at first had thought of a combined military and naval assault, came to accept the view of the Admiral in command of the squadron off Dardanelles that forcing the Straits by ships alone was feasible. Kitchener, maintaining that in any case no British troops were available for this expedition, as well as the War Council, agreed that the attempt should be made. This was the first of the mis-assessments that made the Dardanelles campaign a perennial subject of inquest for military historians.*

The campaign lasted close to a year. It fell into four broad stages. In each one, British forces enjoyed initial surprise. Only in the last stage –

*For the genesis of the Dardanelles expedition see Martin Gilbert, *Winston Churchill*, III, 202ff.

that of withdrawal – did they fully exploit it. On 25 February, British and French ships succeeded in silencing four of the outer forts. Small landing parties attacked the others. Some historians feel that a single division of troops could at this time have successfully taken control of the Straits. There were then only two Turkish divisions dispersed around the area. On 26 February, and in the first days of March, the ships shelled the inner forts at long range. They could not get close because of the mines, and the minesweepers, under fire from mobile howitzers, could not clear the way. An all-out naval offensive was launched only on 18 March. Sixteen British and French battleships were involved. The Turks had used the month since the initial bombardment to replenish their artillery and to extend and thicken the minefields. The combination again proved an effective defence. Three battleships were sunk. Other ships were put out of action. The naval force withdrew. A further immediate attack might still have carried the day. Turkish ammunition was exhausted. Constantinople was in panic. Its imminent fall was predicted by foreign observers in the city, including Germans.

The naval chapter was, however, at an end. The emphasis moved to primarily a land operation. General Sir Ian Hamilton had reported the need for a 'deliberate and progressive military operation, carried out in force, in order to make a passage for the navy'. He was now charged with supreme command of the Dardanelles expedition. Kitchener told him that if he took Constantinople he would win 'not only a campaign but a war'. Despite the Western school, Kitchener now found for him five divisions – four British, one French – for the amphibious landings. They were late in assembling for action.

By the time Hamilton was ready to act, more than a month later, six Turkish divisions were deployed in the area. The defence of the Straits and Constantinople were in the hands of Liman von Sanders, a German general, whose appointment to the Turkish Army in 1913 was an augury of the coming German-Turk alignment. Von Sanders had to disperse his troops widely, awaiting every eventuality, his communication lines were indifferent. Tactical surprise was still British. It was again squandered.

On 24 April, the expedition, brimming with joy and pride, set forth from the Island of Lemnos. (The 'Zion Mule Corps', raised in Egypt mainly out of Jewish Palestinian refugees, formed part of this expedition.) One force headed for five beaches near Cape Helles, with the object of gaining control of the southern part of the Gallipoli Peninsula. Another force of Australian and New Zealand troops was assigned to the beaches near Gaba Tepe (later known as Anzac), some fifteen miles up the western coast of the Peninsula. This was the western edge of the narrow waistline of the Peninsula. From the heights of nearby Sari Bair, the longed-for objective, the Narrows, were only four to five miles away. A French division was to make a temporary diversionary landing at Kum Kale on the Asiatic coast, opposite Cape Helles. The landings were all successfully carried out. The first precious forty-eight hours, however, were not fully utilized. Turkish reinforcements rapidly reached the heights. The British did not have sufficient force to dislodge them. A bloody stalemate set in. The ghost of the western front appeared in Eastern dress.

The first political repercussions occurred in mid-May. Fisher resigned. He did not concur with the War Council's decision of 14 May to press on with the campaign. Churchill was transferred from the Admiralty to the more restricted functions of the Duchy of Lancaster. Later he left the government under the shadow of Gallipoli. A renewed offensive on the western front had also failed. In order to stifle mounting criticism, Prime Minister Asquith drew Conservatives into his government.

The third stage of the Dardanelles campaign took place in August. British strength had been increased to thirteen divisions, while the Turkish had reached sixteen divisions. Rallying from Anzac, invading forces had as their objective the mountain ridges of Sari Bair whence, across the Peninsula, the hills controlling the Narrows could be reached. Simultaneously, a further landing was to take place in Suvla Bay, a few miles to the north. After taking the surrounding hills, this force would join the action on Sari Bair. Both operations commenced on the night of 6 August ; by 10 August they failed. True, initial success had again been achieved. But again, the determined resistance of the Turks, coupled with the rapid movement of their reserves, blocked the British ascent of the heights. At Suvla Bay, British troops, after a successful landing, were held up by dilatory command and by inadequate maps. Two precious days were lost, during which the hills were reinforced by a Turkish force under the command of Brigadier Mustafa Kemal, the future founder of modern Turkey. A last attempt to scale the hills was made on 21 August. Its failure brought down the curtain on the Gallipoli Campaign.

Hamilton asked for further large reinforcements, but was refused. Serbia was being knocked out of the war by a determined German offensive in the Balkans, and available British and French troops had to be sent to Salonika. In any event, to dispatch them to Gallipoli was pointless now that, with Bulgaria's adhesion to the Central Powers, a direct munition line was open between Germany and Turkey. Von Sander's problem was solved ; Britain's remained. To withdraw in face of public opinion seemed almost as difficult as to advance in face of the Turks. The British Cabinet hesitated. Hamilton, who opposed evacuation, was dismissed. Sir Charles Munro, who took his place, recommended evacuation. His recommendation, received in October, was not followed. Finally, in November, Kitchener was sent out, to make up the Cabinet's mind. He, too, supported evacuation. On 8 December, the decision fell. Within ten days the last of the troops in Suvla Bay and Anzac were withdrawn, together with most of the animals, vehicles and supplies. Night after night the ships succeeded in loading their human and other cargo from the ill-fated beaches without the Turks realizing what was happening. Again, ruses worked. In early January the beaches at Cape Helles were also vacated. The withdrawal was a masterpiece of planning and execution.

Gallipoli cost the British Empire a quarter-million casualties. The lists of killed and wounded by Turkish fire or bayonets were supplemented by those ravaged in the summer from exposure to the merciless sun without adequate water and in the winter to icy gales without adequate clothing. The price was high, even by the counterfeit currency of human life in World War One. Gallipoli seems to hold a special place amongst the lingering traumas in British consciousness. It is a mixture of violently contrasting colours : brilliant vision countermanded by strategic miscalculation ; supreme courage set at nought by tactical procrastination ; probably a decisive turning-point in the whole war lost because of the reluctance to endanger a few more ships or to commit a few more divisions in time.

Turkey remained in the war. The vital sea lane to Russia remained closed. Russia remained largely inaccessible to large-scale and regular military supplies from her allies (this was one cause of the breakdown of the Russian armies in 1917). The threat to Suez increased. Over one million British troops were committed to Egypt and Mesopotamia.

As was previously stated, Gallipoli set in motion the map-drawing between the *Entente* Powers of the future Middle East. However, before it started, Russian claims had to be satisfied by Britain and France. This, in turn, obliged the latter two respectively to define their claims. The abyss opened by Gallipoli swallowed up the last possibility of Britain agreeing to even a shell of the Turkish Empire remaining in Asia. It quickened and broadened an incipient British-Arab dialogue, which led to further hypothetical map-drawing. The defeat in the East came on top of *Entente* failures on the western and eastern fronts, as in Italy and the Balkans. Desperately, Britain cast about for further support, particularly from the United States. She sought an ally in the Jewish people. This lent an urgency and new dimension to inchoate thoughts on the value to British interests of a Jewish presence in Palestine.

On 6 March 1915, the British and French governments received an aide-mémoire from their Russian ally : 'The course of recent events,' it opened, 'leads His Majesty Emperor Nicholas to think that the question of Constantinople and of the Straits must be definitely resolved according to time-honoured aspirations of Russia.' Russia's claims were to the possession of Constantinople, the long coveted ancient Byzantine capital, the European coast from the Black Sea to the end of the Dardanelles, the Asiatic shore of the Bosphorus, the Sea of Marmora, as well as the islands of Imbros and Tenedos in the Aegean. In this area, continued the aide-mémoire, the special interests of France and Great Britain would be scrupulously respected. Moreover, Russia would view with sympathy the implementation of her allies' claims in other parts of the Ottoman Empire. In 1913 Sir Edward Grey, Britain's Foreign Secretary, had explained that if Britain abandoned her policy of opposing the partition of Asiatic Turkey, the question of the possession of Constantinople would arise and the probable result would be a European war. The sequence had been reversed.

What Britain had denied Russia for a century, she now acceded to within days. The decision was taken at a special meeting of the War Council on 10 March 1915. In Winston Churchill's words it was 'a convulsive gesture of self-preservation'. In conveying Britain's acceptance of Russian claims, the British Ambassador Buchanan in Petrograd was instructed to point out to Sazonov, the Russian Foreign Minister, that this was 'the greatest proof of friendship that it is in our power to give'. Russia was getting a 'definite promise in her favour as regards the greatest prize of the whole war before we have had time to consider what our own desiderata would be elsewhere in the eventual terms of peace'. Before formulating these desiderata, Britain would consult with France and Russia. However, Britain had already served notice that it would ask for commercial freedom for merchant vessels in the Straits, for a free port in Constantinople and for the inclusion within the British sphere in Persia of the area marked as the neutral sphere under the Anglo-Russian agreement of 1907. Buchanan was also instructed to inform the Russians that as soon as it becomes known that Russia is to have Constantinople at the conclusion of the war, Sir E. Grey will wish to state that throughout the negotiations His Majesty's Government had stipulated that 'the Mussulman Holy Places and Arabia shall under all circumstances remain under independent Mussulman dominion'.

By this latter statement Britain was apparently taking out an insurance policy against any allegation that in agreeing to Russian control of Constantinople she was countenancing the extinction of Moslem independence in the Middle East. Britain was already negotiating with Sharif Husain of the Hejaz and with other Arab chieftains in the Arab Peninsula. She had thrown out to Husain the promise of independence from the Turks, together with the bait of the Khalifat. It was not clear if he could rally the necessary Moslem support to seize it. In any case, Russia would know that by her control of Constantinople she would not be allowed to supersede Britain as the Christian protecting power of Islam. Russia agreed to approximately all the British requests, accepting that Moslem Holy Places should remain under independent Moslem rule and throwing out the thought that the Khalifat be separated from Turkey.

The French were more businesslike. They agreed to Russian claims, but only after Russia gave her views on French claims. The French claims were : Cilicia up to the Taurus and all Syria as far south as the Egyptian border, including Palestine and the Christian Holy Places. Russia unofficially agreed to the French package on Cilicia and Syria proper. It withheld agreement on Palestine. As traditional guardian of the Orthodox interests, it could hardly cede exclusive control over Palestine to the guardian of the Catholic interest. The ghost of the

Crimean War had not yet been laid to rest. Palestine was on the international dissecting table.

In this solution all strands of thought met, all options were retained and at a minimum cost. The liberal conscience of Asquith and Grey revolted against Britain partaking of war spoils. Except for Basra, Britain would acquire no new territory. The breadth of existing imperial obligations cautioned against adding to them. 'Our Empire is wide enough already,' says the introduction to the report of an interdepartmental committee under the chairmanship of Sir Maurice de Bunsen, set up by the Prime Minister in April 1915 to consider Britain's desiderata in Asiatic Turkey. 'It is then to strengthen ragged edges that . . . we have to assert our claim to a share in settling the destiny of Asiatic Turkey.' Basra fitted the description. At the same time, the essential strategic option would remain open. The amended Kitchener line from Acre on the Mediterranean to Rowanduz on the Mesopotamian-Persian frontier would remain Britain's northern defensive tier in the Middle East. In the event of a breakdown of the Ottoman Empire, Britain would act to affirm this line. In the meantime, she would ensure her influence south of the line in Palestine and Mesopotamia.

The Indian Government had opposed the dismemberment of the Ottoman Empire because of Indian Moslem feeling. Others also considered that final conclusions should not be drawn from what might after all be merely a temporary defection of the 'good old Turk'. He might yet resume his traditional role of buffer against Russian expansionism, and weak buffers were not healthy.

Decentralization had been recommended by Britain in the past. An Arab congress held in Paris in 1913 had urged that Constantinople adapt the policy of decentralization under overall Turkish rule. Decentralization meant reform of the Ottoman system of government. In vain, Britain urged this on the Porte for over a half-century. If achieved now, Britain would be relieved of the stigma on her imperial record, which the past alignment with the repressive Turk had involved. The de Bunsen Committee proposed that the Turk should remain in three Arab provinces and in Armenia, but he would be a restricted Turk. He would, however, have to clear out entirely from areas where even a restricted presence could not be tolerated by British interests. These were, apart from Basra, the Kaza of Kuwait and the Senjak of Najd in Arabia giving on to the Persian Gulf. From the beginning of the war, British representatives had been promising the assorted Arab rulers that Arabia and its Moslem Holy Places would, in a post-war settlement, be independent. These promises had been given to enlist support against the Turks. The Arab response was varied. Anyway, Arabia was not one entity. Apart from Kuwait and Najd, the other chiefs and their areas, including Hejaz and its ruler Sharif Husain, would be granted virtual independence, short of a complete sundering of the Turkish nexus from Arabia and the Holy Places.

Another school of thought conceived the future British stake in the Middle East as interlocked with the Arab. In his memorandum of 16 March 1915, Kitchener wrote that in the event of a partition of Turkey, it was in the British interest to see 'an Arab kingdom established in Arabia under the auspices of Britain bounded on the north by the valley of the Tigris and Euphrates and containing within it the chief Moslem Holy Places, Mecca, Medina and Karbala . . . this in our position as the greatest of Moslem States would greatly enhance our prestige amongst the many millions of our Mohammedan subjects'. The grand design of replacing the Turkish Moslem with an Arab Moslem Empire had been forming in Kitchener's mind for some time before the war. In a sense, Kitchener was the architect of pan-Arabism.

In Cairo, the pro-Arab school of British experts was enthusiastic. Ronald Storrs, the Oriental Secretary, in exultation envisioned 'A North African or New Eastern Vice-royalty including Egypt and Sudan and across the way from Aden to Alexandretta . . . comparing . . . with India itself.' In one dramatic move Britain's problem not only in India but also in Egypt and Sudan could be taken care of. In Simla, the British Indian experts neither liked the prospects of the extinction of the Turkish Empire nor, as they believed, the constitution of an Arab one. The first course they believed would upset the Indian Moslems, the second would only accentuate their aroused passions. After all, Britain's future in India was the paramount issue at stake. Let the Cairo novices leave it to the experts. In 1915 they still seemed to agree with what Palmerston had written in 1833 on the route to India : 'His (Muhammad Ali's) real design is to establish an Arabian kingdom including all the countries in which Arabic is the language . . . as this would imply the dismemberment of Turkey we could not agree . . . Turkey is as good an occupier of the road to India as an active Arabian sovereign would be.'

On the future Arab political dispensation, the decentralization plan left open all options. It similarly took into account the conflicting views of the Cairo-Khartoum school and of the Simla school on the future of the Khalifat, leaving each with its hope, neither with decision.

The Turkish Khalif would remain. The question was where. With Constantinople ceded to the Russians, Turkey would need a new capital. A member of the de Bunsen Committee thought this might be Damascus, which should be constituted as a separate province insulated from Great Power zones of interest. The hope was expressed that 'Russia having gained so great a prize as Constantinople and posing as a Christian Orthodox and not as a Moslem Power, would acquiesce in the establishment of the capital outside her zone.' The Turks, of course, might be reluctant to remove themselves to the Arab city of Damascus lest the Turkish Khalifat be supplanted by an Arab one. They might, however, be brought to agree by a promise of guaranteed pensions for the 'great hordes of officials and their dependants who are now employed in Istanbul' and for whom Turkey in Asia would have neither funds nor work.

At the same time, Britain would maintain a reserve account in Mecca. The political status of the Sherif of Mecca would be enhanced. This, joined with his inherent status deriving from his family and physical connection with the Holy Places in Arabia, might create a fitting background for some future assumption by him of the title of Khalifa. In any event, non-Ottoman Sunni Moslems would have alternative addresses for their loyalties. The choice would be entirely theirs. Nobody could accuse Britain of being deficient in concern for the religious feelings of the Moslem subjects of the Empire. She herself would retain her options. The Arab in Mecca was attractive. Still, as Sykes reminded the Committee, an Arab Khalif in Mecca would be on territory forbidden to Christians ; a Turkish one in Damascus, on the other hand, would be within reach of 'Christian arms'.

In March 1915, the promise of Constantinople to Russia seemed real and close indeed. France had received unofficial Russian support for her Middle Eastern demands, except Palestine. Britain had been reluctant to engage in the map-drawing. Opinions differed on the subject. Why not allow the evolution of events to pose its pragmatic counsel ? But time was not given. Hence the appointment of the de Bunsen Committee. It presented its report on 30 June 1915. One of its members was a British Conservative MP, Sir Mark Sykes, an abullient and visionary expert on the Middle East. A Lt-Colonel on active service, but enrolled by the War Office to work with the Director of Military Operations and Intelligence, Sykes was attached to the committee at the personal request of Lord Kitchener, the War Secretary. Next to Lloyd George, he was destined to play the most prominent role in affirming, on the highest international level, the historical connection of the Jewish people with Palestine.

The de Bunsen report might have been written in the mid-nineteenth century had Palmerston then accepted Czar Nicholas' diagnosis that euthanasia was the only cure for the 'sick man of Europe'. It certainly could have been written in the latter part of the century when Prime Minister Salisbury expressed doubts about the traditional policy of maintaining the integrity of the Ottoman Empire. Now, at long last, the 'sick man' was on the dissecting table. Yet in contemplating his demise, which had made the operation possible, British 'doctors' spoke as if the momentous struggle then in progress was but a temporary stilling of traditional rivalries with their French and Russian colleagues. The de Bunsen report referred to the 'known or understood aspirations of those who are our Allies today, but may be our competitors tomorrow'. Kitchener was more direct. In a memorandum of 16 March 1915, he wrote :

We have in fact to assume that, at some future date, we may find ourselves at enmity with Russia, or with France, or with both in combination, and we must bear this possibility in mind in deciding how, when the time for settlement comes and the question of the partition of Turkey arises, our interests can best be safeguarded.

Thus the lines of peace had to be drawn in a manner that would provide depth and strategic manoeuvrability in the event of future war, particularly with Russia. The underlying theme was a fatalistic acceptance that the Middle East, cross-roads of three continents, could hardly be insulated from Great Power rivalries.

Britain's strategic line had to embrace on all sides her vital interests in the area. Kitchener knew them from personal preoccupation as Commander-in-Chief in India and, subsequently, as Agent-General in Egypt. For years he had been planning British defence in the Middle East in the event of war and thinking of the permanent lines of British influence in the event of the disappearance of the Ottoman Empire. He had felt the clouds gather. A visit to Constantinople in 1910 convinced him 'we are out of it altogether and the German is allowed to do as he likes'. And as he wrote in 1915, 'In consequence of Russia having become a Mediterranean power . . . and of France being established herself in Syria in close proximity to the Nile Delta, the strategical situation in Egypt will be considerably influenced . . . our communication with India by the Suez Canal might be seriously endangered and Egypt itself might be placed in considerable jeopardy . . .' Egypt was already in British hands ; Mesopotamia had now to follow suit. 'If we do not take Mesopotamia, the Russians undoubtedly will sooner or later. This would give them an outlet into the Persian Gulf . . .' Mesopotamia, Kitchener further explained, would be important for Britain because of its potential agricultural resources, as an ideal colonization field for the surplus population of India. 'Its possession is also necessary to guard our interests in the Persian oil-fields and to control the land route from the Mediterranean to the Persian Gulf, which will eventually become our most direct and quickest line of communication with India.'

Egypt and Suez needed a cover on the eastern Mediterranean coast. The most feasible point, in Kitchener's view, was Alexandretta. As he explained to the War Council, 'With Russia in Constantinople, France in Syria and Italy in Rhodes, our position in Egypt would be untenable if any other power held Alexandretta.' Alexandretta's importance for the defence of Mesopotamia is set forth in the 16 March memorandum. British reinforcement could reach Mesopotamia by rail from Alexandretta in a fortnight less than it would take them to get there by sea via the Suez Canal, Red Sea and Persian Gulf. Any attempted advance southwards of Russian forces from the highlands of Armenia and Kurdistan would have its flank exposed to a British advance from about Aleppo. British occupation of Mesopotamia would, it is true, offer the Russians a prolonged flank for possible attack from Armenia and Kurdistan. It was to be hoped that from the remains of the Ottoman Empire, a buffer Turkish or Armenian state from Anatolia to the Persian border would interpose. 'But even a frontier coterminous with Russia, with all its grave drawbacks, would be preferable to a Franco-Russian domination of the line from the Gulf of Iskanderrun to the Persian Gulf . . . Alexandretta is quite outside Syria so that the French have no real established . . . claim to the place . . . Syria alone will well repay them.'

The broad structure of Kitchener's strategic concept was accepted by the de Bunsen committee and became British policy. But with one major difference : Haifa was substituted for Alexandretta. Alexandretta was a better port, but the French would resent their zone of interest in Cilicia and Syria being sundered by a British presence. The railway from Alexandretta would be at French mercy and would approach closer to Russian territory than was desirable. Haifa, on the other hand, could be developed into a good port and could be connected by railway with Mesopotamia. Moreover, as the de Bunsen report noted, 'if Alexandretta were acquired by Great Britain, France could not be refused the southern part of Syria, which would bring her frontier into Arabia, a situation which we could hardly tolerate'. Haifa had been suggested by Committee of Imperial Defence before the war as a point for the landing of British troops to block a large-scale attempt to invade Egypt. Sykes, who supported Haifa against Alexandretta, wrote that this was the 'only real point of difference' between Kitchener and himself. He claimed that Kitchener was 'reluctantly reconciled to Haifa'.*

In sum, then, the de Bunsen report defined British desiderata, in the event of partition of the Ottoman Empire, as the annexation of the vilayets of Basra, Baghdad and the greater part of Mosul, with a port on the eastern Mediterranean, at Haifa, and British railway connection between this port and Mesopotamia. The floor of the British zone would be from Aqaba to the Persian Gulf, the sides running from Acre on the west and Basra on the east to Mosul on the apex. The report drew on military, political and economic reasons (including oil considerations) to explain why it would not be feasible to hold the Basra vilayet without taking the Baghdad vilayet to the north, and why, once the latter was in British hands, the greater part of the Mosul vilayet was required.

At the outbreak of war with Turkey in November 1914, Asquith declared publicly that 'it is the Ottoman Government . . . not we who have rung the death-knell of Ottoman dominion not only in Europe but in Asia . . . the Turkish Empire has committed suicide, and dug with its own hand its grave . . .' Lloyd George described the Turk as 'a human cancer, a creeping agony who was to be called to final account . . .' Brave words, indeed, yet a little hasty. In the spring of 1915 the de Bunsen committee considered partition of the Ottoman Empire as one of four possibilities for the post-war settlement. It did not recommend it. There were several reasons. If the Ottoman Empire in Asia were dismembered,

*On Kitchener and the question of Palestine in 1915, see also M. Vereté, *Middle Eastern Studies*, May 1973.

the Turks would continue to fight even after the fall of Constantinople, which it was hoped would shortly be the result of the Gallipoli campaign. Also, the destruction of the political power of Islam, as represented by Turkey, coupled with British annexation of Mesopotamia, would spell for all Moslems the end of the hope for an Arab Khalifat in a significant Moslem state. Besides, Britain would have to increase her direct responsibilities and expenditure for defence.

The committee considered three alternatives to partition : to maintain the Turkish Ottoman Empire as a state, with zones of interest assigned to each of the Allied Powers ; to leave unimpaired the Empire's status in name and in fact, as before the war ; or the latter proposal modified by a decentralization of government on federal lines. Under all proposals Turkey would have to yield Constantinople to Russia, probably Smyrna to Greece and the Basra vilayet, whole or part, to Britain. All three plans would be a basis for negotiations immediately on the fall of Constantinople, thus freeing British forces from the Turkish front. In all three plans the Turkish Moslem state would survive and thus Indian Moslem feeling would be soothed.

Loosely defined zones of interest by nature lead to friction. They would be considered by the other powers to be temporary and provisional, and the inherent effectiveness of the Turkish Government would compound the instability of the arrangement. On the other hand, if left untouched, the Empire would become a playground for Russian political intrigue and for France's 'Levantine' financial machinations, 'and in Turkey these are the only means by which political or financial power is to be achieved or maintained'. The third plan of a decentralized system of administration thus seemed to the de Bunsen Committee to be the most feasible from the British standpoint. Turkey in Asia, the Committee pointed out, falls ethnographically and historically into five great provinces – Anatolia, Armenia, Syria, Palestine and Iraq-Jazirah. Since anyway Constantinople would leave Turkish control, it would be necessary to replace the centralized machine of government. A decentralized scheme would be in harmony with the aspirations of large sections of Ottoman subjects in all regions. Should it fail, there was always a good chance that several autonomous states might arise – Turkey proper in Anatolia, an Armenian and an Arab federation under the nominal suzerainty of the Sultan. Britain would be free from any immediate military responsibility. If the scheme were successful, Britain would pursue her enterprise in Palestine and Iraq-Jazirah (the areas of British influence under plans of partition or zones of interest) free from military obligations ; should the Empire fall to pieces, Britain could declare the two areas as independent states under British protection, annex them, or declare them to be British.

Palestine was another major calculation in bringing the de Bunsen Committee to recommend the maintenance of the Ottoman Empire in a decentralized form. In the planning of Britain's strategic future in the

Middle East, Palestine came more and more into focus. In the words of one of the military experts whose analysis was considered by the committee : 'Mesopotamia and Egypt – with Palestine as the connecting link between the two – are British interests.' France's claim to the Holy Land was historically entrenched in the traditional guardianship of the Catholic interest. It was part of the broader claim to Syria, of which Palestine was the southern province under the Ottomans. In 1840 Britain had blocked a French take-over of the whole of Syria by proxy through Muhammad Ali who had come up from Egypt supported by the French. France's acknowledgment, early in this century, of Egypt belonging to the British sphere of influence, only spurred on her effort to assure for herself a predominant status in Syria. In Syria, including Palestine, France was at once the major foreign investor, the patron of education, the emissary of religion. Just before the war she had received concessions from the Turks for further development of her investments in the railways in Syria, planning an extension southward to link up with the French-owned Jaffa–Jerusalem railway, but meeting with British opposition when she projected a further link southwards to El Arish. Haifa and Jaffa were to join Tripoli as beneficiaries of French port development. The railroads might give France access to Egypt, the ports enhance her naval power in the eastern Mediterranean. As the Chairman of the Foreign affairs Committee of the French Parliament put it in October 1914, 'The Mediterranean will not be free for us . . . unless Syria remains in our sphere of influence. By Syria must be understood, not a Syria mutilated . . . but Syria in its entirety . . . from El-Arish to the Taurus.' In 1912 the French became suspicious that Kitchener from Egypt was dabbling in Syria. Britain's Foreign Secretary, Sir Edward Grey, assured the French Ambassador in London that Britain was not engaged in 'intrigues in Syria and we had no intentions or aspirations respecting it'. However, once Britain decided it had to have Haifa as the hub of security for both Egypt and Mesopotamia, it could not tolerate France in possession of Palestine south of Haifa. France would then be a neighbour of Egypt and Arabia : the future danger was clear. The present alliance restricted the possibilities of obviating it – but not for Mark Sykes. He suggested to the de Bunsen Committee that in the event of partition, the British region comprise in the west the territory from Acre to Egypt. In a division of spheres of interest in a surviving Ottoman Empire, this area would be included in the British sphere. In order to counter-balance French pressures, he added a suggestion on the establishment of a special Russian administration in an enclave comprising the regions of Jerusalem, Bethlehem and Jaffa. A Catholic was espousing the Orthodox interest for Protestant Britain's strategic needs !

The proposal to claim Palestine for Britain had already been advanced by Lloyd George. At the first Cabinet meeting that considered the future of the Ottoman Empire, on 9 November 1914, he had spoken of the 'destiny of Palestine'. The following March, at a War Council meeting, he suggested the occupation of Palestine by Britain and was known to support Samuel's scheme for a British protectorate over the country. He and Sykes had to wait two years till the interlocking of Lloyd George's personal destiny with the tides of the war assured British control of Palestine.

In 1915 the de Bunsen Committee did not consider feasible a claim for the retention of Palestine by Britain. At the same time, the Committee consoled itself with the thought that 'the forces opposed are too great for France ever to make her claim good'. Britain could count on 'Russian support in return for sympathy for Russian views in regard to Palestine'. In view of the unique universal character of Palestine, the Committee proposed that 'the country's destiny must be the subject of special negotiations, in which both belligerents and neutrals are alike interested.' This was a hint of possible internationalization. In his memorandum to the Committee, General Sir Edward Barrow of the Indian Office had suggested that Palestine be administered as an autonomous province of the Turkish Empire by an international commission under the protection of the Allied Powers. His memorandum contained the interesting observation that 'any attempt by one of the powers to acquire a special privileged position [in Palestine] would be resented by the rest . . . and would speedily lead to that Armageddon in the Valley of Esdraelon which has terrified the imagination of the world for ages past'. The Committee felt that one of the advantages of the decentralization scheme, which they favoured, was that it could put off the need for a decision on Palestine. 'By granting local autonomy in Palestine the question of the Holy Places would be left in an unprejudiced position.' Palestine would become an Arab province under Turkish suzerainty. Britain, they must have thought, would have time to buttress her sphere of interest there in preparation for all eventualities. Should the consensus of the Allies be against decentralization and in favour of either partition or the scheme of zones of interest, the French at any rate would be denied exclusive control of Palestine.

III   Britain And The Arabs

During its deliberations in the spring of 1915, the de Bunsen Committee had before it the Russian and French maps. On 30 June the Committee submitted its proposed British map. A few weeks later, Sir Henry McMahon, the British High Commissioner in Egypt, transmitted to London the Arab map for a post-war settlement in the Middle East. It was dated the second day in Ramadan 1333, that is 14 July 1915. It was submitted by Husain Ibn Ali, the Grand Sharif of Mecca, of the noblest Arab stock, whose linear affiliation extended back directly to the daughter of the prophet, at the dawn of Islamic history. Husain under the Turks was the ruler of the Hejaz, an inhospitable desert running north-west 800 miles from Hali on the Red Sea and Mecca to Aqaba and Ma'an. To the south lay the province of Asir controlled by the Idrisi, beyond that the Yemen of the Imam, where the Turks for decades had been facing fitful insurrections against their attempt to impose their authority. The interior fastness of Yemen proved its impregnability to the Turkish Sultan then, just as it was to defy Nasser of Egypt fifty years later. To the east, on the Persian Gulf, the dynasties of Rashid and Saud battled with each other, the redoubtable Abdul-Aziz Ibn Saud commencing his career of military conquest, which ultimately was to make the whole of Arabia his province. From Kuwait at the head of the Persian Gulf to Aden on the south-west tip of the peninsula, the coast was studded with several Arab principalities with which the Indian Government had entered into treaty relations in the nineteenth century, Aden having been occupied by British forces in 1839 as Muhammed Ali of Egypt was making his northwards thrust into the heart of the Ottoman Empire. The paltry existence of some of these territories was supported by British subsidies. When their sun-scorched terrain laid bare liquid treasure, they were to subsidize Britain's balance of payments.

Husain had returned to Mecca from Constantinople in 1908 endowed with the title of Grand Sharif, enshrining the guardianship of the Holy Places. He had gained permission to return from the Young Turks, after Sultan Abdul Hamid had brought him from Mecca and kept him at his side for fifteen years in distinguished confinement. He had been suspected by the Sultan as being a possible rival in Islam. Shortly after his return to Mecca he was seen as an obstacle to the Young Turk policy of centralization. He opposed the extension to Mecca of the Hejaz railway from Damascus to Medina. This railway line was opened in 1908. It had been ostensibly undertaken by the Sultan to provide a short route for the pilgrimage to Mecca instead of the long route by caravan, or by sea through the Suez to the Red Sea coast. Its strategic purpose was to draw Arabia closer to Constantinople. Paradoxically, it emphasized the physical, as well as other, distances between Damascus and Mecca.

Husain was watched closely by the Turkish *vali* or governor. He feared the Turks were planning to depose him. His fears were not without basis. In February 1914, Amir Abdullah, the second son of Husain, opened his half-century involvement with Britain by a visit to Kitchener at the British Residency in Cairo. He wanted to enquire on the availability of British support for the resistance his father and his followers would evince should the Turks try to depose Husain. Kitchener was non-committal. Mecca interested him, as did the Red Sea coast of the Hejaz, from which, in war, Turks and Germans could threaten

British shipping and despatch agents into Egypt and Sudan. It was dangerous and premature to add to the existing strain in Turco-British relations. Storrs was instructed to maintain discreet contact with Abdullah for every eventuality. They played chess together ; in the small, dapper, poker-faced scion of the prophetic house, whose retiring demeanour was more subtlety than spirituality, Storrs may have seen a future pawn. Abdullah may have seen himself as a future king on the British chess-board. Both would have been right.

Their game became serious as, with the outbreak of the war in Europe, the shuddering barometer in Constantinople forecast an early Turkish alignment with Germany. With Kitchener's approval from London, Storrs, at the end of September, sent a secret message to his chess partner in Mecca. It contained an enquiry as to where the Arabs would stand if Turkey joined the conflict against the Allies. The reply in late October 1914 was non-committal, but not negative.

The Turco-Arab relationship was complex. For five centuries they had been interwoven in the common tapestry of Islam against the successive encroachments of alien Christian powers. Throughout the nineteenth century and up to the war, revolutionary fires against Ottoman rule ignited each other across the Balkans. In the years immediately before the war, Turkey had suffered violent haemorrhages of blood and territory in the Balkan wars and in the Italo-Turkish war in North Africa. Except for the mutterings of a few secret societies in Syria and for the claims of open societies for more constitutional understanding, the Arabs, who constituted half the population of the Ottoman Empire, had not stirred. Their grievance was against the lack of Turkish regard for the Arab language and against the devious methods by which Arab representation in government and parliament was restricted. George Antonius, in *The Arab Awakening,* dates the birth of the Arab nationalist movement to the last quarter of the nineteenth century. It was slow and limited in growth. Arab nationalist consciousness became acute in the measure that the Young Turks pressed their programme of centralization on the non-Turks of the Empire. The Arabs sought reform and autonomy within the Turkish framework, not its sundering apart. In 1913 they were talking of local autonomy or of a joint Turco-Arab Empire. With the proclamation of general mobilization by Turkey in August 1914, existing Arab ranks in the Turkish Army were replenished, and new Arab divisions were formed. Arab soldiers fought at the side of the Turks throughout the war on all fronts ; defections were minimal. Until the last days of the Ottoman Empire, Arab nationalism never assumed comprehensive proportions. By 1914 there were, however, seeds of estrangement in Arabia and in Syria which held out hope for the British.

With Husain of Mecca, personal fears and ambitions found self-justification in the general bitterness of the non-Turkish subjects of the Ottoman Empire. The theme of pan-Turkism, increasingly preached in

Constantinople, made it easier to identify pan-Islam with reservations about Turkish rule, particularly as the Young Turks combined their policy of centralization with a lack of emphasis on the tenets of Islam. A Constantinople régime riddled with European ideology could hardly be the standard-bearer of an Islamic revival. Above all, Husain knew that if the Turks were defeated, his dynasty would be safe. Their defeat would not be a blow to Islam if Arab hegemony filled the vacuum. Still, to go it alone might end in traitorous isolation, to say nothing of the awaited reprisals by the Turkish forces in Husain's bodyguard. Hamlet-like, he held counsel with his three sons in their Mecca fortress. He needed to consult with fellow chieftains in Arabia and with the incipient nationalist movement in Damascus.

When Turkey finally threw in its lot with Germany, the conflicting pressures on Husain grew. The Turks requested the adherence of Mecca to the jihad proclaimed by the Sultan from Constantinople. Husain sent the prophet's standard from Mecca to Damascus to symbolize his identification with the offensive being planned against the Suez Canal. From Damascus it was ceremoniously transferred to the Al-Aqsa mosque in Jerusalem, where it remained indefinitely, awaiting transportation on the victory march to Egypt. Husain's signature on the jihad did not reach Damascus with the standard. The lacuna was explained by fear of a blockade of the Hejaz coast by British warships. Conversely, Kitchener's appeal to Husain for adhesion to Britain did not elicit a final positive response, on the grounds that precipitate action would result in crushing Turkish reprisals.

From March to May 1915, Feisal, the youngest and most cautious of Husain's three sons, paid an official visit to Damascus and Constantinople. He explained to the Turkish rulers his father's hesitations regarding formal adherence to their cause. At the same time, he discussed with the leaders of the two Arab secret societies, al-Fatat and al-'Ahd, the terms that would make it worthwhile to abandon hesitations on formally joining Britain. He returned to Mecca with the Damascus Protocol. If this were accepted by Britain 'the Arab divisions in Syria would rise to a man' in revolt against the Turkish oppressors. But the Arab divisions continued to fight on the side of Turkey, and the Syrians acclaimed Allenby's troops as they passed through Syrian cities and deliriously welcomed Lawrence when he led Feisal into Damascus. They became adept in fomenting tension and war in which others had to live and die.

The Damascus Protocol called for the recognition by Britain of the independence of the Arab countries within a rectangle whose extreme north-western point was Mersina in Asia Minor and whose extreme north-eastern point was Amadia on the Persian frontier, the eastern frontier stretching down to the Persian Gulf, the southern being on the Indian Ocean, but excluding Aden, the western on the Red Sea and the Mediterranean. In return, a defensive alliance between Britain and the future Arab state was offered, together with an assurance of economic preference for Britain.

On 14 July 1915, Abdullah wrote to Storrs, enclosing a letter from Husain to McMahon, the British High Commissioner in Egypt. In it was set forth the Damascus Protocol with some additional points, including particularly the request that Britain agree to the proclamation of an Arab Khalifat for Islam. There was no need to mention the candidate, for his signature was on the enclosed letter. In London, the Arab map for the post-war settlement of the Middle East was thrown into the hamper to rub shoulders with the Russian, French and British versions.

The tribal chieftain of Hejaz was to become Britain's partner in dialogue on the future Middle East. He transmitted overall Arab demands and was to be the recipient of the overall assurances. He, and others, became convinced that he and his family should be their rightful beneficiaries. Kitchener's second message of 31 October 1914 had merely promised the integrity of Husain's position and territory. In April 1915, the Sirdar of Sudan, through the Sudanese Moslem leader Sayyed Ali el-Mirghani, had transmitted assurances that the 'Arabian Peninsula and its Moslem Holy Places should remain in the hands of an independent Moslem State', adding, 'Exactly how much territory should be included in this State it is not possible to define at this stage.' Guarantees of support against external aggression enabled the Indian Government to conclude agreements with other chieftains in Arabia – the Idrisi of Asir and Ibn Saud of Najd.

In June 1915, the de Bunsen Committee noted the absence of any dominant government or chief in Arabia. It proposed independence for some chieftains, autonomy under the Turks for the others, one of whom was Husain. This certainly did not relate to the Arabs in Syria and Mesopotamia. By then all strands of British thought and assessment had been taken into account. Husain was not bound by the evolution of British imperial thought. Kitchener's message to him of October 1914 had also pan-Islamic and pan-Arab undertones, with Husain implied as the first Arab Khalif in five centuries who was invited to proclaim the 'good tidings of the freedom of the Arabs'. In the aftermath of the war the paradoxical outcome was that the Hashemite dynasty lost the Hejaz and was expelled from Arabia, finding its continuity under British auspices in Iraq and Jordan. Arab nationalism from the start became entangled in the triple circle of the nation-state, pan-Arabism and pan-Islam.

When Husain's message of July 1915 reached London, additional British divisions were converging on the Aegean for the final act of the Gallipoli drama. The heights that defied them were manned in comity by Arab and Turkish troops. The Arab troops showed no recognition of the Turks as oppressors or of the British as liberators. If the heights had yielded to British arms, Husain's message would probably have remained an exotic wartime episode. At Gallipoli the Turks won the battles, but lost their Empire. Turkey remained in the war. There could be no peace with an Ottoman Empire. Once the hope of knocking off the head of the Ottoman Empire vanished, there remained only the long road of hacking away at the body, limb by limb. The Arabs lay astride the limbs. The British-Arab dialogue entered its crucial stage.

IV   Britain and the Jews

The Jewish claim to Palestine was voiced during the first stage of map-drawing, alongside French, Russian, British and Arab claims. Its protagonist was unexpected. On 9 November 1914, a few days after Turkey's entry into the European war, the British Cabinet held its first discussion on the hypothetical post-war disposition of the Ottoman Empire. After the meeting, Herbert Samuel, then a member of the Cabinet as President of the Local Government Board, spoke to Grey, the Foreign Secretary, of 'the opportunity for the fulfilment of the ancient aspiration of the Jewish people and the restoration there of a Jewish State'. Samuel prefaced his suggestion by observing that the 'jealousies of the great European powers would make it difficult to allot Palestine to any one of them'. A Jewish state in Palestine, Samuel pointed out, might become a 'fountain of enlightenment'. It would inspire the Jewish people throughout the world to raise their standards and character, thus adding to 'their usefulness to the peoples among whom they lived'. He suggested 'that British influence ought to play a considerable part in the promotion of such a state because the geographical situation of Palestine, and especially its proximity to Egypt, would render its goodwill to England a matter of importance to the British Empire.'

The creation of a new state would be a most formidable undertaking, but Samuel was convinced that Jewish communities throughout the world would provide the funds to 'buy out existing interests of individuals and to lay the foundation of the State'. Samuel thought that Russia's cooperation might be forthcoming, as her support for the 're-establishment of the Jewish State' would gain for her the loyalty of her Jewish subjects, those in Russia proper and those recently brought within her orbit by the advance of her armies into Poland. This loyalty could, of course, be obtained by the granting of equal rights to Jewish subjects, but Samuel doubted if Russian public opinion would allow the Russian Government to take this course.

Grey declared himself 'favourable to the proposal and . . . prepared to work for it if the opportunity arose', adding that 'if any proposals were put forward by France or any other Power with regard to Syria, it would be important not to acquiesce in any plan which would be inconsistent with the creation of a Jewish State in Palestine'.

Three months later, in February 1915, Samuel spoke again to Grey. The tenor on either side had changed. Instead of turning Palestine forthwith into a Jewish state upon its liberation from the Turks, Samuel spoke of constituting it as a British Protectorate, with active encouragement for Jewish colonization and cultural development. Grey was 'indisposed to assume for the British Empire fresh military and diplomatic responsibilities'. He spoke of neutralizing the country 'under international guarantee', with the Holy Places under an international commission and the government vested in a Jewish council. Alternatively, the suzerainty of Turkey might continue with a régime on the Lebanese pattern but with a governor appointed by the Powers. Samuel 'expressed a doubt whether the Arab population, who numbered five-sixths of the inhabitants, would accept such a government' and also pointed out 'the risk that an international government might end in some European State becoming dominant . . . If Germany had possessed Palestine before the outbreak of this war, she could have prepared a most formidable attack on Egypt.'

In January 1915, Samuel had set forth his ideas in a memorandum, which he transmitted to the Prime Minister and Grey. In mid-March he circulated a revised version to members of the Cabinet. By then, the Dardanelles campaign was gathering momentum and Britain had acknowledged the Russian claim to Constantinople. The internal British debate on British desiderata in a post-war Middle Eastern settlement was moving from general theorizing to precise map-drawing. Samuel's memorandum ruled out three prevalent alternatives for Palestine : (1)   annexation by France ('a great European power so close to the Suez Canal would be a continual and formidable menace . . .') ; (2)   retention by Turkey ('unthinkable') ; (3)   internationalization ('a stepping-stone to a German protectorate'). He also discarded a fourth alternative, which he himself had advocated only a short time previously. This was 'the establishment of an autonomous Jewish State'. He explained that 'it is certain that the time is not ripe for it . . . to attempt to realize the aspiration of a Jewish State one century too soon might throw back its actual realization for many centuries more'. A few weeks later, in a conversation with the representative of the Conjoint Committee of British Jewry, he explained that 'something would have to be done . . . the Jews would seem to be insensible to their great traditions if they did nothing . . . immediate political privileges would be impossible, partly because the Jews were in a minority in Palestine and partly because any attempt at a Jewish State would at this moment fail with very great scandal to the whole of Jewry'. Thirty years later, in his *Memoirs,* Samuel recalled his thoughts in early 1915 :

At some time, perhaps, a Jewish State might come about in the course of events ; but so long as the great majority of the inhabitants were Arabs it was out of the question . . . At the same time, it was not necessary to accept the position that the existing population, sparse as it was, should have the right to bar the door to the return of a people whose connection with the country long antedated their own, especially as it had resulted in events of spiritual and cultural value to mankind in striking contrast with the barren record of the last two thousand years.

Samuel's solution was a British Protectorate for Palestine with facilities for Jewish land purchase, for the founding of colonies, for the establishment of educational and religious institutions, for cooperation in the economic development of the country ; 'and that Jewish immigration, carefully regulated, would be given preference, so that in the course of time the Jewish inhabitants growing into a majority and settled in the land, may be conceded such degree of self-government as the conditions of that day might justify'.

Samuel was a liberal thinker and liberal imperialist. The thesis of the first was that with patient and gradual treatment the ills, stresses and conflicts of mankind could be progressively cured ; the thesis of the second was that imperial interests required a moral justification. The Jewish people was viewed against the canvas of the great patterns of universal history. If alone of all peoples it was to be denied self-fulfilment, the aim of universal justice would be impinged upon. This fulfilment could not be achieved by emancipation alone. In any event, emancipation seemed remote from the great masses of Jewry in Eastern Europe, while in Western countries there was growing irritation at the large number of Jewish immigrants from Eastern Europe. Moreover, the image of the Jew in Western countries had little relevance to his historical birthright and memory, and to his potentialities for mankind. It could be assumed that the peoples of the Middle East would take the gradual course to natural self-expression, sustained and guided by the shield of a benevolent imperialism. The Arabs were considered one racial and religious entity across the vast expanses of the Middle East. As they were liberated from centuries of Turkish subjugation, they surely would not begrudge the Jew his return to that small piece of territory on the eastern coast of the Mediterranean, which had been linked with him from time immemorial and apart from whom it had never achieved national identity or association. Wedded to the moral impulse, the imperial interest found justification ; in the union, the former acquired an overriding quality, and the assessment regarding the development of Arab reaction and the comity of British and Jewish interests were rapidly to founder. The moral assessment has survived sixty years of ceaseless debate on the conflicting claims of Arab and Jew.

Samuel was a Jew. Under his urbane, unflappable, passionless, pragmatic, characteristically British demeanour, there were deep strands of Jewish religious sentiment and historical involvement. 'If Palestine was to be given a new destiny,' he wrote in his *Memoirs,* 'Great Britain, with her important strategic interests in the Middle East, was directly concerned . . . for myself the matter had an additional and special interest. The first member of the Jewish community ever to sit in a British Cabinet (Disraeli having, when a child, been withdrawn from the community by his father) it was incumbent upon me at least to learn what the Zionist movement was . . .' His family background, four generations in Britain, his total integration into British political and intellectual life, his apparent freedom from passion and sentiment, hardly seemed to cast him among the seekers of the peace of Jerusalem. On receipt of Samuel's memorandum, Prime Minister Asquith expressed wonderment at the 'lyrical outburst proceeding from the well-ordered and methodical brain of H.S.', seeing in it an illustration of Disraeli's maxim that 'race is everything'. At the other pole of the incipient dialogue, Weizmann, coming in December 1914 to try to convert Samuel to a Zionist approach, found himself being upbraided for the modest nature of his demands and being told that 'big things would have to be done in Palestine . . . the Jews would have to bring sacrifices, and he [Samuel] was prepared to do so . . . He also thinks that perhaps the Temple may be rebuilt as a symbol of Jewish unity – of course in a modernized form . . .' Stupefied, Weizmann replied that if 'I were a religious Jew I should have thought the Messianic times were near. . .'

Six years later, Samuel, as first British High Commissioner in Palestine, read in the Hurva synagogue in the Old City of Jerusalem the weekly section of the Prophets. He and the thousands of Jews present were overtaken by fraternal emotion as he read the passage in Isaiah 'Comfort ye, comfort ye my people, saith your God. Speak ye comfortably to Jerusalem, and cry unto her, that her warfare is accomplished, that her iniquity is pardoned' (40 : 1 – 2). Samuel himself, in later describing the scene, wrote that 'One could almost hear the sigh of generations.' Comfort indeed was to come to Zion, but tragically and not without warfare. Much of this might have been avoided had the policy of Britain in Palestine followed Samuel's original initiative in November 1914 and not his second thoughts of 1915.

It should be added that the demand for a Jewish State – raised by Samuel in November 1914 – did not become the official Zionist programme till 1942 in the throes of World War Two. It was then termed the 'Biltmore programme', after the New York hotel in which, in 1942, David Ben-Gurion formulated it. The theme of gradual evolution to Jewish self-rule or sovereignty in one form or another, under the auspices of a Great Power, with the interests of the latter simultaneously served – on which Samuel's 1915 memorandum was based – formed the framework of thought in which in 1917 the Balfour Declaration was to be moulded and on which the Zionist's presentation of their case between the two world wars was built. Whatever the final judgement of historians on Samuel's tenure as High Commissioner, he deserves a significant place in Zionist history for having been the first, on the outbreak of the war, to actively espouse the Jewish return – a service which has received scant attention among the chroniclers.

In the period under discussion, 1914–15, Samuel's initiative had little impact. It is not clear if it was ever discussed in the Cabinet. No reference at all is made to it in the de Bunsen Report of June 1915, which recommended British desiderata in the event of Turkey being knocked out of the war. Nor did the report refer to any Zionist activity at that time ; in fact there was not much to which to refer.

With the outbreak of the war, the Zionist Organization was caught off balance. The central office was in Berlin, and the German Zionists believed in a German victory. In any event, Germany was looked to as the Power that could exercise effective good offices with its Turkish ally to safeguard the Jewish community in Palestine, many of whom, as Russian citizens, were suspect to the Turkish authorities. In Russia, Jews secretly hoped that a German victory would release them from Czarist oppression. In neutral America, a provisional committee for Zionist affairs was set up, headed by Louis Brandeis, later to become an outstanding member of the Supreme Court of the United States. Weizmann unsuccessfully suggested that the central responsibility for Zionist activities be transferred to this committee. A meeting of the General Zionist Council at Copenhagen in December 1914 decided to leave the central office in Berlin and to establish an adjunct in neutral Denmark. It was further decided to draw the American Provisional Committee into activity in the interests of the Jewish community in Palestine. Nahum Sololow – a member of the Zionist Executive – was dispatched to England for political activity. As a general principle, it was laid down that no negotiations could be undertaken by the Zionist executive with the government of any country at war with Turkey.

Weizmann was in England. He had been there since 1904 as a lecturer in chemistry at Manchester University. He was a member of the Zionist General Council but not of the executive, having become prominent at Zionist congresses through his espousal of 'practical Zionism'. With the outbreak of war he was convinced of ultimate Allied victory and that this would bring Palestine within the sphere of England. 'We – given more or less good conditions – could easily move a million Jews into Palestine within the next fifty to sixty years, and England would have an effective barrier [betwen the Suez Canal and the Black Sea] and we would have a country . . . ' He began to weave his contacts with leading personalities, including C. P. Scott, the influential editor of the *Manchester Guardian,* Samuel, Lloyd George, then Chancellor of the Exchequer, and Mr and Mrs James de Rothschild, who opened for him the doors to the British hierarchy. However, he was operating without official Zionist authority, his access was limited, and his preoccupation with his personal problem of becoming absorbed (as a scientist) in the British war effort limited the time he could devote to Zionist activities. Moreover, he had no knowledge of the British Government deliberations, in the spring and into the summer of 1915, on British policy in the Middle East in the event of a successful Gallipoli offensive and Turkey forced into making a separate peace. During those crucial months neither Weizmann nor any other Zionist representative apparently met Kitchener, Grey or Asquith, the decisive Cabinet figures in formulating a new Middle Eastern policy ; nor was a Zionist memorandum submitted to any address for circulation. Had the Gallipoli Campaign succeeded, and had Turkey then made a separate peace, Palestine, under the de Bunsen Committee's recommendations, would have become an autonomous Arab province of the Turkish Empire, or an internationalized area if the Empire were dissolved. In either event the Zionist hope would possibly have been quenched. In 1915 the Zionist leadership could have been no more aware of the paradoxical fact that the Zionist dream hung on the failure of British arms to break through the six miles on the Gallipoli Peninsula to the Narrows, than their forefathers at the end of the eighteenth century could have realized that Napoleon's invasion of Egypt and Palestine had first stirred Britain to a realization of the crucial importance of the Middle East, including Palestine, to the imperial interest. It was this realization that, over a century later, finally matured into a British determination to hold on to Palestine in the post-war settlement, which, in turn, made British patronage of Zionism at the time part of the Pax Britannica.

V   Palestine and the 'Pax Britannica'

By the spring of 1917, a British decision had been taken that Palestine should be under British control in any post-war settlement as part of Pax Britannica in the Middle East. At the same time, the nexus between British control and Zionism was established. This development, during the years 1914–17, went through two distinct stages : first, from the outbreak of the war with Turkey to June 1915 ; second, from the summer of 1915 till the spring of 1917, when British troops were poised to enter Palestine.

As soon as war broke out with Turkey, the British official mind became occupied with the question of assuring, in any post-war settlement, a land route to India, the defence of the Suez Canal and a land link from the Mediterranean to Mesopotamia. This concern was already reflected in British actions during the very first few weeks of the war. British interest in the Middle East hinged on the Suez Canal and Mesopotamia, and this spelled exclusion of attempted German control and prevention of Russian incursions into the area. This was the background to Disraeli's acquisition of Cyprus in the Congress of Berlin (1878) and Grey's near-ultimatum to the Sultan in 1906, to move Egypt's frontier in the north-east to the Rafa-Aqaba line : he feared possible attack from the north. The importance of Palestine for Egypt's defence had apparently been fixed in British minds by 1914.

Concern with Palestine was not entirely new in British imperial thinking : as far back as 1840, Palmerston, the Foreign Secretary, had urged the Sultan to allow the settlement of Jews, among whom he had detected a 'strong notion' that 'the time is approaching when their nation is to return to Palestine'. The question in 1914, however, was what Britain ought to do about the country, and several strands of thought were found in conflict.

Under Gallipoli, the 'Indian school', which opposed the dismemberment of the Ottoman Empire, was in the ascendancy. Its thinking – also accepted to a considerable extent by the Foreign Office – was reflected by the de Bunsen Committee Report. By the summer of 1915, this 'school' seemed to have won the policy battle with the decision to maintain the Ottoman Empire intact – after the fall of Constantinople and the conclusion of peace. Palestine – as it has already been pointed out – would then become an autonomous Arab province, like Syria and Mesopotamia, with Arabia alone remaining semi-independent. The Jewish case was almost completely ignored.

The *débâcle* in Gallipoli set in motion the second stage of the nexus between British control of Palestine and Zionism. It saw the defeat of the Indian by the Cairo-Khartoum school. The rationale of the latter approach was hinted at by Ronald Storrs, who wrote in a letter of March 1915 of 'A North African or near eastern [British] Vice-royalty, including Egypt and the Sudan and across the way from Aden to Alexandretta'. In a letter dated August of that year, Reginald Wingate, Governor of the Sudan, explained to the Foreign Secretary in London and to the Indian Viceroy that British-sponsored pan-Arabism would serve as an antidote to the Ottoman rulers' pan-Islamism. Acknowledging difficulties, he nevertheless foresaw 'in the dim future a federation of semi-independent Arab States . . . under European guidance and supervision, linked together by racial and linguistic bonds, owing spiritual allegiance to a single Arab primate, and looking to Great Britain as its patron and protector'.* He therefore urged support for the Sharifian cause, agreeing with Colonel G. F. Clayton, chief of intelligence in Cairo, that the Sharif possessed most of the attributes considered by Moslems essential for the Khalifat and was also the most suitable from the British point of view.

Both quotations are from Eli Kedourie, *The Chatham House Version,* 17.

The case was put succinctly, in operational terms, by General Sir John Maxwell, Officer Commanding in Egypt, in a cable dated 12 October, urging Kitchener, the War Secretary, to meet the Sharif's wishes :

> A powerful organization with considerable influence in the [Ottoman] army and among Arab Chiefs (viz : The Young Arab Committee) appears to have made up its mind that the moment for action has arrived. The Turks and Germans are already in negotiations with them and spending money to win their support. The Arab party, however, is strongly inclined towards England . . . . If their overtures are rejected, or a reply is delayed . . . the Arab party will go over to the enemy and work with them . . . On the other hand, the active assistance which the Arabs would render in return for our support, would be of the greatest value in Arabia, Mesopotamia, Syria and Palestine.

This assessment was based on imaginative reports of an Arab officer, Muhammad al-Faruqi – a member of the above-mentioned young Arab 'powerful organization' – about Arab intentions and potentialities,* and it led directly to the dispatch of McMahon's crucial letter to Sharif Husain in Mecca twelve days later. This, in turn, made imperative an arrangement with France for a division of spheres of influence and control in the area : indeed, three days earlier (21 October) discussions to that end were already proposed by Grey to the French Ambassador. The result, in May 1916, was the Sykes-Picot Agreement. It represented a heavy concession (in Syria) by France whose representative started the talks by demanding the entire area from the Taurus mountains in the north to El Arish and Aqaba in the south – an area in which the British Foreign Secretary, only three years back, had indicated, albeit somewhat vaguely, political 'disinterest'. The winner, ostensibly in the name of Arab national aspirations, was Britain. It obtained less than what Sykes had schemed for : control of Palestine from Acre to Aqaba, save for a small Jerusalem enclave with an outlet to the sea. But it still obtained a great deal.

The little that was left of the grand French design for 'la Syrie intégrale' was in recognition of Britain's need to have France's cooperation in the struggle against Germany. A strong incentive for the quick conclusion of the Accord, as it was, was information that the Russian Government was flirting with the idea of a separate peace with a new Turkish Government to be headed by Djemal Pasha, which would have kept both Britain and France out of the entire area carved up by Sykes and Picot : Palestine, Syria, Mesopotamia and the Arabian Peninsula. A last-minute French attempt to obtain Russian support for their claim of right to Palestine led only to Russia's extracting some French concessions in Anatolia.

*More about al-Faruqi's mission on page 223 ; Maxwell's cable, in F.O.371/2486 in the Public Record Office.

From the British viewpoint, however, the Agreement was by no means entirely satisfactory. When a general outline of the forthcoming Accord (initialled by Picot and Sykes) was ready in early January 1916, Sykes was taken to task by a number of people in the government for yielding too much to Picot. The Director of Naval Intelligence, Reginald Hall, questioned the need for any agreement with France on spheres of influence in Syria and Iraq in order to get the cooperation of the Arabs. Assuming, however, it was necessary, he still thought France should have been allowed no footing in Palestine. 'South of Tyre', he said, 'she has not so good a claim . . . as . . . ourselves.' He pointed out that Jews throughout the world had not only 'a conscientious and sentimental interest' in the future of Palestine, as mentioned in the Picot-Sykes document, but a 'strong *material* and a very strong *political* interest', and were likely to oppose 'Arab preponderance in the southern Near East'. He therefore suggested that 'In the Brown area [of Palestine, earmarked for international administration] the question of Zionism . . . be considered'.* A Jewish presence, in other words, would fill up the lacuna left by the Sykes-Picot agreement in terms of the defence of Egypt, both from the French and the Arabs.

Between mid-1915 and the spring of 1917, Britain asserted vital imperial interests in any post-war allocation of the Ottoman Empire : she yielded any thought of continuing the traditional policy of banking on the Turks ; reached agreement with France whereby Paris conceded exclusive control of Palestine, while Britain assured herself of a presence in the greater part of the country ; and entered into an alliance with the Arab world under which she gained permanent influence in evolving Arab statehood ; at the same time, she began to take a direct interest in a Jewish presence in Palestine. The key to the final abandonment of the age-old link with the Ottoman Empire lay in the fortunes of the Gallipoli Campaign. The course of the campaign also created a vital and immediate British interest in supporting nascent Arab nationalism.

Towards the end of the summer of 1915, it became clear that British chances of retrieving success from the continuous failure of the Gallipoli operations were rapidly receding. Sir Ian Hamilton, the British Commander in Gallipoli, pressed for further reinforcements and also appealed for action to detach the Arabs from the Turks – about half of the Ottoman troops facing the British in Gallipoli were Arab, and in Mesopotamia, they were nearly all Arab. In September, Sir Ian's appeal achieved credibility from the appearance in Cairo of an Arab officer by the name of al-Faruqi, who had defected from Turkish lines in Gallipoli to come over to the British.

Al-Faruqi was associated with dissident Arab officers in Syria and Mesopotamia. The message he brought to Cairo was : that if Arab demands for a British promise of independence were fulfilled, a general uprising of Arab soldiers there could be expected. Several months later,

*See M. Vereté, *'The Balfour Declaration'* in *Middle Eastern Studies*, January 1970, 54.

he became the emissary in Cairo of Sharif Husain, whose July message to the British was, at first, treated with scepticism. Added to the urgings – both in the Mecca message and in Al Faruqi's – was the threat that unless British support was forthcoming, the Arabs would openly side with Germany and Turkey. (In fact, the Arabs were already by then fully engaged in battle on the Turkish side.)

All this took place against the background of disillusionment in Khartoum and Cairo over the failure, until then, of London to adopt the concept of the Khartoum-Cairo school that the British interest would be best served – not in the short-term alone but also in the long-term – and Britain's position in the Middle East would be best assured by a combination of a British military presence coupled with the effective direction of an Arab state or a confederation led by some outstanding Arab-Islamic figure. All these considerations combined led to a swing away from the de Bunsen recommendations of June 1915 to maintain the Ottoman Empire in Asia intact, with local autonomy in Armenia, Mesopotamia, Syria and Palestine. In the new circumstances, frantic messages were exchanged between Cairo, Khartoum, Simla and London.

The lapsed British-Arab negotiations were renewed. On 24 October, 1915, the British High Commissioner in Egypt, Sir Henry McMahon, with guidance from the Oriental Secretary (Storrs) and the Chief of Military Intelligence (Clayton), wrote to Sharif Husain the famous 'McMahon letter', which was later to be described as a 'Balfour Declaration for the Arabs'. Although London had by then come to favour action with the Arabs, and on the whole approved in principle, albeit with some reservations, the assurances to the Arabs submitted by Cairo, the final text of the McMahon letter was drawn up without the Cabinet's specific endorsement. McMahon was later both praised and criticized for having acted without formal authority. His explanation was that time was running out and that, anyhow, he had Grey's 'authority to act without further reference'.

As events proved, the British acted from a mis-assessment of the situation. The assumption in the autumn of 1915 about the advantage to be gained from an Arab alliance was as unfounded as the assumption, in 1917, of the measure of Jewish capacity to influence the outcome of the war in Britain's favour.

In his message, McMahon told Husain : 'I have . . . lost no time in informing the Government of Great Britain of the contents of your letter, and it is with great pleasure that I communicate to you on their behalf the following statement, which I am confident, you will receive with satisfaction.' The letter then declared Britain's readiness to accept 'the limits demanded' by Husain, but with the exception of 'the two districts of Mersina and Alexandretta, and portions of Syria lying to the west of the districts of Damascus, Homs, Hamma and Aleppo [which] cannot be said to be purely Arab', as well as 'without prejudice to our existing treaties with Arab Chiefs'. Within the remaining frontiers, McMahon's message continues, 'Great Britain is prepared to recognise and support the independence of the Arabs'; but this assurance can only be applicable to 'those regions lying within those frontiers wherein Great Britain is free to act without detriment to the interests of her ally France'. Another reservation respecting the assurance of independence relates to 'the vilayets of Bagdad and Basra', with regard to which McMahon states 'the Arabs will recognise that the established position and interests of Great Britain necessitate special administrative arrangements . . .'

The question whether the accepted frontiers included Palestine hung on the interpretation of the phrase 'west of the districts of Damascus', etc., an area that McMahon excluded from the limits demanded by Husain. Years later, the Arabs were to claim that the meaning of district was no more than district, implying the territories adjacent to the cities, and that Palestine, which lay to the south of the district of Damascus, was accordingly *not* within the area excluded by McMahon. But the British, the Government as well as many officials,* argued that in the 'district of Damascus' a far larger region was meant to be included, in fact the territory south of the city and east of Jordan – thus clearly excluding also Palestine from those western 'portions of Syria . . . [which] cannot be said to be purely Arab', while both McMahon and Sir Gilbert Clayton (who had 'made the preliminary drafts of all the [McMahon] letters to Husain) stated that they never 'intended . . . to include Palestine in the area in which Arab independence was promised'.

In any event, the rider on French interests was crucial. This was also the contention of Lord Maugham, the chairman of the British team of an Arab-British Committee set up by the British Government in 1939 to consider the McMahon-Husain correspondence. 'If there is anything which is certain in this controversy [over the meaning of McMahon's pledge],' he stated, 'it is that Great Britain was not free in October 1915 to act in Palestine without regard to the interests of France.' Accordingly, 'the reservation in respect of French interests . . . not only did exclude Palestine [from the area in which Britain undertook to recognise and support the independence of the Arabs], but should have been understood to do so . . .'

Just as the agreement to yield Constantinople to the Russians in March 1915 set in motion a British definition of her interests in any carving out of the Ottoman Empire, so McMahon's message to Husain was followed by Britain's negotiations with France on the limitations of spheres of control and influence in an ultimate post-war settlement.

On 21 October Grey invited the French Ambassador to begin discussions on the subject, but only a month later did François George-Picot, French ex-Consul-General in Beirut, start his talks with Arthur

---

* The notable exception of Arnold Toynbee, of the Intelligence department of the Foreign Office during the war, must be mentioned.

Nicolson, the Permanent Under-Secretary of the Foreign Office. Nicolson told Picot in general terms of McMahon's negotiations with Husain, proposing that France too recognize the independence of the Arabs. Picot refused, firmly claiming for France northern Iraq and all Syria, down to El Arish and Aqaba. The conference thus came to a dead end, and it took the French Government a month to change its position. Now, at the second meeting, just before Christmas, Picot was forthcoming with substantial concessions, and the parties seemed to agree in principle on the respective areas under their direct control or under their influence, where independence of the Arabs would be recognized. This break-through in the negotiations having been achieved, the next phase was handed over by Nicolson to Sir Mark Sykes who, together with Picot, had still to settle the question of Palestine as well as to work out a proposal for an Agreement between the two Governments.

Sykes had originally hoped to hold Palestine (on both sides of the Jordan) – from, approximately, the Acre-Dera line in the north down to the Egyptian frontier – for Britain. But France too was claiming the whole country. Within a few days of the discussions, the future of Palestine was decided. The country was to be partitioned under four headings : (1)   Britain was to hold Haifa and Acre Bay with the right to build a railroad to Mesopotamia ; (2)   Northern Palestine was to be placed under direct French control, linking up with the Lebanese-Syrian littoral in a line up to Mersin ; (3)   The inland region of western Palestine, on a line from, approximately, Acre-Tiberias down to Gaza and the Dead Sea, was to become an international area ; (4)   Southern Palestine, the Negev, was to become part of an Arab state stretching across Transjordan and up to Mesopotamia under British aegis. Apart from direct French control of a line from Acre north to Mersin, France would directly hold Cilicia in Asia Minor and, indirectly, an Arab state stretching from the four towns of Damascus, Hamma, Homs and Aleppo eastwards through northern Mesopotamia.

Parallel to French control over the littoral and Cilicia (the Blue Zone), Britain would have direct control of southern Mesopotamia up to Baghdad (Red Area). Britain thus managed to bar total French control of Palestine, leaving the inner part under international control, but surrounding it on the west by the Haifa enclave and on the south (the Negev) and east (Transjordan) by an Arab state under British aegis. The British strategic link from the Mediterranean to Mesopotamia was thus assured, while the approaches to the Suez Canal were to remain under indirect British control.

The plan had two major lacunae in terms of British interests. First, the Palestine centre, although not under French control, was to be internationalized and, under certain eventualities, could become a burden o the approaches to the Suez Canal. Secondly, the envisaged Arab state would mean – in the Negev – close Arab proximity to Egypt, and indirect control was not the same thing as direct control.

In sum, Britain yielded somewhat to France in consideration of the war alliance ; but neither Sykes, nor the Cairo school, were resigned, in their inner minds, to Palestine not being under total British control. The Cairo school, in fact, refused to resign itself to the thought of French control, direct or indirect, even in Syria. These reservations were the prologue to the next chapter in forging Palestine's destiny, which opened in 1917.

Having tied up their agreement, Britain and France now had to obtain Russian approval. Sykes proceeded to Petrograd at the end of February 1916. Before leaving, he, apparently for the first time, took interest in the Jewish stake in Palestine. He met with Samuel to discuss the latter's memorandum on the subject, and in Petrograd he spoke to Picot of the great advantage that would accrue to the allied war effort from gaining Jewish support.

In London, on 11 March, Sir Edward Grey sent messages to the British Ambassadors in Paris and Petrograd, underlying the importance of gaining Jewish support for the war effort. He told them that 'it has been suggested to us that if we could offer to the Jews an arrangement in regard to Palestine completely satisfactory to Jewish aspirations, such an offer might appeal strongly to a large and powerful section of the Jewish community throughout the world.' He then proposed a formula for a Jewish commonwealth in Palestine, to be published by the three allied powers, which went beyond the terms of the later Balfour Declaration. It clearly held out the prospect that 'when in the course of time the Jewish colonists in Palestine have grown strong enough to cope with the Arab population, they may be allowed to take the management of the internal affairs of Palestine (with the exception of Jerusalem and the Holy Places) into their own hands.'*

The origins of this initiative are as yet not altogether clearly defined.† Grey was acquainted with the Samuel memorandum, to be sure, but seemed not to have been committed to it. In the Sykes-Picot draft, moreover, the Jewish national stake was ignored, as it had been by the de Bunsen Committee. Strangely enough, it seems to have been a suggestion made in February 1916 dispatch from McMahon, who, four months earlier, had given Britain's pledge to Husain, which sparked off Grey's proposal. For it was reported in that dispatch (received on 23 February) that Edgar Suares, the head of the Jewish community in Alexandria, was convinced that 'with a stroke of a pen, almost, England could assume to herself the active support of the Jews all over the neutral world if only the Jews knew that British policy accorded with their aspirations for Palestine'. This hit a nerve, since, before the war, the British Residency in Cairo, the British Embassy in Constantinople and the Foreign Office were under the impression that the Jews and Zionists were generally pro-German and pro-Turk.

*L. Stein, The Balfour Declaration, 224.
†But see M. Vereté, op. cit., 55-7.

Apart from the possible influence of the Suares proposal, there was also the impact of the Foreign Office's contacts with Lucien Wolf. Although anti-Zionist himself, Wolf was honest enough to comment to the Under-Secretary of State, Robert Cecil, that the way to obtain American-Jewish support in the war was to publish a Zionist declaration on Palestine. He also suggested a formula of a declaration in somewhat guarded language. Grey, in his message to the ambassadors, amplified it to mean evolution towards a Jewish commonwealth in Palestine.

In Petrograd, Sazonov raised no objections to Grey's proposal, so long as the rights of the Orthodox Church were protected. Buchanan, the British Ambassador, explained that a Jewish national home in Palestine would require that British troops occupy Palestine in order to protect the Jews from the Arabs. In such an event, Jerusalem would be internationalized, despite the desires of the Jews to the contrary.* Sazonov even indicated sympathy for the Jewish colonization idea. Briand, however, was not in favour – for reasons never fully clarified. One may suspect that just as some elements in British hierarchy, while endorsing the Sykes-Picot agreement on Palestine nevertheless continued to hope that the country would eventually come under complete British control, so certain elements in France continued to strive for total French control of Palestine. In any case, the Grey proposals seemed to have died at birth. The Sykes-Picot Accord, after some adjustment of the proposed frontiers in Asia Minor, became a British-French-Russian Agreement. The Jewish stake in Palestine was shelved for the time being.

In retrospect, however, the Grey proposal may be viewed as the preamble to the Balfour Declaration of close to two years later. As in relation to the de Bunsen Committee deliberations, there was no record of Zionist activity, the Grey proposals came into being without any direct Zionist prodding. They apparently reflected the dual British desire to gain American-Jewish support for Britain's war effort and the use of a Jewish presence in Palestine as a buffer against both the French presence in the north and the Arab presence in the south. The next chapter opens in 1917, when Britain's posture in the East reached the point where a bid for exclusive control of Palestine could be made.

* C. J. Smith, *The Russian Struggle for Power, 1914–1917*, 419.

Background to Sinai

From an Interview with Shabtai Teveth, Ha'aretz,
11 November 1966

An important element in the background to the Sinai Campaign was the
personal rivalry between Nasser and Prime Minister Nuri Sa'id, which
reflected the national rivalry between Egypt and Iraq. The efforts to
integrate Egypt into the Western defence system had failed. After the
conclusion of the Baghdad Pact in 1955, Nasser went to Bandung.
According to one account, it was Chou En-Lai who advised Nasser at
Bandung to approach the Soviet bloc for arms. In the summer of 1955,
Dimitri Shepilov, then editor of *Pravda,* visited Cairo ; he was followed
by the Soviet Foreign Minister. And in December 1955, the Czech-
Egyptian arms deal was signed.

Anyone who follows international developments can perceive that
Nasser was already moving away from the West in the autumn of 1954,
after the signature of the agreement for the evacuation of the Canal zone
by the British forces. Nasser wanted American arms without an accompanying American military delegation, but, in keeping with their policy,
the Americans insisted on a delegation going with their armaments, as
they did with other countries in the Middle East. The Soviets, on the
other hand, supplied Nasser with arms 'unconditionally'. With his
approach to the Soviet bloc, Nasser began his political game. Although
he had failed in every one of his external efforts in the Middle East (with
Syria, Lebanon, Jordan, Iraq, Yemen, etc.), he succeeded in strengthening his international position by playing East and West against each
other. At one and the same time, he convinced the West that if his régime
fell it would be replaced by a Communist one, and the East that an
extreme rightist régime would emerge from the ruins of his own.

In view of these developments, little importance should be attached to
the Israeli raid on Gaza at the beginning of 1955 [in retaliation for
sabotage and killing committed by terrorists from bases in Gaza, an
Israeli paratroop unit attacked an Egyptian base near Gaza on 28
February 1955 ; thirty-eight Egyptian soldiers and two civilians were
killed and many were wounded], despite the views of those, including
some Israelis, who regard it as the main reason for Nasser's appeal for
arms to the Soviet bloc. The Gaza raid may have somewhat stimulated
the process, but it may be assumed that, even without it, Nasser would
have made the same change in his policy.

If Nasser had only asked for defensive arms against Israel, the Americans would probably have been prepared to supply them. In fact, the

United States was very eager to establish the Western defence system with a base in Egypt, or at least with her participation, and this aroused serious anxiety in Israel. Against the background of Nasser's inter-Arab activity and the international position he adopted for reasons that have no particular connection with Israel, Israel was the touchstone in the inter-Arab struggle. Each side wanted to prove that its international policy would serve Arab interests against Israel. The more Nasser denounced Nuri Sa'id as an agent of Western imperialism, the greater was Nuri's pressure on his partners in the Baghdad Pact – especially Britain and the United States – to reduce their support for Israel.

The Western attempt to establish a defence system in both the north and the south of the Middle East aroused the Soviet Union to look for a way to penetrate into the region. The Czech-Egyptian deal was signed as a counter-balance to the Baghdad Pact and a 'prize' for Nasser's non-adhesion to the Western defence system, and not in order to give him arms superiority over Israel – although this was the inevitable result.

It is possible that Nasser aspired from the beginning to neutralism as he understood it, a fact that was not perceived in 1953-4 by the Americans, who had great hopes for him. This trend facilitated the growth of Indian influence, especially in view of the establishment of the Baghdad Pact. Nehru's influence was considerable at the time and the Indian Ambassador in Cairo influenced Nasser to adopt the neutralist position in the inter-bloc struggle.

On the Israeli side, a main feature of the background to the Sinai Campaign was concern at any strengthening of Egypt, whether by plans that did not come to fruition – such as MEDO (Middle East Defence Organization) and Dulles' plan to base the Western defence system on Egypt – or through the Czech arms deal. Foreign Minister Moshe Sharett's journey to Geneva (where the first Summit Conference was taking place) at the end of 1955 was meant to bring home to the Powers the gravity of Israel's position as a result of the upsetting of the balance of forces. Later, Sharett and Eban (then Israeli Ambassador to the US) had talks in Washington with Dulles about the supply of arms – especially planes – to Israel. If the Secretary of State had responded to Israel's request in December 1955, it is highly possible that the Sinai Campaign would not have taken place. Ultimately, he agreed to arrange to have Israel supplied with planes by other countries.

Why was US action in this regard delayed for several months more ? Sharett believed that the Kinneret Operation at the end of 1956 was the reason. [On 11 December 1956 Israeli forces attacked Syrian army posts east of Lake Kinneret, from which Israeli farmers and fishermen had been harrassed.] True, the operation did not make Washington's efforts any easier, but there can be no certainty on this subject. In the US State Department there was a conflict between various evaluations. Some took the Czech arms deal as proof that Nasser had fallen victim to Soviet influence, while others – headed by Henry Byroade, the American Ambassador in Cairo – argued that the deal was a one-time event and that Nasser had made it in despair. Byroade claimed that Nasser could still be saved from Soviet influence.

In November 1955, shortly before the Geneva Summit Conference, Dulles summoned Byroade and the late Edward Lawson, then U S Ambassador in Israel, to Paris. He agreed to wait six months to test Byroade's view that Nasser could still be won over for the West. As part of the effort to repair relations with Egypt, negotiations continued during the following months for American aid for the building of the Aswan Dam. Dulles did not believe that Israel was in any immediate danger. He apparently thought that from Israel's point of view action on aircraft supply could be put off, thus avoiding a step that might have interfered with the process of testing relations with Nasser. At the same time, Washington did not give up the hope, which it had cherished since 1954, that somehow or other it would be possible to prevent a deterioration on the Egyptian-Israeli borders and perhaps to improve relations between Cairo and Jerusalem. In fact, during the first few months of 1956 there was some American activity to this end. President Eisenhower sent a special envoy to the area, who met several times with Ben-Gurion and Sharett in Jerusalem and Nasser in Cairo [see 'The Anderson Mission', page 237].

During the critical period of early 1956, the United States was thus operating on three levels at one and the same time : examining the possibilities of improving her diplomatic relations with Egypt, including continued talks on an American grant for the building of the Aswan Dam ; attempting to persuade Israel that she was in no immediate danger, while promising to work for the satisfaction of her immediate requirements in aircraft through France and Canada, but without taking energetic steps to speed up these supplies ; and a last and supreme effort to find out whether it was possible, despite the growing tension, to arrive at a reconciliation between Egypt and Israel. If I am not mistaken, the question of the agreements for the supply of planes from France and Canada – twenty-four Mystères (for which American approval was necessary) from the former and twenty-four F 84s from the latter – was on the way to settlement between March and May 1956. During the same period it became clear that there was no hope of an improvement in Cairo's attitude to Israel.

In July 1956, two successive crises broke out : the first over the Aswan Dam and the second over the Suez Canal. Various accounts have been published of the reasons for America's ultimate withdrawal from the Aswan project. According to one version, it was doubtful whether Congress was prepared to budget the enormous sum required ; according to another, the United States found out that the Egyptian Government was conducting parallel negotiations with the Soviet Union to finance the dam. In any case, it may be assumed that by this time Washington had come to the conclusion that Ambassador Byroade had been mistaken in his evaluation of the situation. During that summer, tension in Israel grew. In the face of the threat to our security, France agreed (after negotiations in which Shimon Peres, then Director-General of the Ministry of Defence, played a major role) to supply Israel with arms. The nationalization of the Suez Canal and the failure of the efforts to reach a political settlement that would satisfy France and Britain intensified the crisis in relations between these two countries and Egypt.

Israel felt that she was engaged in a race with time. The operations of the *fedayun* [terrorists based in Egypt, Gaza and Jordan who raided Israeli territory] intensified and there was growing concern at the unknown dimensions of Egyptian power and the pace at which new Soviet arms were being absorbed by the Egyptian Army. In addition, the situation deteriorated in Jordan : on the one hand, pro-Nasserist forces were attempting to overthrow Hussein's régime and, on the other hand, the Iraqi Army stood ready to enter the country. In October, pro-Nasserist elements gained a majority in the Jordanian parliament, and the unification of the Egyptian, Jordanian and Syrian armies under Egyptian command was proclaimed. Jordanian-Israeli relations were extremely tense, and Britain warned Israel against any military action in case of the entry of Iraqi forces into Jordan. It was clear in Jerusalem, however, that the real focus of danger was in Cairo.

The Sinai Campaign, which began on 29 October, and the accompanying events were no mere episode. They were of historic significance for Israel, the Middle East and the world as a whole. From Israel's point of view, the campaign led to a fundamental change in her regional and world position, as well as in political and military thinking both in Israel and in the Arab States. For the Middle East as a whole, the campaign strengthened the trend towards greater independence of the countries of the region as against the doctrine of Nasserist hegemony under the mask of Arab unity. For the Great Powers, the campaign emphasized the consequences of a local outbreak in the Middle East for the relations between them. From the international point of view, the events of 1956 were followed by a transformation in the system of external influences over the area.

In the United Nations, 1956 marked the beginning of the appearance of the Afro-Asian bloc, which was then relatively small, as a force of great international importance. In the maelstrom of the 1956 crisis, the United Nations international police force [United Nations Emergency Force], which has since played its part in foci of international tension in Africa and elsewhere, was born.

The direct results of the Sinai Campaign – the crushing of the threatening Egyptian force, the stoppage of *fedayun* activities and the opening of the Straits of Tiran to free navigation – were perceptible immediately, but in the course of the years it transpired that the campaign also had demonstrated that Israel is a permanent factor in the Middle East. This recognition has since struck roots in the international consciousness and has also begun to penetrate the Arab consciousness. At the end of the War of Independence, it was believed that the armistice agreements would be a preface to peace in a few years, but it became clear that Arab hostility had not only not declined, but was steadily growing, and peace was still far away. Israel suffered from isolation and discrimination. In the various proposals for international military arrangements in the region, there was no place for her. She found it difficult to get defensive arms in face of the growing threats from the Arab countries. From the international point of view, the solution to the Israel-Arab problem appeared to involve concessions by Israel, including border revisions to which Israel could on no account agree. In the eyes of the Powers, Israel was regarded, in a way, as a nuisance.

The Sinai Campaign was a turning-point in the relations between Israel and the Powers. When, a few months later, the Eisenhower Doctrine for the Middle East was enunciated, Israel was recognized equally with the Arab countries. Until a few months before the Sinai Campaign, the tripartite declaration by the Powers, issued in 1950, calling for the maintenance of the balance of forces in the Middle East, was still on record, but it was never carried out in practice. Before the campaign, the arms embargo was broken in regard to France. During the succeeding years, diplomatic struggles were needed to ensure the opening of significant sources of arms in other Western countries. Today it is generally agreed that a careful balance of forces is the most effective guarantee against war in the region. Without such a balance, Israel is liable, whenever the Arabs receive large quantities of arms, to find it necessary to take action in self-defence. Since the Sinai Campaign, the voices that called for Israeli territorial concessions have died down. True, the Israeli Army returned to the armistice lines, but since its return it has made them permanent, and none of the Western Powers has expressed any reservations regarding them.

It is also true that the Sinai Campaign exacerbated the relations between Israel and the Soviet Union, but against the background of Soviet activity in the region, which was then in its earliest stages, it is doubtful whether the relations would have improved very much even had the campaign never taken place. Today, ten years later, it appears that it is not the memory of the campaign that is the major reason for the lack of progress in improving relations between Israel and the Great Powers.

It is a fact that since 1956 Israel's relations with the non-Arab countries in and around the Middle East have improved. It seems that the campaign has been followed by a growing recognition in these countries that Israel is strong and her position in the area is firm. Against the background of the serious clash in the United Nations between Israel and the Afro-Asian bloc, many were anxious lest the campaign and the charges that were flung against Israel might in the future raise a barrier between ourselves and the peoples of Africa and Asia, many of which were then on the threshold of independence. In reality, the African and

Asian peoples were not influenced for long by Arab propaganda about Israel's motives in the Sinai Campaign. Friendship and real understanding between them and Israel continued to develop and was strengthened on the practical plane by the opening of the sea routes from Israel to these two continents.

Most critical of Israel's moral position in connection with the campaign was the Government of India, and for many years Prime Minister Nehru continued to rebuke Israel for her reaction. He saw the campaign against the background of his fundamental prejudice, regarding Israel as a foreign body in the region, and even without the campaign it is doubtful whether his attitude would have been any different.

According to Zionist political thinking during the decades preceding the establishment of Israel's independence, Arab hostility to the Zionist enterprise was not fundamental, but was the consequence of Arab social structure, local interests, a temporary failure to understand the Zionist contribution to the progress of the entire area and continual mischief-making by external factors. A historian who studies the history of the Zionist effort may reach the conclusion that a more accurate and comprehensive perception by the Jews and world public opinion might have made greater difficulties for the realization of the Zionist idea.

In any case, it is very doubtful whether many people could have foreseen in 1947 that, after almost twenty years, Israel-Arab relations would be as they are today. With the signature of the armistice agreements it was believed that peace was around the corner, though this faith was gradually undermined as the years went by. However, the alternative, the continuation of a prolonged state of war, was in such glaring contradiction to the original assumptions that it seems there were psychological barriers to its acceptance in Israeli consciousness.

From 1954 to 1956 there were, therefore, two schools of thought about the prospect of settlement with the Arabs. After the Sinai Campaign, out of a feeling of strength, it was easier to absorb the idea that we should have to stand firm for many years to come with our deterrent force in the hope that historical processes would have their effect on Arab consciousness. It transpired that even the shattering of a threatening Arab military force does not necessarily mean peace. The hope, which was born after the military victory in the first week of the campaign, that we might get direct negotiations for peace in return for the evacuation of Sinai was not realized. Arab thinking was not ripe for peace. Nor were the Great Powers ready to sacrifice world interests on the altar of Israel-Arab relations. Israel, therefore, adapted herself to the thought that peace would be the result of a slow and gradual process, which must be carefully watched and stimulated whenever possible. In the meantime, Israel must protect her security and prevent war by strengthening her deterrent force.

Arab hostility to Israel is founded on a failure to understand the true nature of Israel and the spiritual and historical roots that bind the Jewish people for all eternity to its homeland. Just as the Jews did not understand the Muslims, so they did not understand us. This lack of understanding still dominates Arab consciousness, but Arab thinking today is not the same as it was ten years ago. The change was emphasized after the Summit Conference, which was convened in 1964 under the same banner of hostility that was brandished in 1948 and in the framework of the same crude thinking that called for the immediate crushing of Israel by force. If this were so at the beginning of the Summit Conference, however, three main trends were apparent in Arab thinking during the course of it. The first trend, for which Syria was the spokesman, called for the launching of war against Israel without delay and with no concern to the relations between the forces. This trend recalled the Arab thinking that was dominant on the eve of Israel's independence and that was revived during the years 1954-6. The second trend, which was expressed by Nasser, might be called 'Arab Zionism'. It called upon the Arabs to continue to cherish the ardent conviction that Israel is a foreign growth in the area. In order to uproot her, the Arab world must first achieve unity, strengthen its military forces, improve the international position of the Arab countries and consolidate the Arab economies. In the course of time, all these endeavours would endow the Arab countries with superiority over Israel and at the same time tighten the siege against her. Time and logic would inevitably have their effect. This trend, then, calls for patience and the long view. The third trend is publicly represented by President Bourguiba of Tunisia. It argues that the Arabs have lost the opportunity to solve the problem of Israel by war. Hence they must try to realize their claims, or part of them, by negotiations and international pressure. (The Tunisian President's ultimate goal is still wrapped in obscurity.)

We cannot exclude the possibility that the changes and differences in the Arab approach during the past few years are ultimately due to the shock caused by the Sinai Campaign. The campaign proved that there was no basis for oversimplified Arab thinking about the prospect of overwhelming Israel by force, which reigned previously. The fruitless efforts to achieve Arab unity and Nasser's attempt to dominate the Arab world continued, in stages, also after the Sinai Campaign. The fact that the other countries did not rush to give Egypt military aid during the campaign did not remain without effect on the Arab consciousness. Though this cannot be stated with certainty, it may be assumed that the shattering of the legend of Egyptian power dwarfed Nasser's image to some extent in the eyes of the masses, at least outside Egypt, and released the other Arab rulers from the complex of Nasser's exclusive supremacy in the region. It is possible, therefore, that the Sinai Campaign made an important contribution to the inculcation of the principle that the Middle East is a pluralistic region, in which there is room for various peoples, each with its own political character and its sovereign independence.

The events of 1956 also shook international public opinion. Rightly or wrongly, the conviction grew that the grave tension among the Middle East countries involved the danger of an international conflagration. There is the impression that the Powers are interested in preventing a major outbreak in the region ; but if there is some contradiction between the desire to prevent war and the Powers' acts of commission or omission that lead to an increase in tension, it is due to the fact that the Powers are more influenced by global considerations than by the interests of the peoples in the region.

In 1956, the United States took vigorous action to stop the fighting. In the political struggle that followed, it pressed relentlessly for the evacuation of the Israeli forces from Sinai, thus perhaps saving Nasser's régime. This intervention not only aroused among Americans the feeling that perhaps the United States had not given fair consideration to Israel's situation before the campaign, but also led to the conclusion that, just as America had not allowed Nasser's régime to be overthrown by force, so it should not allow Nasser to overthrow other régimes by force. Only a year and a half after the events of 1956, American marines landed in Lebanon to protect Camille Chamoun's régime against pro-Nasserist forces, and British troops, with American encouragement, were sent to Jordan to save Hussein's régime from Nasserist subversion. Anyone who was intimately familiar with the situation in the Middle East during the period before the Sinai Campaign will find it difficult to imagine any such American action at that time. This development was not only a paradoxical result of 1956 ; it also symbolized the appearance of the United States as the major Western factor in the Middle East.

The Anderson Mission

In January 1956, Robert Anderson, United States Secretary of the Treasury, was sent to the Middle East by President Eisenhower to mediate between Israel and Egypt in the hope of reducing the dangerous tension between the two countries. After talks with President Nasser in Cairo, he came to Jerusalem and met with Prime Minister David Ben-Gurion and Foreign Minister Moshe Sharett. Also present were Teddy Kollek, Director-General of the Prime Minister's Office, and Yaacov Herzog, Director of the United States Division at the Foreign Ministry. Anderson paid two further visits to each country, at the end of January and in the first half of March, after which the mediation effort was abandoned. Following are Dr Herzog's recollections of this mission in an interview over a decade later.

My impression at the time – and it is not contradicted by anything I have learned since – was that the mission was doomed to failure from the beginning. It came a year and a quarter after the beginning of the deterioration in the relations between the Egyptian revolutionary régime and Israel. At that time, Nasser was starting his efforts to undermine Arab régimes that, in his view, were anti-revolutionary and pro-Western, and he appeared to be advancing towards the realization of his dream of Egyptian hegemony throughout the Middle East. At the same period, Nasser also embarked on his policy of 'neutrality' leaning to the Soviet Union, and, after the Czech-Egyptian arms deal of September 1955, extensive Soviet arms supplies began to flow into Egypt.

His first aim was absolutely fundamental to the Egyptian revolutionary outlook on the place of the Land of the Nile in the Arab world. Nasser's attitude towards the Cold War – the chilly winds of which had started to blow in our region before the Egyptian revolution – was either the result of his world outlook, a reaction to the inclusion of Baghdad in a Western defence treaty (in January 1955), or an expression of his quest for status, prestige and the international and regional advantages involved in manoeuvring between the two blocs. Possibly a combination of all these considerations made up Nasser's motives.

From 1953 (when the American Secretary of State, John Foster Dulles, visited the area) until the beginning of 1955, the United States hoped to base a Western defence treaty on Egypt, and it was this consideration that led it to press Britain to respond to the Egyptian revolutionary régime's demand for the withdrawal of the British forces from the Suez Canal zone. When America despaired of this possibility, she started to work for the 'Northern Tier' treaty, in which she included Baghdad in response to the demands of the British. The Soviet Union wanted to outflank the Baghdad Treaty by jumping over the Northern Tier into our region. It met with a response from Nasser, who had already started to draw inspiration from the neutralist policies of Nehru and Tito and saw himself as a potential partner in the leadership of the 'non-identified' world bloc. The feelers between the Soviet Union and Egypt over the arms deal started, apparently, in the spring of 1955 at the Bandung Conference, with Chou-En-Lai – strangely enough – as the go-between. In September 1955 the Czech-Egyptian deal was born, opening a new chapter in the history of the Middle East. Into this new situation President Eisenhower's emissary made his entry at the beginning of 1956.

The struggle between pan-Arabism, or Arab unity under Nasser's leadership, and the independence of the Arab states, became intertwined with the Cold War, each struggle influencing the other, with the focal points of the combined struggle at Baghdad on the one side and Cairo on the other. An outstanding example of the combination of the two tensions was the violent outbreak in Jordan in November 1955, when the visit of the British Chief of the General Imperial Staff, who came to discuss the inclusion of Jordan in the Baghdad Pact, ended in failure. Five months later, early in 1956, Glubb Pasha, the British Commander of the Jordanian Arab Legion, was dismissed.

While he was still struggling for supremacy in the Arab world as the chief spokesman and leading representative of the region on the international scene, it is difficult to see how Nasser could have let go of the Israel-Arab problem, even had he so wished, especially as the problem was connected with the two other struggles in the Arab world. Nor are there any grounds for the assumption that at the time of the mission, at the beginning of 1956, he really had any such intention. Had he wished, even without taking the risk of direct contact with Israel, he could have discussed proposals for a settlement in the region as put forward by [John] Foster Dulles in the summer of 1955 and Anthony Eden, the British Prime Minister, in his Guildhall speech towards the end of that year. Both involved an Israeli withdrawal from part of the Negev to enable a direct link to be established between Egypt and Jordan. It seems, therefore, that even the political isolation of Israel was not so important in Nasser's eyes as his dream of subduing her by force. It is clear, at any rate, that the emissary himself, at the end of his mission, did not have the impression that there was any sense in continuing to attempt to arrive at a settlement, and his opinion was shared by his superiors in Washington. In any case, we have never heard any accusation that Israel was to blame for the failure of the mission.

Although the emissary concentrated on Egyptian-Israeli and Arab-

Israeli relations during his discussion with us, it may be stated with confidence that with Nasser he also tried to clarify all the aspects of US-Egyptian relations after the Czech-Egyptian deal. It was my impression that the emissary made no greater progress in this matter than he had in connection with an Israeli-Arab settlement. In any case, a few months after the end of the mission, the United States announced the withdrawal of her financial support for the building of the Aswan Dam and informed Egypt accordingly in quite an offensive fashion. Even on the limited question of border pacification, with which the emissary dealt, together with his quest for a fundamental settlement, he did not receive satisfactory replies from Nasser.

The Secretary-General of the United Nations visited the Middle East during the same period and came again in April 1956 for the purpose of finding some arrangement, even a temporary one, to stop the killing on the borders. His attempt also ended in failure. The argument that Nasser repeated to various visitors, including the emissary, that it was very difficult for him to impose his authority on the *fedayun* in the Gaza Strip, was proven baseless after the Sinai Campaign : between 1957 and 1967 he was perfectly capable of preventing the murderous infiltration.

To sum up, during that period Nasser was trying at one and the same time to undermine the pro-Western régimes in the region, to gain advantages from the Cold War in the Middle East and to appear as the standard-bearer of 'the liberation of Palestine', first through the *fedayun* and later by all-out war. When we come to analyse Nasser's attitude during his talks with the emissary, it should be remembered that at the time of the mission – from January to March 1956 – Nasser still hoped to get American finance for the Aswan Dam project. He was apprehensive of the increasing influence of Nuri Sa'id, the Iraqi Prime Minister, through Western support. He also wanted to convince the United States that the Czech-Egyptian deal, which had been born four months previously, did not mean that he was sliding into the Soviet sphere of influence. Nasser's policy was based on the desire to balance – if only in appearance – his relationships with the Great Powers.

His great success in this regard was the support he received from both the United States and the Soviet Union after the Sinai Campaign. The break came in the summer of 1958, when the US Government landed marines in Lebanon, and Britain sent troops to Jordan to prevent Nasser from gaining control over both countries. From 1958 to 1960, Nasser was out of favour with Washington. But when Kennedy became President, Nasser renewed his hopes to balance his relations with the Powers and indeed gained American recognition for the revolutionary government in Yemen. The failure to achieve a solution in Yemen over a period of five years again disturbed his relations with Washington, though not completely. Even in our own period, the quest for balanced relations, if only outwardly, continues to be an element in Egyptian policy.

This is not the place for an extensive analysis of Nasser's place in the Israel-Arab dispute, but anyone who follows the course of events cannot escape the impression that he added to the conflict a new historic dimension in that it was his contention that so long as Israel existed there could be no complete success for Arab nationalism. During the entire period of Nasser's rule, some argued that he was the only man who was capable of making peace with Israel. This view has evaporated, I believe, since his death.

It was not only to the emissary, but to Western visitors in general, that Nasser alleged that the Gaza raid was the turning-point in the prospects of a settlement with Israel and even hinted that this was what compelled him to appeal for arms to the Soviet Union in order to wipe out the stain on the honour of the Egyptian Army. This story gained currency in the Western literature on the period. Without belittling the shock that the operation caused to the Egyptian Army, and without analysing the political situation at the time, it is difficult to regard this argument of Nasser's as sincere. Nasser was a master of calculated moves. He was perfectly capable of restraining his emotions and refraining from changes in basic policy under the impact of emotional impulse (until May 1967). His numerous failures were due rather to mistaken evaluation of the effectiveness of his military strength then to lack of planning and cold calculation. It is hardly conceivable that because of the Gaza raid – which the Egyptian people did not even hear about – he decided overnight to change Egyptian policy if, indeed, he sincerely wanted a settlement with Israel (especially as the Israeli-Egyptian border had already been in a ferment for many months). Moreover, in considering his allegation that it was the Gaza raid that drove him to contact the Soviet Union, it is impossible to ignore the fact that the same month in which the raid took place also saw the signature of the Baghdad Pact, which Nasser regarded as a fundamental Western challenge to the prospects of his leadership in the Middle East. The rivalry between Egypt and the Northern Tier countries over the fate of the Middle East goes back to the beginning of its history.

The Arab world at the time was convinced of two fundamental axioms : that time was on their side and that Israel's doom would be sealed in a much shorter period than that of the Crusaders. Moreover, many of the world's capitals had grave doubts about the long-term survival of Israel. In my opinion, the Arab world lived on this plane of thought until after the shock it received in the Six Day War. True, the axiom has not been abandoned, but it is burdened with doubts, which have even been uttered in public by Arab spokesmen. In 1956 no Arab leader dared use the name of Israel expressly in public. It was as if Israel were a leper among nations, or some kind of nightmare that would soon vanish. To talk of peace with Israel was certainly impossible, if only for emotional reasons ; and, with the exception of a remark by President Bourguiba of Tunisia, this situation continued until 1967.

In 1956 Israel was faced by a multi-dimensional siege : the attacks of the *fedayun* ; the Egyptian blockade of the Straits of Tiran and the Suez Canal ; Egypt's military preparations for war ; the West's wholehearted support for part of the Arab world and the Soviet Union's for the other part, with no one favouring Israel ; the danger of Nasserism gaining control over the Middle East ; the American and British plans for a settlement, which would have weakened Israel's prospects of independent survival ; and, above all, the lack of response to Israel's desperate requests for defensive arms. In 1955 and 1956 Israel felt more isolated than at any other period since the establishment of her independence. Without underestimating the dangers of today, it is hard to see how anyone can argue that time has worked to Israel's disadvantage. Despite the more extensive Russian support, the Arabs themselves are not sure that time has been and still is on their side. Our great challenge today is to protect our security while seeking every crack in Arab consciousness that may lead to peace.

At the beginning of 1956, Washington believed – or wanted to believe – that there was still some possibility of an Israeli-Egyptian settlement. Not only had Jerusalem stopped believing in such a possibility at that stage, but it was afraid that the pursuit of a settlement would have only one result : namely, a prolonged delay in meeting Israel's urgent demand for defensive arms. On the one hand the emissary was busy for a few months shuttling between Cairo and Jerusalem. On the other, the hands of the clock moved on : the Czech arms were being absorbed into the Egyptian Army, and the threat of an unannounced air attack on Israel's cities cast a lengthening shadow. The late Moshe Sharett, then Foreign Minister, believed that but for the Kinneret Operation, which was carried out in December when he himself was in Washington for talks on the supply of arms, our request would have met with a positive response at the time. I believe there was no solid basis for this view, though the operation undoubtedly served as an excuse for delay. For fear of injuring her position in the Middle East, the United States did not want to become a supplier of arms to Israel, but after the failure of the 1956 mission she tried, for lack of any alternative, to help us get arms from Canada and France. Her efforts in this direction were not totally effective ; in a few months we concluded an extensive arms agreement directly with France.

If the United States had responded in time to our demands, the history of the Middle East might have been different. In the course of time, it appears that the lesson that Israel must not be left defenceless – both for fear that she might be driven to take desperate action and because her deterrent power is a central factor in the prevention of war – began to make an impression on the American consciousness. The process was gradual and passed through several stages. The principle won full recognition in President Johnson's public statement in 1968 about America's responsibility for the preservation of the balance of forces in the region, and the measures that President Nixon took with this end in view.

The mission of the US President's emissary to Jerusalem and Cairo between January and March 1956 was indeed one of the most unsuccessful attempts to break the fifty-year deadlock in Arab-Israel relations, but I believe the historian will have to designate it as one of the central events and turning-points in the development of the Middle East in our time.

With Ben-Gurion in 1956–7

A day before the start of the Sinai Campaign, on 28 October 1956, Yaacov Herzog was seconded by Mrs Golda Meir, then Foreign Minister, to the staff of Prime Minister David Ben-Gurion as political liaison officer. He worked closely at the Prime Minister's side for over four months, during the military operations and the diplomatic struggles that followed. The following account of this period is adapted from an interview with Ya'acov Reuel, published in The Jerusalem Post *on 8 October 1971*

Ben-Gurion never gave a precise date for his decision to launch the Sinai Campaign. However, from the time the Czech-Egyptian arms deal was announced in September 1955 – to our complete surprise, incidentally – I sensed in him a growing anxiety about Israel's isolation and the threat to her very survival. Remember the time : *fedayun* raids and border clashes a daily occurrence ; the Suez Canal blockaded and Eilat sealed off, Nasser's bid for hegemony in the area moving to a peak, East and West vying for Arab favours, and increasing Arab strength.

I recall Ben-Gurion speaking to US Ambassador Edward Lawson, in November 1955, about the danger to Israel's cities from sudden Egyptian attack with newly acquired Soviet jet aircraft. He now expected the worst from Nasser, whom he had once welcomed as a possible harbinger of better relations with Israel. Now he was utterly disillusioned. In November 1955, Ben-Gurion in fact proposed immediate military action to break the Egyptian blockade of the Straits of Tiran. He did not succeed in getting Cabinet approval, but he kept brooding over the need for action.

In large measure I think this was the cause of Ben-Gurion's break with the late Foreign Minister Moshe Sharett. I remember in May 1956 I asked him why he was forcing Sharett's resignation – I had the greatest respect for both men – and after pondering the question for a few minutes, he said he could not tell me the reason. Later, in November, after the campaign, the late Randolph Churchill, who came visiting, asked the same question. Ben-Gurion's answer at that time was that Sharett was an outstanding Foreign Minister for peacetime, but not for wartime. He clearly meant that Sharett would not have gone along with his idea of a Sinai campaign – and, therefore, Sharett had to go.

The last straw that led to his decision was the military alliances against Israel between Egypt, Syria and Jordan in September and early October 1956. Ben-Gurion viewed them as a most ominous development. But there were some favourable developments that presented themselves at the time and that he was determined not to let pass. First, the weapons that Israel began to receive from France that summer helped rectify somewhat the military imbalance created by the Czech arms deal. And, secondly, Nasser's break with the Western powers, particularly with Britain and France, over the nationalization of the Suez Canal seemed, in some measure, to correct the political imbalance. I doubt very much whether the campaign would have been launched if Ben-Gurion had not been at the helm. Sooner or later, given the existing situation and Dayan's and Peres' pressure for action, a clash of arms was virtually inevitable. But, if it were not for Ben-Gurion, the decision might well have been delayed until 1957, or even 1958. Then Israel's position *vis-à-vis* Egypt would probably have been much weaker, and Nasser might have attacked in the meantime. Ben-Gurion alone had the authority and prestige in matters of defence, both in the Cabinet and among the people – and not merely because he was Prime Minister and Minister of Defence – as well as the unwavering detemination to swing the decision in October of 1956.

If ever there was a formal document setting out the aims of the war, I am not aware of it. But I think he knew pretty well what he was after. As far as I can judge – and, mind you, I only learned about the war plans at the last moment, when I joined his staff – he hoped to reopen the Gulf of Aqaba to Israeli shipping and safeguard it by an Israeli presence on the Gulf ; to put an end to *fedayun* incursions from the Gaza Strip, and in the process to break the back of the Egyptian Army so completely as to remove a growing threat of attack on Israel. The Gaza Strip presented a bit of a problem : Ben-Gurion wanted to put an end to Egyptian control and to replace it with Israeli control, but he was by no means eager for outright annexation, which would have meant the addition of several hundred thousand Arabs to Israel's population.

After the occupation of Sinai, he seemed to change his mind somewhat. In his address to the Knesset on 7 November, his first public report on the successful campaign, he implicitly laid a historical claim to the island of Yotvata, better known as Tiran. He even quoted Procopius, the ancient chronicler, to support the claim. From this statement, one could also draw the inference that he intended to retain control of the land approaches in Sinai to the Gulf of Aqaba. The general tone of this euphoric speech was vague on Sinai generally. It aroused violent reaction across the world ; it left a long shadow in Israel's memory. The following day (8 November), under international pressures, he retracted. But I do not think that he really meant more than control of Yotvata and the land approaches to the Gulf of Aqaba with a view to safeguarding freedom of Israeli shipping to and from Eilat.

His sudden illness had no effect whatsoever on the progress of the campaign. It started, as I recall, on Sunday night, 28 October. The American Ambassador had brought President Eisenhower's urgent message expressing concern over Israel's mobilization to Ben-Gurion's home in Tel Aviv. After the meeting, Ben-Gurion instructed me to draw up an immediate reply and, after clearing it with Foreign Minister Meir, who was then in Jerusalem, to bring it to him. He insisted only that it not contain any assurance not to start military action, as he did not wish to mislead the President. Then he said he felt he had a temperature. Next morning, when I brought in the draft, my entry was blocked by Paula, the late Mrs Ben-Gurion, who said Ben-Gurion was running a high fever and that no visitors were being allowed – period! It was only through the 'good offices' of his attending physician, Prof. Zondek, that I was finally permitted to come in. Ben-Gurion read the draft and approved it. He was in control of his faculties, but also visibly ill.

By the same afternoon, however (this was Monday, 29 October, the day the campaign started), he was already well enough to hold a bedside war-council, attended by, among others, Chief of Staff Moshe Dayan. He had me read out the points for the Foreign Ministry's statement, prepared for issue as soon as the fighting started, instructing that particular stress be laid on the danger of the *fedayun*. He did not come to his office for several days afterwards. He was, however, in constant touch with events – military and political – from the little room on the first floor of his home in Sderot Keren Kayemet. (He had been moved from his regular room on the second floor in consideration of the possibility of air raids on Tel Aviv.)

That was where I saw him Tuesday night (30 October) close to midnight, when I hurriedly brought in the text of the Anglo-French ultimatum – to Israel and Egypt to cease and desist from hostilities around the Canal and a reply drawn up by Mrs Meir. I found him in an ebullient and meditative mood surrounded by stacks of books, on Jewish and general subjects. The ultimatum was to expire in but a few hours – the deadline was 6 a.m. Wednesday morning – and I expected him to give his full attention to the business of state. Instead, to my utter stupefaction, he embarked on a discussion of Maimonides' Code of Laws ; I think it was on the chapter on slaves. I answered his questions as well I could, all the time impatiently trying to urge him to relate to the papers I had with me, but he simply ignored my importunities. After some ten minutes, a glint appeared in his eyes. He perked up abruptly and snatched the papers from my shaking hands, making a few changes in the draft. As he was reading it, it struck me that what he had been attempting to do during those seemingly endless ten minutes was to assure himself that he was on top of the situation so that he would be able to peruse the state papers in absolute calm and composure.

Then came the political crisis over the demand for Israel's withdrawal from the occupied territories. His address to the Knesset on 7 November, a series of variations on a note of triumph, was based on a gross misassessment of the international situation, which had grown extremely acute with the landing of British and French troops on Egyptian territory on 5 November. In going over the text of the speech the day before, I had raised the question of its impact abroad. But Ben-Gurion was in no mood for discussion. He was, of course, fully aware of Israel's near-total isolation at the UN from the very start of the campaign, but then he did not take the UN very seriously ; he made the point - quite rightly - that General Assembly resolutions were only recommendations. Although taken aback, he did not seem to consider the threatening note of Soviet Prime Minister Bulganin on 5 November - with the British and French landings in Egypt - as requiring immediate action on our part.

I suppose the root of his miscalculation lay in the erroneous assumption that with its NATO allies, Britain and France, engaged in combat with Egypt, the US would flinch from taking too hard a line towards Israel. He was therefore entirely unprepared for the vehemence of President Eisenhower's backing of the General Assembly's call for immediate and unconditional Israeli withdrawal. What the US did then was to remove Israel's - as well as Britain's and France's - protective shield against possible Soviet retaliation, leaving them all exposed. How vulnerable this actually made Israel was something that could not be determined with certainty at the time. Perhaps it was over-estimated ; but as a responsible national leader, Ben-Gurion could not afford to underestimate it. The fact was that a regional conflict between Israel and Egypt - and that is how Ben-Gurion still viewed it in his address to the Knesset - escalated overnight into a potential global war. The limited Sinai Campaign was suddenly caught in the vortex of world tensions. Realizing this, Ben-Gurion still briefly hoped he could persuade Eisenhower at a private meeting to see things his way. When the Ambassador to Washington, Abba Eban, advised him by phone on 8 November that in the ugly atmosphere prevailing in the US capital it was hopeless even to suggest the *tête à tête*, Ben-Gurion courageously bowed to reality and agreed to withdraw - without a peace agreement. He was, of course, greatly disappointed.

Ben-Gurion was determined to phase the withdrawal so as to gain time for the crucial battle over Israel's right to free passage through the Straits and control of the Gaza Strip. The international mood was by then progressively relaxing. As soon as total withdrawal of British and French troops was completed, at the end of December, the phased pullback of Israel was in progress, and UNEF began taking over in Sinai, war hysteria all over the world subsided. Public opinion in the US was beginning to balk at any idea of sanctions on Israel, especially as the Soviets, the aggressors in Hungary, were being let off scot free. But on 19 January 1957, when the withdrawing Israeli forces reached the international frontier with Egypt, leaving only a salient leading down to Sharm el-Sheikh and the Gaza Strip in Israel's hands, the heat at the UN for total pullback was on again - and again with US support. American-Israeli relations were deeply strained, and Ben-Gurion at one point considered Israeli resistance to world pressure, even in the face of sanctions. He called the then Finance Minister, Levi Eshkol, to find out how long the state could hold out with the available stocks of food and fuel. Eshkol, after half-an-hour's calculations, reported five months. Ben-Gurion was satisfied.

As it turned out, sanctions were never voted, but the American pressure was tremendous. Late in February I took the text of Eisenhower's last personal message to Ben-Gurion – there were six in all during this period. It was past midnight, and I had to wake him up. He read it and was greatly perturbed. He rose and paced the room for a while, pondering. He was bitterly disappointed with the President. He had fond personal memories of General 'Ike', the Allied Commander in Europe, and his compassionate treatment of the Jewish survivors of the Nazi death camps after the war. He could not understand Eisenhower's failure to understand him. He said he understood that the Americans were operating on the global view of their interests – the consideration of possible Soviet involvement and of Afro-Asian disaffection if the U S supported the 'aggressors' ; but he could not stand – and he bitterly inveighed against – their smug moralizing. He had no doubt that Eisenhower and Secretary Dulles would have done exactly the same had they been in his place.

However, when he became convinced, towards the end of February 1957, that the best possible terms under the circumstances were final Israeli withdrawal in return for American assurances to support Israel's right of free navigation through the Straits and of self-defence in case of violation, as well as her liberty of action should Egypt attempt to reoccupy the Gaza Strip, he called the Cabinet in to ratify the deal with Washington. When I learned of his decision, I said to him that he was courting a Cabinet crisis. He replied that he didn't care a hoot for the composition of the Cabinet, he only cared for the welfare of the Jewish people. He won, and Mrs Meir then made her famous statement of 1 March to the General Assembly in full agreement with Dulles.

This, however, still did not settle the matter. On 2 March, I was summoned to Ben-Gurion's home. He was violently agitated. U S Ambassador Henry Cabot Lodge, in addressing the Assembly, had departed from the agreement with Dulles on the language relating to the Gaza Strip. Ben-Gurion was prepared to go immediately on the radio and announce cancellation of the entire accord. I asked for time to study Lodge's actual statement. Ben-Gurion then bade me close my eyes, and when I reopened them I realized he had pencilled out the offending passages in the text. It was the Sabbath, and he did not want me to watch him writing. Then he proceeded to call the first emergency Cabinet session on the Sabbath. The rest is familiar history.

Following the campaign and its aftermath, he had absolutely no regrets. At the time he might have been enraged by the Americans, puzzled by the British, deeply worried by the Russians. Certainly mistakes had been made. But there was no attempt that I can recall at after-the-fact criticism or, for that matter, rationalization. And I think he had good reason to feel proud of the success his strategy had scored. The campaign was by no means a failure. It helped remove the immediate Egyptian military threat to Israel, assured freedom of shipping through the Straits and a more-or-less tranquil frontier with the Gaza Strip. In addition, it established Israel in world public opinion as a permanent feature on the Middle East scene for the first time since the War of Independence.

All this persisted, it is true, for only ten years, until Nasser moved in May 1967. Israel's right to self-defence against violation of her freedom of navel passage was by then generally accepted ; she was no longer branded an aggressor for acting to break a renewed stranglehold. With the U S no longer teaming up with the Soviets, the principle of no withdrawal without a peace agreement, which Ben Gurion hoped for back in 1956, was written into internationl consensus, and the maintenance of the regional balance of arms became a fundamental principle of U S global strategy.

John Foster Dulles

Transcript of an unrehearsed interview in Jerusalem with Professor Louis L. Gerson for the John Foster Dulles Oral History Project of Princeton University, 27 May 1964

I served in Washington as Minister of the Israeli Embassy from October 1957 until June 1960. Thus, for about a year and a half I was in Washington while Secretary of State John Foster Dulles was in office. I also had close contact with United States-Israeli relations in previous years. From 1954 I was head of the United States Division in the Foreign Ministry, and in 1956-7 – that is, during the Sinai Campaign and during the political negotiations following the military campaign – I was on Prime Minister Ben-Gurion's staff, dealing with political matters, and I was also in charge of United Nations affairs.

As for my impressions of the Secretary of State, I would say in the first place that one immediately felt in his presence the force of his personality and the vigour of his determination. He seemed to be a man with a deep sense of mission, a higher spiritual mission, apparently, in relationship to the forces of materialism, of Communism. He felt it, apparently, to be his duty to block Communist penetration across the world and to rally forces throughout the world against any Communist infringement of territory or régimes. You felt simultaneously, in talking to him, the keen legal mind, the sense of mission, a touch of great experience in world affairs.

At the same time, I must say one did not feel so much the sense of history that one might have expected to be associated with a person in that position. I always felt that he was a great man, Dulles, and that he may not have been fully appreciated in his own country, particularly by the press. On a number of occasions when he was fully right in his analysis and his action, he did not get the proper appreciation in press editorials and comments. He had a concept of world affairs that I would say was very simple and to the point, although it may not have been simple in execution.

It came home to me at one meeting I attended with Ambassador Eban. It must have been either in August or September 1958, after the Lebanese and Iraqi crisis in July. Ambassador Eban brought the Secretary of State a letter from Prime Minister Ben-Gurion (I think the letter was addressed to the President ; it was brought to Mr Dulles) in which Ben-Gurion set forth his views on the Middle East and what he thought the United States could do in the Middle East and also in relation to the situation in other continents. Mr Dulles was deeply impressed with the letter. After reading it through, he called in his secretary and said, 'Get this to the President immediately.' He then turned to us, and he said that lately certain liberal people have had the ear of the President. 'Now, they talk of the tide of history. I never know exactly what they mean, but in any event, my policy is to erect effective sandbags, if this tide seems to be flowing against us, and they are effective sandbags.'

I thought that that summed up a lot of his world approach. I have often thought, myself, that Western statesmanship over the past decade or two decades divided, broadly speaking – and this is very rough and superficial – into two main groupings ; what I would call the Conservative school, that is those who believe that firmness (I don't like to use the word 'rigidity' so easily because it has a derogatory sense, and I'm not taking sides in this), is the only course. One must, of course, understand the background of the Communist thrust. One must understand the motives for the conduct of the new nations. One must not ignore the ways and possibilities of improving relations, but one must not get too excited. After all, in their opinion, it is the West that still guides the world and sets its tone, and both the Communists and the new nations must bear this in mind. I do not say they don't want good relations with the other side. On the contrary, they certainly do, but theirs is a certain pattern of approach. They are not easy to stampede, let us say.

Now, there is another group of people who take a line that there is a background to what has happened in the world over the past decades ; that you have to bear in mind this background ; you have to understand the complexities from which it developed ; there must be a readiness to reappraise policies, not without giving up, of course, any basic position of yours. This is no difference between the two schools ; it is a question of attitude as it influences policy – attitude, style and, probably, an intensity of search for the negotiating point.

I always felt that Dulles epitomized the first school. Just as, say, Stevenson would epitomize the second – or Humphrey, too. And I felt that his statement on the tide of history, as he made it, sort of summed up the approach of that school. This is a general impression.

I had one personal encounter with the Secretary of State, which was a very interesting one and which indicates something. It was some time in 1958. Probably the spring of 1958. Ambassador Eban had gone in to speak to him of some question. I had accompanied him, and the Ambassador congratulated the late Secretary on his seventieth birthday. The Secretary was, I wouldn't say morose, but somewhat disturbed. He said, 'Yes, I was reading the Bible. I often read the Bible with my brother, Allen. And I reached the passage in Psalms : "A man's years are three score and ten – and if with great strength, four score." And I didn't like that too much, so I turned to Robert Browning's poem, "To Rabbi Ben Ezra".'

Rabbi Ibn Ezra, as you know, was a famous Jewish commentator on the Bible whose work was translated into English. Robert Browning, in writing this poem and dedicating this poem to him, wished to express his tribute to his biblical commentary. That opens, as you remember :

> Grow old along with me ;
> The best is yet to be . . .

I then said to the Secretary that the Jewish masters of biblical interpretation, as far as I could recall – some of them, at any rate – did not view this in a physical sense. In other words, a man physically lives, in the regular norm, until seventy, and if he is of great physical strength until eighty, but they viewed it in a spiritual context.

The Secretary looked very grim, you know, when he met with foreign representatives. Many ambassadors and ministers in Washington felt it quite a trial, a trial of endurance to go in to the Secretary of State and to emerge unscathed. He used to sit there with his yellow lined-pad making notes, and now and then he would look up through or above his glasses – it was quite a confrontation. So, he just looked at me, and I thought, 'Heavens, I must have made a mistake to inject something personal, and I'd better shut up' – which I did.

But about two weeks later (if I'm not mistaken, it was at the Ambassador's home on the occasion of a dinner for Israel's tenth anniversary, which the Secretary of State attended), he mentioned this to me (we were talking of biblical interpretation) and he said, 'Now, look here. You said something about this verse in the Bible. What exactly did you mean ?' 'Well,' I said, 'as far as I understood – some of the masters explained this to me – a man lives to seventy in the sense that after seventy the drive, the passion, the search for power, for money, for career seems to fade and thus, although he continues physically living after seventy, unless he has had higher spiritual motives throughout his life, his life in a way comes to an end. Whereas, if he has had this motive, then a new life opens for him. In other words, "with strength" means with spiritual balance and strength. Then he moves on to eighty, and then he begins to see life and human destiny in a higher sense, because he is not burdened by the day-to-day press and rush of mortal existence, the pressure of making a living and holding his status and all that.'

He said, 'Well, is there any further proof of this approach ?' I said, 'Yes, there is. In the *Ethics of the Fathers,* the sages give each age its attribute : they say thirty is strength ; forty is wisdom ; fifty is counsel (that is, you counsel others) ; sixty is age ; seventy is old age ; and eighty again is strength. Now, the strength of eighty couldn't be the strength of thirty ; that of thirty is physical, that of eighty is spiritual.'

He was deeply interested, and he said, 'Look, Mr Minister, would you please send me a memorandum on this, quoting me in detail what the Masters said on this ?'

Well, that was quite an assignment, you know. I went off to New York and went through the library there, the commentaries on the Psalms, and I drew up a memorandum, which I assumed would be quite an unusual one in the State Department, that is, for foreign representatives. I sent it through the State Department to the man dealing with Israeli affairs at the time, Donald Bergus, and wrote that in accordance with the request of the Secretary of State, I was sending him a memorandum on the Jewish viewpoint on man's destiny and age, and would he please send this on to the Secretary. I got a very nice letter back from the Secretary of State, and last year, when I was in Washington, Mr Allen Dulles, the brother of the late Secretary, asked me to record, to set down in writing the circumstances of the meeting. You see, they had a copy of the memorandum, I assume, in the papers. I did. I sent it to him, and I would be happy to let you have it, if you are interested [see page 258].

Well, this was a personal thing. This, I think, shows a lot. I think he felt, probably, that when he turned seventy, having had his cancer operation, that his prospects for a long life were rather dubious. And he certainly had this presentiment. He was concerned, certainly, about this in his last year, which I think is highly interesting.

Now, on the United States-Israeli relations, I would like to say a word. There were misunderstandings, I would say, in the first years of his office. Quite grave at times. And, of course, there was the big difference of opinion in the Sinai Campaign, to which I will refer later on, if you are interested.

I would say that over the years we in the diplomatic field, certainly – and I am sure that you will hear this far more comprehensively from the Deputy Prime Minister, Mr Eban, who had a close personal relationship with the Secretary of State, quite an interesting relationship, as you will hear from his appraisal. But we certainly felt that over the years he showed more and more understanding of Israel's needs and her policies on the basic issues of Israel having deterrent capacity. I think I am quoting one of his secret notes to the Prime Minister : 'Israel should have the capacity to withstand any indigenous attack in the Middle East.' On the question of arms balance, on the question of economic aid – generally in major issues – he developed a very positive attitude and one of deep understanding.

I remember, by the way, that at that dinner in Eban's home, to which I referred earlier, he spoke. And it was interesting. He said, this was the tenth anniversary, and his mind went back to 1948. He recalled that he had supported Israel at the United Nations Assembly in Paris in 1948. In other words, his understanding, his approach, was not something new. He then spoke very warmly of the Judeo-Christian heritage, of what the Jewish people had given to the world, of Israel symbolizing this message down through the ages. You could clearly see that his attitude to Israel did derive, apart from every political interest, from a spiritual approach. It certainly had a spiritual element in it. Of that I have no doubt. But he didn't talk too much about these things, and on this occasion he did. So, I would say that, all in all, despite the difficulties of the early years, his record on Israel, I think, was quite a good one.

Now in the Middle East, generally, he took one action, I think, for which he must be remembered, which at the time was crucial, which halted Nasserism in the area and which strengthened the sense of integrity and independence of the countries of the area. I refer to the landing of American troops in Lebanon in July 1958. As far as I understood in Washington (I was there at the time), he took this decision almost spontaneously. He recommended to the President, he urged members of the Senate – with him, it was self-understood that when Chamoun [then President of Lebanon] appealed for help, the United States acts. This would probably fall into the category of the sandbag – erecting effective sandbags – and I must say, in tribute, this was a most effective sandbag.

I noticed at the time that he was heavily criticized, which upset me. Well, it wasn't my business to look out for the Secretary of State, but I felt I could be a little objective in these things. He was heavily attacked at the time of the landing, but when the American troops came out totally unscathed, and when the independent state of Lebanon had been upheld, and when Nasserism had been halted in the area – deterred at any rate at the time – after all, this operation was a great success. I would say that since Korea, if I am not mistaken, there has never been a landing, certainly not on that scale, of American Marines in a foreign country. And this had been taken by spontaneous decision. A right decision, carried out effectively. And still, once the thing passed off safely, Dulles got no credit. None of those newspaper people who had written against him retracted what they had said.

I spoke to some newspapermen. It was hardly my job to look after the Secretary of State's prestige in the United States, but from the standpoint of the Middle East, I asked a number of newspapermen, 'Is this fair? You criticize the man when he took a risk. Surely you should give him credit when the risk works out. This is a thing not only of Middle Eastern significance, it is of world significance – this action taken by the United States.' Well, they half agreed, but there was a problem – a problem, I think, that the Secretary of State never managed to get his personality across.

Now, of course, it is not for me as an Israeli to talk of the relationship of the Secretary of State with the American people, or even with people throughout the world. But this is a private recording, and if it was ever published I would want to see what should be published. But I'm talking frankly here. I thought he didn't manage to get his personality across. His external style, what you call in the United States 'the image' – I think the image was a very sound one, and I think the image reflected something very deep in the American people – but somehow or other it didn't click with the American people. There was a paradox there.

I remember a man, very high in the American government, dealing with public relations, and he said to me, 'Look, if they gave me a billion dollars a year, I couldn't sell Foster to the world.' And he was, I think, an admirer of the Secretary of State. That was the problem there. Those

who knew him intimately felt the sense of mission and force and drive –
I would say, almost an element of greatness. But the vast public, particularly the people who saw the image in Europe and abroad – there
seemed to be something rigid there. The Communists, of course, also
distorted his image – and with some success, I should think – sort of a
Wall Street lawyer, and that form of thing. People also didn't like his
manner. They called it 'preaching at them'. Now, there was in him
something of a preacher. He was a lawyer and diplomat and a preacher.
He was a church man, but deeper ; I think he would have very much
enjoyed sermonizing. He may have been a frustrated preacher, for all I
know. But there was that element in him. Now when you give that to
diplomats and others, since usually the preaching is not to their liking,
they don't take it in too positive a form.

To come back to the Middle East. I suppose that what will be studied
in terms of his record in the Middle East for many, many years will be the
question of Sinai-Suez. As I said earlier, the Lebanese action was an act
of great statesmanship on his part and will be recognized as such. As far
as the rest of the relations in the Middle East ; I suppose there can be
differing views on Aswan. I know that the Secretary of State, from the
time in 1953 when he came out to the area, really believed he could bring
some settlement in the area. He believed this from 1953 to 1955. He
believed that he could work with Colonel Nasser at the time. He believed
he could build up an effective Western defence posture, that is, an
alliance with the Middle Eastern peoples, based in the North, on the one
hand, but based primarily in Egypt around the Suez Canal, on the other.

I think that he played a considerable part as Secretary of State, im-
pressing the British to get out of Suez in 1954, if I am not mistaken. It
was the agreement of September 1954 on the Suez evacuation. And the
Secretary had a lot to do with that. He pressed the British. The concept
there was that with the British out then Egypt would feel its national
aspiration satisfied and would fall in line with the Western defence
framework. And, of course, ultimately, the Baghdad Pact developed –
that I know was not the Secretary of State's planning in terms of Iraq
being inside. Your State Department wanted it with Turkey, Iran and
Pakistan. They did not want Iraq in, but the British insisted because they
had their direct defence commitment there and bases. But the idea of the
Egyptian régime, the Nasser régime, being at the Middle Eastern core of
a new defensive set-up, to be established after the declaration – that was
definitely in Dulles' mind from the time, I would say, he took office until
1955.

I think he probably gave up that hope only about the spring of 1955,
after Nasser had gone off to Bandung and begun to flirt with Chou
En-Lai and to move very close to the Indian concepts. My impression
was that around November 1954 your people still felt that Nasser might
be influenced to come in somehow or other into a defensive framework.
In any event, that was a mistake in assessment, definitely a mistake. And

then out of the blue in September 1955 came the Czech-Egyptian arms deal, which was a landmark in the whole record of the area over those years.

I think Dulles was deeply upset by that deal for a number of reasons : (1) It meant the Soviet leapfrogging into the area : (2) It meant his whole dream of this Western defensive system, deeply in the Middle East, was vanishing ; and (3) was his great disillusionment with Nasser.

From what I understood then from the late American Ambassador to Israel, Edward Lawson, when Dulles came to Paris at the time, to the Summit Conference, which took place in Geneva about November, if I am not mistaken, of 1955 (he called to Paris at the time Henry Byroade, the Ambassador in Cairo, and Edward Lawson), apparently the Secretary took the position that he was going to give sort of a probation period to Nasser. There were those who argued that this was a one-time deal, that Nasser was under great pressure and that they must understand his impulsiveness. This form of apologetics, of which we heard a lot over the years, is again part of the Western world-Nasser relationship.

Be that as it may, the Secretary finally decided to give him a probationary period, and that period ran out probably about April or May of 1956. By that time the Secretary, first of all, I assume, understood this was not a one-time operation – this arms deal. Second, he probably learned that the Egyptians had been negotiating with the Soviets, too, on the Aswan Dam. Third, he was running into his Congressional difficulties. And fourth, he had a certain position . . . I mean, neutralism for him was not a middle way, it was a moral evil. You have to live with it if you had no alternative. But I would say this jump from his expectations in 1954 to what happened in 1955 and 1956 disturbed him, and he felt no reason why he should battle in Congress to put through the Aswan Dam project, and he cut off the Dam and that, of course, in turn, brought on the Suez Canal nationalization.

I always felt that there were differing views in the State Department. The Secretary of State was very firm on Nasser. There were always those who, apparently, without saying so, seemed to say that he was wrong. I felt there a certain dichotomy of approach between the Secretary on the one hand and his officials on the other, who certainly did have the tide-of-history concept in the Middle East, right or wrong, and were trying to work with it, whereas Dulles' policies were clear and sharp. We at times even felt that at meetings with the Secretary. You can ask Ambassador Eban on that ; he would know more, but I had that impression.   In any event, I am not at all sure the Secretary's policies always – I'm sure they were carried out faithfully – but whether right down the line there was this same sense of approach as with him. I was not sure of that.

Now, we come to the Suez crisis. The Secretary's relations at that time with the British and the French and other maritime users – well, naturally you'll hear much from them, I suppose. It is not for us to talk about. We were so much in the centre of the picture. We had our issue with Suez at the time, but far more important were the *fedayun* raids, which were going on now since 1955. You see, Nasser went through three stages in the Middle East. He finished with the British – or so he thought – in 1954. He turned on us in 1955 and 1956 and simultaneously on Jordan. After we managed to hold this business with the Sinai Campaign, he turned to other Arab countries. He goes through cycles, but we are not talking of Nasser now.

Our position, in relation to Nasser, was getting very, very grave. I would say that after the Czech-Egyptian arms deal, the Secretary did make arrangements for arms to be delivered to Israel – that is planes, F-86s. Well, he first confirmed the permission for the delivery of Mystères, being made in France under American control. I don't remember the details. First twelve and then twelve in April and May of 1956. And then he pressed hard on Lester Pearson in Canada, and it was about August, I think, that the Canadians came through with their offer of twenty-four F-86s.

So certainly the Secretary was faithful to his view of maintaining the arms balance. Where he, of course, erred was that he didn't take fully into account our sense of anxiety at this great Soviet military arms build-up in Egypt. I can remember those very dark months throughout the winter of 1955 and into the spring. Our deep anxieties, our impatience at not getting the arms. Ultimately, I think it was around May or June, we began to get arms from France. I would say that had the Secretary come through with the arms in December of 1955, many things might have been different. But it is no good now going into the 'ifs' of history. We had help with the Mystères, and we were offered the Canadian arms – heavy planes – but that was too late.

Nasser's pressures on the area were increasing in September or early October. He concluded a tripartite agreement with Jordan and Syria under which their armies had come under the unified command of Egyptian forces. We were getting very apprehensive. If you know the geography of Israel, one snap and you can cut across it ; nine miles and you can snap the country apart with one sudden thrust. That, together with the possibility of heavy bombing with the Soviet planes, caused grave concern. And the Sinai Campaign developed.

I would say one word now on the campaign, before I finish. The Secretary of State was very violent in his reaction in the beginning, but, I would say, he seemed within a week or so to have understood the motives for what we did. While not necessarily accepting them – not necessarily acknowledging them – he understood them. I don't think he ever understood the motives of the British and the French. I think much of his anger and reaction against the whole business was that he lumped all three together. Later on he began to differentiate.

Now, in that period, right through December and January, until the famous 11 February 1957 statement that the Secretary issued, in which he guaranteed or expressed American support of the freedom of passage through the Gulf of Aqaba for Israeli shipping and said that American ships, too, would visit there – I think that in all that period he showed growing understanding. It took some time before he came around. But on that, of course, Ambassador Eban is the expert ; he conducted negotiations with him.

I certainly would say that, as I have mentioned earlier, there were various contributions that he made. He also will always be remembered in connection with the freedom of passage, because were it not for the American position, certainly internationally, it would not have been easy to get the position that we did get on that. And, of course, with his legal training he buttressed it in legal form.

So, to sum up. There were differences of opinion with the late Secretary. There was considerable disagreement at times. I think on the essentials of Israel's security and her progress, understanding her deeper spiritual motive, he was very positive. I think he made great contributions towards the Middle East. Two outstanding things, I would say, would be Lebanon and assurance of passage through Eilat ; these were the two outstanding things he did for the area. In addition to giving it the sense of integrity and independence and of a firm American commitment of support, he also developed very much the commitment of the Eisenhower Doctrine, which came into being, though it was never spelled out fully and never developed, but at least there was this seed of thought, which may ultimately flourish into something more substantive. Be that as it may, his name, I think, will ultimately be set down by historians in very positive terms in the Middle East, despite the violent passions that have not been assuaged up to the present day on his attitude to the Sinai-Suez campaigns.

I can only speak personally. I think we were right in doing what we did. I'm not at all sure – I want to be absolutely honest – that if I were in his place I would not have taken the position he did. I might have acted earlier. I might have tried to prevent this thing happening. I might have been more persistent in my line with Nasser. In other words, once you take a firm line go right through with it and make sure all this rot stops. But his position, as I understood it, was against the crossing of frontiers, which he felt would have a great significance on a global scale.

At the same time, I understood from people in Washington that towards his death he often sort of reiterated that he was right on Suez, and they felt that he was saying it so much that it may be that he had second thoughts. I think this was, with him, a question mark, particularly after 1958 when, of course, in totally different circumstances (I am talking of the legal situation) he did, in fact, what the British and French did. And again I emphasize the difference – the British and French moved in for one purpose, and the American troops moved at the request of a friendly government – Lebanon. The fact, however, is that in 1956 British and French troops moved into the Middle East, and then in 1958, two years later, American troops moved in. With all the differences in the two cases, they are not entirely without a certain common roof. This happens. And I think that by that time the Secretary must have had second thoughts : 'Heavens, I halted the British and the French and the Israelis, and if I hadn't, maybe I wouldn't have had to move into Lebanon.' But I think that his concept in 1956 was linked to a global approach.

As I said, I am not sure what I would have done, but weighing all things concerned, you must understand him, too. Such is life. We in the Middle East would have been far better off if the campaign had fully succeeded. I am sure we were right. We were morally right. We had no alternative but to act. I think any country in our position would have acted the same way. I think Dulles would have acted the same way, exactly the same. I realize the paradox. Although, as I say, if I were in his position, I might have acted the way he did. I'm sure that if he were in our position, he would have acted as we did. But you have these barriers between nations at the moment. Ours was a distinctly Middle Eastern approach. He had world responsibilities. I think he exaggerated the whole business of the danger of world war – afterwards it transpired he exaggerated. His assessment was wrong on that, but on the question of crossing frontiers and all that, he had his point there, although we don't think he was right legally or morally, as far as we were concerned. I remember Mr Ben-Gurion during the campaign always saying, 'Well, I don't mind Dulles' political position. I understand it. He's got a global approach, and I can understand that. But I cannot tolerate him lecturing me morally, because were he in my position, he would have done exactly what I did.'

Memorandum for Secretary Dulles, 13 May 1958

Psalms, Chapter 90, verse 10, reads : 'The days of our years are three-score years and ten ; and if by reason of strength [*gevurot*] they be four-score years, yet is their strength labour and sorrow . . . .' The Hebrew term '*gevurot*,' strength, is conventionally interpreted in the physical sense. An alternative interpretation, however, relates the expression, and with it the context of the scriptual passage, to the province of the spirit.

According to Rabbi Simon b. Zemach Duran (1316–44), who was of the Spanish school of commentators, the meaning is that a steady moral balance carries one to the age of eighty. Rabbi Menachem Meiri (1244–1306), of the French school of commentators, observes that from

eighty onwards one is vouchsafed a deepening of spiritual consciousness. Both commentators indicate that what the verse wishes to convey is
that in the seventh decade and thereafter man becomes increasingly
aware of the lasting moral significance of human destiny in contrast to
the ephemeral nature of material impulses and impressions. The seventh
decade is thus a period of maturity of conscience the impact of which
begins to be grasped with the opening of the eighth decade. (It may be
noted that at the ripe age of eighty Rabbi Simon Duran wrote a substantial commentary on certain parts of the Talmud).

The *Ethics of the Fathers* (chapter 5, verse 24) would appear to have
read the Biblical verse in this sense. For in detailing the attributes and
capacities associated with various stages of mortal life it describes the
eightieth year as signalling strength, using the same expression as
appears in the above verse in Psalms : 'At twenty, one pursues a vocation ; at thirty, one has full vigour ; at forty, one has ripe judgement ; at
fifty, one is fitted for counsel ; at sixty, one has age ; at seventy, one has
ripe age ; at eighty, one has strength (*'gevura'*).'

Similarly, the opening lines of Robert Browning's famous poem,
Rabbi Ben Ezra would appear to have been inspired by the concept of the
higher insight gaining emphasis with age.

> Grow old with me!
> The best is yet to be . . .

In conclusion, it may not be irrelevant to observe that in view of the
fateful crisis affecting human destiny in our time, international diplomacy is ever-increasingly a test of spiritual understanding and assessment.

Reply From Secretary Dulles, 20 May 1958

Dear Mr Minister :

Thank you for your letter of May 13 and for the extensive research
you undertook with regard to the words of the Psalmist. I found the
commentary most interesting and am greatly impressed by your knowledge of these matters.

Sincerely yours,

John Foster Dulles

Part Four: In Retrospect

The Land And The People

An Address Delivered at the Ramban Synagogue in Jerusalem on the Inauguration of the Observances of Israel's Twentieth Anniversary Year, 24 October 1968

This simple place of worship that we are dedicating today in reunified Jerusalem is the synagogue established by Rabbi Moses Ben Nahman, the Ramban, 700 years ago, and this ceremony marks the beginning of the celebrations of the twentieth anniversary of the State of Israel. The foundations of the synagogue are being gradually uncovered before our very eyes and the foundations of Jewish history are being uncovered in the depths of our souls.

In his commentary on the Scriptures and the Oral Law, the Ramban analysed for the benefit of generations to come the spiritual character of our people, the character of this land and the link – to which there is no parallel anywhere – between the people and the land. On the verse 'because Abraham . . . kept my charge' (Genesis 26 : 5), the Ramban comments that the Patriarch Abraham fulfilled the entire Torah only in the Land of Israel. And on the verse 'and Jacob lived in the Land of Egypt seventeen years' (Genesis 47 : 28), he says that the son of Jacob went down to Egypt to escape from the famine and hoped to return when it had passed, but they did not go back to the land and the exile was long, so that Jacob died in Egypt and they brought back his bones. So it was in later years, when Rome laid siege to Jerusalem and its people were beset by famine, 'And the exile has pressed long upon us, and, unlike our other exiles, its end is not known and in it, we are like unto the dead : they said of us, "Our bones are dried and our hope is lost," ' (Ezekiel 37 : 11). And the Ramban concludes : 'We shall be lifted up above all of the nations as a gift to the Lord and a deep mourning will fall upon other nations as they behold our glory. May the Lord establish us, that we may live before him.'

In his commentary on Leviticus, the Ramban says that the essence of all the commandments is for those that dwell in the Land of Israel. He quotes the dictum of the *Sifri* that the commandments are observed in exile so that we shall not find them strange when we return to our land, and he goes on to join this dictum with another from the *Sifri* : that in dwelling in the Land of Israel is deemed equal in merit to the observance of all the other commandments in the Torah. He explains the passage in Deuteronomy (11:21), 'that your days may be multiplied, and the days of your children, in the land which the Lord sware unto your fathers to give them,' as meaning, 'that you may return from exile and live in the land forever.' These interpretations are given *halahic* expression in the Ramban's statement in *Sefer Hamitzvot* ('The Book of the Commandments') that the duty of dwelling in the Land of Israel abides in all generations. We shall never abandon the land to any other nation, he says, or to desolation. We shall never abandon the land to a present conqueror or to any other among the nations in the generations to come.

In connection with this imperishable definition of the centrality of the Land of Israel to the total spiritual experience of the Jewish people throughout the generations, the Ramban describes the character of the land in commenting on the verse 'and your enemies which dwell therein shall be desolate in it' (Leviticus, 26 : 32). 'These are good tidings. They tell us, throughout our exiles that our land does not suffer our enemies. And indeed since we left, it has suffered no other people or nation.' Elsewhere, he says, 'this land is the heritage of the Lord, dedicated to His Name ; he has set no lord or stewards or governor over it.'

In these formulations of the bond between Israel and its land, we see before us the epitome of Jewish history. Over a millennium after the destruction of the Second Commonwealth and 700 years before the reunification of Jerusalem under Israeli rule, the Ramban pointed to two fundamental phenomena to which there is no precedent nor parallel in the annals of mankind : when the Jewish people returns to its land, it will return full of the vigour of life and the whole era of exile will be like a perished age ; and that the Land of Israel has never been historically identified with any other people. These are the two basic features of our right to this land. Sixteen conquests have taken place in this land, and they are as if they had never been. Nor may the presence of other nations here be called an indwelling in the land.

In commemorating this immortal thinker, we recall his introduction to his commentary on the Torah : 'May he vouchsafe us the day of good tidings, as it is written : "How beautiful upon the mountains are the feet of him that bringeth good tidings, that publisheth peace" ' (Isaiah 52 : 7).

As our sages have said, 'Even in death the righteous are called living' so, too, the soul of the Ramban, bound up in the bonds of everlasting life, senses today the reality of the beginning of the good tidings with the return of Israel to Zion and to Jerusalem reunited.

The Day of Atonement

From an Address on the Day of Atonement at Bet-Shalom Synagogue, 1961

Yom Kippur has many attributes: it is a day of fasting, of self-abnegation, of prayer, of atonement, of forgiveness. But the central theme is summed up in the concept of *teshuvah,* 'return' – return to oneself, to one's spiritual personality, return to the sources of inspiration, to the Jewish code of life and rigid discipline, return to one's family, to one's people, to one's land – all leading up to the return of the Jew to his Maker.

Year after Year, on this most sacred day of the Jewish calendar, the dialogue between the Jew and his Maker continues. We are not alone in our prayer for life. Throughout the length and breadth of Israel reborn, in every continent on the globe, in great and small countries, in affluent and poverty-ridden surroundings, in groups with deep religious content and in groups almost assimilated from their tradition and faith, in lands of freedom and behind the Iron Curtain, whether overtly or covertly – wherever there is a group of Jews at this moment, the prayer for life is heard.

Just as this religious experience knows no social barrier, just as it cuts across every geographical boundary, it is also beyond the limits of time. The dialogue is age-old; it is with us today as it was with the High Priest in the Temple thousands of years ago. It reforms and uplifts the record of Jewish experience in every age and clime and circumstance, in pain and triumph, in torment and fulfilment. It looks ahead, almost beyond the scan of mortal vistas, to envision the ultimate spiritual destiny of man. Its content is likewise all-embracing, touching on the interlocked aspects of many relationships: we pray each for himself or herself, we pray for our family and dear ones, we pray for our people. And in the Temple the High Priest likewise sought atonement for himself, his family and the entire House of Israel (Leviticus 16 : 17). In addition, we pray for mankind – for peace and for spiritual fulfilment.

As I stand before you, I cannot but recall Yom Kippur in Jerusalem, the city of sanctity, of prophecy and the fountain-head of enduring inspiration. It was my custom on Yom Kippur in Jerusalem between prayers to walk the streets and to contemplate the stillness of the atmosphere, the tranquillity of the city's spirit. Jerusalem seemed also to belong to the process of return, to *teshuvah.* It seemed to be returning to itself and to its native context, to its harmony, its prophets and to God. In almost every street I would hear the chanting of prayers by Jews from every corner of the globe, each group bearing the background and accent of its origins. These people had returned to their homeland after thousands of years of separation of land from people and had renewed their partnership with Jerusalem. They groped on Yom Kippur for the path of return, of *teshuvah*.

From the dawn of history man has groped after his spiritual essence and his relationship with his Maker. It has been a search afflicted by doubt, suspense, fear, a sense of basic loneliness, the feeling of temporariness and of nothingness against the endless panorama of universe, history and existence. David expressed it when he said : 'When I consider thy heavens . . . the moon and the stars . . . what is man, that thou art mindful of him?' (Psalms 8 : 3–4).

This search has been frustrated and retarded by excessive and unbalanced material impulse. It has been derided by free-thinkers. The efficacy of prayer, Providence, the prophetic pattern of history and the problem of faith and freewill have been debated from all angles throughout the course of the search. But it has also been uplifted by flashes of insight, by a yearning and dedication resulting in spiritual contact, by a flash of higher inspiration sometimes vouchsafed to ordinary mortals. The affirmation of this inspiration and contact is the theme of Yom Kippur. In intuitive faith the Jewish soul rises to its heights on this most sacred day. Today the spiritual category asserts itself, it balances and refines material impulse and seizes the human being. Thus the return is sought and consummated. Jonah the Prophet, whose record we shall read this afternoon, balked before the command to participate in the return but gave expression to it in an immortal passage :

> When my soul was overwhelmed within me
> I remembered the Lord :
> and my prayer came in unto thee,
> into thine holy temple (Jonah 2 : 7).

Return, then, is the theme. And in the Torah and the Prophets the same word is used both for the spiritual return of the individual and the people and for the spiritual return from dispersion.

> And [thou] shalt return unto the Lord thy God . . . that then the Lord thy God will turn thy captivity, and have compassion upon thee, and will return and gather thee from all the nations, whither the Lord thy God hath scattered thee. If any of thine be driven out unto the outmost parts of heaven, from thence will the Lord thy God gather thee, and from thence will he fetch thee (Deuteronomy 30 : 2–4).

Two Synagogue Homilies

'The Moment of Departure', Hechal Shlomo, Passover 1965

> Stand still, and see the salvation of the Lord, which he will show to you today : for the Egyptians whom ye have seen today, ye shall see them again no more for ever (Exodus 14 : 13).

This is the boundary line between bondage in Egypt and wandering in the wilderness ; above all, between the physical and spiritual perception of freedom. The bondage of Israel ended with the submission of Pharaoh's house to the divine command : 'Let my people go!' But in preparation for the giving of the Law on Sinai, for the people's hour of solitude with its God, for the acceptance of the divine yoke, it was necessary to undergo the experience of the Red Sea, when, as the sages said, a simple handmaiden saw what Ezekiel the Prophet never saw.

The labour of winning freedom from Egypt was the labour of Moses and Aaron ; the people were passive, not active participants. Moses now wished to endow the people with the perception that he had been granted when he saw that the bush 'was not consumed'. At the banks of the Red Sea, the entire people stood face to face with its masters of yesterday – with all the chariots of Pharaoh – and the imminent salvation of the Lord. Then they perceived that God works neither by might nor by power, but by the spirit. Without this vision, the people lacked the sense of eternity without which they were not capable of receiving the eternal Law. Here they were required to be active themselves, to be transformed into the soil in which it would be possible to plant the eternal life that springs from the law of truth.

It was this inner vision that enabled the Jewish people throughout the generations to endure its oppressors and tormentors, to confront all the challenges of civilizations that sought to annihilate it, to preserve the purity of its soul in the expectation of deliverance. In the face of every challenge in the history of Israel, there were some of our people who cried, like our forefathers as they stood before the Red Sea : 'Let us alone, that we may serve the Egyptians,' but the people as a whole, time after time, manifested its inner vision : 'Ye shall see them again no more for ever.'

And indeed today, at the beginning of our redemption, when we look back over the millennia, we see clearly the meaning of the biblical command : 'Remember the days of old, consider the years of many generations' (Deuteronomy 32:7). There is no other people that has preserved its national and spiritual continuity intact for thousands of years ; there is no other people that in its dispersion has preserved such extraordinary unity. 'And what one nation in the earth is like thy people . . . Israel (II Samuel 7 : 23). So that he may preserve this memory, the Jew is called upon at Passover to obey a unique injunction : 'In every generation, a man must regard himself as though he himself had come out of Egypt.' Memory alone is not enough ; there is a need for each and every Jew, and of the nation as a whole to attain the inner vision. This is the eternal historic drama of the departure from Egypt.

'The Breaking of the Tablets', Hechal Shlomo, 1966

The weekly portion of *Ki Tisa* (Exodus 30 : 12 - 34) was written 4,000 years ago, but it relates the tale of the history of Israel until our own day : the affirmation of the eternal uniqueness of the Jewish people ; the description of its meeting with its Maker ; the acceptance of the yoke of the Law and the Commandments ; the concept of Divine Providence as an axiom in the life of the individual, the nation and all mankind ; the ascent of the people from the morass of materialism to the perception of sanctity, purity and eternity ; liberation from both the burden of idolatry and the fatalistic approach ; the recognition that there is a Master in the world ; the affirmation of the eternal quest for a spiritual ideal under the protection of Providence. This historic experiment of the moulding of a pure, spiritual personality is permanently engraved in the weekly portion named after Jethro, which tells of the giving of the Law (Exodus 18 - 20). This is the story of the unique moment of inspiration in which the world was joined to Providence and the Divine Spirit and in which was moulded the character and image of the Jewish people for all generations. As the sages said, our nation is not a nation except in its Law.

This week's portion, however, is also a description of a process that continues and is ever-renewed in the heart of the individual and the nation over the entire expanse of Jewish and human history. Here is a description of the fall after the ascent, and with it the promise that even the fall takes place only in order that there may be an ascent.

The story of the golden calf is identical to the annals of a people : there is no period in Jewish history in which the tablets were not shattered ; there is no generation, no period, in which they were not revealed anew. In every generation, tablets and fragments of tablets lie together in the Ark. Judaism believes in the supremacy of spirit over matter, but it does not believe in a flight from matter. Rather, it is engaged in the eternal effort to purify and sanctify matter, to reunite the two worlds in order to return to the inspiration of the giving of the Law. Here, too, lies the riddle of the unity of Israel throughout the generations, despite all its divisions. Had the tablets not been shattered, the Babylonian Talmud tells us, no nation could have ruled over Israel. Commenting on the statement that the writing was 'graven upon the Tablets', '*Harut al Haluhot*', the sages suggest that we should not read '*harut*', graven, but '*herut*', freedom. And indeed, after the profound shock of the making of the calf, Moses was concerned lest the people of Israel should be able to endure the trials of future generations in the pursuit of its special mission in the history of mankind. 'And he said unto him, If thy presence go not with me, carry us not up hence' (Exodus 33 : 15). And what was his prayer? 'For wherein shall it be known here that I and thy people have found grace in thy sight? Is it not that thou goest with us? So shall we be separated, I and thy people, from all the people that are upon the face of the earth' (Exodus 33 : 16).

Even if it is not in the power of a people always to rise to the heights of the complete and unbroken tablets, nevertheless, 4,000 years after that extraordinary dialogue with the Almighty on the heights, we can still see that we are indeed separated and distinguished from all the peoples. There is no other people whose spiritual and national continuity has persisted through four millennia ; there is no other people that, in exile, has maintained an unbreakable bond with the land it loved, without being able to see it.

In Memory of My Father

*Memorial Assembly, 29 June 1964, for Isaac Halevy Herzog
(1888–1959), Chief Rabbi of Palestine (later of Israel) from
1937*

The memorial assembly on the anniversary of the passing of my father,
of blessed memory, has become a matter of tradition. The term 'memorial', however, is both incomplete and inadequate. It denotes part of the
truth, but not the whole truth ; it is a description that is not quite accurate ; it does not fully distinguish or define the occasion. Perhaps we shall
be more faithful to our perception of its significance if we define it as a
symbol of continuity, for the man and his work have insured themselves
a permanent place in the fabric of the spiritual continuity of the House of
Israel. His life has been integrated in the continuity of the past, while his
memory and his vision persist as part of the continuity of the future. Our
sages interpreted the verse, 'The righteous shall flourish like the palm
tree' (Psalms 92 : 12), as the palm tree casts a long shadow, so the
righteous cast a long shadow.

This traditional assembly is being held for the first time in an institution of great importance for learning and scholarship, a centre of higher
Torah studies for Israel and the Diaspora ; an institution that, since the
memorial assembly a year ago, has been given the name of my father, of
blessed memory. The institution is worthy of his name and the name is
worthy of the institution, for the man was integrated in the timeless
dynasty of the Torah.

The sages of the Mishnah declared that houses of study and of prayer,
even after their destruction and physical disappearance, retain their
sanctity ; their radiance endures to all eternity. This institution in the
heart of Jerusalem, Israel's capital, recalls the memory of the illustrious
houses of learning and study that arose generation after generation in all
the corners of our exile but that since have disappeared – especially
during the Holocaust twenty years ago. They have disappeared, but they
still live.

All his life my father, of blessed memory, lived in Yavneh, in Sura, in
Pumbedita, with the illustrious sages of Babylon, with Maimonides,
with Rashi in his academy in Worms, with the Gaon of Vilna in his house
of study, in Volozhin and Mir with the great figures of the last generation, with those who were cut down in the Holocaust, even if he never
visited them when they were intact. When he witnessed their destruction, although he wept together with the other survivors of the calamity,
his faith never left him. In the resurgence of Torah scholarship in Israel,

in this house and in other houses of study, the institutions that no longer exist have found their continuity, and my father's spirit endures in them. In his life there was fulfilled the verse : 'he walked with me in peace and equity' (Malachi 2 : 6) ; with our own eyes we witness in him, after his death, the fulfilment of the verse : 'He shall enter into peace . . . walking in his uprightness' (Isaiah 57 : 2). Blessed be the memory of the righteous.

Every year we meditate on his teachings, and every year on this occasion distinguished students receive prizes given by Youth Aliyah in his name. Here is another link, a symbol and example of the continuity, the power of revival, the unending spirituality that has moulded our people and has established its place in the annals of the world. My father believed with unshakable faith that now, after tens of generations have experienced the agony of exile, there is no power in the world that can halt the process of the nation's liberation from bondage. This belief combined the faith in both senses of the term 'return' : to the land and to our origins. This dual faith has merged into the distinctive character of the Jewish people, a distinctive character at which the nations of the world have marvelled – some in praise and some in execration. There is no other people who, for thousands of years, clung to their 'appealing land' and cherished it in memory alone, although they could not behold it. There is no other people who, in their dispersion, found no security anywhere. There is no other people who preserved the spiritual ties between their branches despite all the geographical distance and the differences of background and culture. Both land and people challenged the accepted laws of history, and it is our generation that has been privileged to reap the fruits of that challenge.

As he walked with all the generations, from Yavneh to the *yeshivot* that were destroyed in our time, my father lived with this vision of the future, the integration of spiritual revival with national revival. This vision strengthened his faith both in times of calamity and during the struggle for national independence. This is the vision that he bequeathed to us as a symbol of eternal life. This communion with the memory of the shepherds of Israel dates from the beginning of Israel's annals, at the passing of the foremost of the prophets, the founder of Israel's line of spiritual leadership. Moses was eulogized in two ways : 'The memory of the righteous is blessed' and 'His soul participates in the life of the world to come'. Not only is the memory of the shepherds of Israel preserved in the annals of the nation, but their memory nourishes the faith that their spiritual heritage is eternally intertwined with the eternity of Judaism.

Hechal Shlomo, 1966

It is customary to recall the memory of illustrious men because of their intellectual or spiritual greatness, their leadership, or their work for the general good. But the Jewish people tests its departed leaders, especially in the realm of the spirit, not only from the viewpoint of their contributions in the past but also, and perhaps principally, by the impress of their contribution to the future, by the persistence and ramifications of their influence, generation after generation. Was the person we are recalling integrated into the fabric of his age ? Did he sense its true character and meet its challenges ? Did he fully and profoundly appreciate its ties with the entire spiritual experience of the nation throughout the ages ?

It is not for me, as a son, to speak about the qualities of my father, of blessed memory, about his scholarship, wisdom and piety, his broad experience and the scope of his thought. From what has been said and written about him, there seems to be general recognition and understanding of his greatness, of the fusion in him of mind and heart and, above all, of the harmony of his spirit and personality, in which all his qualities were intermingled. The more time passes, the more the first shock of his departure is alleviated and the deeper and more poignant seems to be the appreciation of his involvement in his age and the impression of his qualities on the future. Not only was his personality itself in harmony ; it was in harmony with the soul of his era, and as the era progresses further, so his spirit marches with it.

The force and significance of the memory of an individual or an event are to be found in the way it is mirrored in the eternity of Judaism, in its bond with the present and the future ; the essence of Judaism means that what lies in the past is not to be sealed there, but that its memory, inspiration and lesson serve the future. In this connection, we can discern a golden thread that runs through prophecy, liturgy and faith : the transition from bondage to redemption, from grief to joy, from destruction to construction. The recognition of this transition is one of the tests of spiritual completeness. With the destruction of the Second Temple and Israel's exile from its land, for example, the completeness of Jewish spiritual experience hung in the balance. So Rabbi Akiva consoled the sages who wept for the devastation of Jerusalem with the solace that as the forecast of desolation had come true, so they could be assured that the prophecy of restoration would also be fulfilled.

Emotional unity and inner harmony were characteristic of my father's personality. As a spiritual spokesman he was called upon to demonstrate this harmony not only as an individual, but primarily in the public realm. He was the last spokesman of the calamity that visited the House of Israel and the first who brought the tidings of consolation at the beginning of the Redemption. In his day, the axe was lifted against the people of Israel ; its distress transcended the limits of human imagination ; it was menaced by the danger of spiritual extinction. In the maelstrom of despair, in the deepest abyss of disaster, how was it possible to find the faith with which to believe that all these agonies were the birth-pangs of redemption, that here was the turning-point, the crossroads in the annals of the Jewish people. I remember how he was shocked and shaken by his meetings with the pitiful remnants snatched from the hellfires of Europe after World War Two. In the plane on his way from Prague to the War- saw Ghetto, he noted in the volume of the Midrash that he always kept with him : 'My pain is without parallel or measure ; the sea will dry up but my eyes will still be a source of tears. Why can I see no consolation and how long will I see no light ?' But if he was sorely pained, his soul was not riven, and from the same volume of the Midrash he continued : 'In Thee we shall be saved, we shall return to Zion from Tophet. Purge us, purify us ; restore us to everlasting life ; to our House of Life restore us. His power reaches to the skies.'

Not for a moment was there any doubt in his heart that the rivers of blood and agony were paths to redemption, that this was the beginning of deliverance, that Zion would not be visited by calamity and that the Third Commonwealth would arise and stand forever. Thus, too, in the days of storm and stress and the struggle for Israel's independence, he believed with his entire being that no power could frustrate the fulfilment of prophecy and that the sons of Israel would return to their borders. He, the last spiritual leader of the destruction, remembered the first leader of the same destruction : Rabbi Johanan Ben Zakkai, who, before his death almost 2,000 years ago, instructed his disciples to pre- pare a throne for Hezekiah, King of Judah, as a tangible symbol of faith that the Kingdom of Israel would surely be restored. In the same way, my father, of blessed memory, found the strength to soothe a bereaved people from one end of the earth to the other with the assurance of consolation and approaching salvation. If his body were bowed by the agony of his people, his soul looked forward with absolute confidence to redemption ; and its burgeoning light, reflected in the mirror of eternity, was a harbinger of its onset.

His perception of the bond between catastrophe and redemption, his conviction that without the resurgence of Israel in its land the last ember might, Heaven forbid, be extinguished, and the significance and truth of this understanding and faith gradually became clear to the entire people. The age left its imprint on him, as did he on it, until each became a part of the other. And just as the age absorbed the accumulated experiences of the House of Israel in all preceding generations, so did his faith maintain the link between past and present and between present and future.

As the Mishnah says in the tractate *Berachot*, 'All those who ended the blessings in the days of the Temple, used to say ". . . to all eternity", but it has been decided that they should say ". . . from eternity to eternity".'

To cherish his memory therefore means not only to recall the past, but also to be identified with his faith for the future. His spirit, which suffered the agonies of faith, became merged with the beginnings of redemption and will always be associated with its manifestations. As our sages said : 'Both these and these say : The memory of the righteous man is a blessing and his soul has life in the world to come.'

Index